HIKING GUIDE TO
Kansas

Text and Photographs by
Catherine M. Hauber

Maps by
John W. Young

Foreword by
Carl H. Ringler
Kansas Trails Council

HIKING GUIDE TO
Kansas

 UNIVERSITY PRESS OF KANSAS

Published by the University Press of Kansas (Lawrence, Kansas 66049), which was organized
by the Kansas Board of Regents and is operated and funded by Emporia State University,
Fort Hays State University, Kansas State University, Pittsburg State University, the University
of Kansas, and Wichita State University

Library of Congress Cataloging-in-Publication Data
Hauber, Catherine M., 1954–
Hiking Guide to Kansas /
text and photographs by Catherine M. Hauber ;
maps by John W. Young ;
foreword by Carl H. Ringler.
p.   cm.
Includes bibliographical references and index.
ISBN 0-7006-0947-4 (pbk. : alk. paper)
1. Hiking—Kansas—Guidebooks.
2. Trails—Kansas—Guidebooks.
3. Kansas—Guidebooks. I. Title.
GV199.42.K2H38 1999
917.8104'33—dc21   98-53813

British Library Cataloguing in Publication Data is available.

Printed in South Korea
10   9   8   7   6   5   4   3   2   1

The paper used in this publication meets the minimum requirements of the American
National Standard for Permanence of Paper for Printed Library Materials Z39.48-1984.

FOR OUR CHILDREN

Erin, Meredith, and Michael Hauber and Bryce Young

Contents

SOUTHEAST REGION

SOUTH CENTRAL REGION

Maps

ABOUT THE MAPS

As we explored these trails, we were struck by the variety and distinctiveness of land-forms we encountered across the state. That variety contrasted with the perceptions of the state held by many of the people we talked with. As a result, we chose to focus attention on the predominant physiography of each hike by matching the background color of each map to a key map of the state's physiographic regions.

The trail maps were developed using a variety of measurement techniques ranging from compass and pedometer to a global-positioning satellite receiver. We used 1:24,000 and 1:100,000 scale U. S. Geological Survey topographic maps throughout this project, and we recommend that hikers use the 1:24,000 topographic maps for long rural hikes. While hiking trails do not appear on those maps, their detail is greater than can be shown on trail maps reduced to fit book format. Take your compass.

The maps are as accurate as we could make them at the time we hiked these trails, but be aware of trail-map limitations. Trails are dynamic. Sometimes little-used or heavily damaged sections are abandoned. High water, fallen trees, and landslides result in relocation of portions of trails. Multiple-use trails with heavy bicycle traffic can change rapidly, in some cases becoming "braided" trails with many branches. In some instances, happily, trails systems are expanded. Little surprises can spawn adventures. Be prepared!

Foreword

Trails loom large in Kansas history—the Oregon, Santa Fe, and Chisolm being the best known. This invaluable guidebook by Catherine Hauber and John Young introduces you to a wide variety of more recent trails—for recreation, not destination—that cross the woodlands, prairie, wetlands, and high plains of the Sunflower State. Hike these trails and observe close at hand the autumnal colors of canopied woods, the undulating waves of big bluestem on a blustery tallgrass prairie, a flock of migrating shorebirds lifting from Cheyenne Bottoms, or the gorges and canyons carved into the Arikaree Breaks.

Walk these trails and see these and many other wonders. Those who follow the author's advice will come to appreciate the space, solitude, wildlife, and natural beauties of Kansas, which the poet Walt Whitman once said possesses "North America's characteristic landscape" and "fills the esthetic sense fuller" than do waterfalls and mountains.

Hiking Guide to Kansas will prove valuable to the experienced and novice hiker alike. Hauber and Young spent three years researching Kansas trails for this book. They have hiked these paths, collected the data, studied the history, and distilled their experiences and knowledge into concise, informative, and tempting trail descriptions. Young's maps, which every user will treasure, testify to his expertise as a surveyor and to his love of hiking. His attention to detail reflects the same spirit that prevails in the design and building of the best trails.

Not so long ago Kansas had virtually no long-distance trails, and its hikers looked to the mountains east and west. At the Old Military Trail Campground at Perry Lake, then ablaze with its legendary fall color, Kansans interested in trails met at the summons of Dorothy Stanley Moore of Merriam. Motivated as much by the looming fossil-fuel shortage and the accompanying rise in gasoline prices as by the scarcity of trails, users across the state answered Moore's call to respond to the need for recreational trails. Moore's initiative led to the formation, in the fall of 1975, of the Kansas Trails Council, Inc. As this book attests, good trails abound today.

The volunteer men, women, and children who have devoted themselves to providing more trails for Kansans have invested much labor and reaped the benefits. Hikers, backpackers, bicyclists, canoeists, equestrians, and just outdoorsy folks have partaken of the recreational opportunities as they groomed trails and collected history. Trails are made by wheels and keels and feet, as one long-time member of KTC's Board of Directors observed. One could add that trails are also made with handsaws, loppers, and clippers as well as judicious scouting and a lot of calloused hands. For example, since 1975, the long trails at Perry, Elk City, Clinton, El Dorado, Toronto, and Tuttle Creek have required thousands of hours of labor contributed by hundreds of volunteers. A gift of the people of Kansas, these trails depend upon maintenance by devoted trail watchers, who emulate the caretakers along the storied Appalachian Trail.

Among those who dreamed of more Kansas trails and helped to create them was George O. Latham, proprietor of Lawrence's Gran Sport, "Outfitter to the Self-Propelled." By education a biologist, George was by persuasion an environmentalist. His loves were the Kaw River, Clinton Lake, and his clients. He was on hand for the first organizational meetings and for the first scouting parties at Perry Lake. His favorite trail through the Woodridge Primitive Area at Clinton Lake is named for him. Even a decade after his sudden death, his devotion to the work of the Kansas Trails Council is sorely missed. But his legacy lives on because his mother, Jane Latham of

George O. Latham

Lawrence, who died in 1990, bequeathed funds to the KTC in his memory that ensured that George's interest in self-propelled Kansans would endure. With this support, the KTC has funded a number of projects consistent with George Latham's goal of providing more and better pathways.

In memory of George O. Latham, then, the Kansas Trails Council is pleased to sponsor this fine book, which will guide the self-propelled to many of the finer trails of Kansas. To those who make, maintain, and use those trails, the KTC salutes you. To Catherine Hauber and John Young, whose book will encourage the use of Kansas trails, the KTC salutes you as well.

Carl H. Ringler
President, Kansas Trails Council, Inc.

Preface and Acknowledgments

As I drove into work on a November morning in 1993, I was preoccupied by a sense of routine. I fought a near-irresistible desire to be outside walking on a warm, sunny, fall day. It was then that the idea of a guidebook on Kansas hiking trails began to develop. That night, I called the Youngs, longtime friends and fellow hikers, to see if they would be interested in working on the book together. Their enthusiastic reaction was the start of a three-year outdoor adventure and one of the greatest escapes from routine that we had ever experienced.

One of our first (and still favorite) hikes was the Konza Prairie, where our children raced up the rocky hills, heads bent into the stiff wind, hands on the bills of their baseball caps. They marveled at the trail tunnels through the tallgrass and the enormous oaks along Kings Creek. At Big Basin, we climbed to the top of a ridge covered with wildflowers and watched the evening sun break through the clouds, lighting a distant valley where a herd of buffalo fed. The wooded 15-mile Elk River Hiking Trail in southeastern Kansas led us under cantilevered rock canopies, through narrow, rock-lined passages, and around huge boulders, seemingly balanced precariously on end. The memories that are indelibly etched in our minds, however, are those of mishaps — Sue Young running the race of her life when a buffalo rose from the ditch next to her at Big Basin; landing in mud up to the axles of our mountain bikes on the Turkey Trail at the Cimarron National Grassland the day after a 5-inch rain; carrying those same muddy bikes for miles on that trail after goathead stickers punctured all of our bike tires and spares; conquering the trails at Clinton Lake in the summer, wrapped like mummies in our endless war against the ticks; spying a copperhead curled at my feet when I looked down to inspect my ankles for ticks; realizing at the end of a long hike at Clinton Lake that I'd left the keys to my truck, parked just yards away, in John's car, parked at the trailhead, where we'd started our hike early that morning.

As we trekked across the state in pursuit of trails, we were repeatedly struck by the beauty and wildness of Kansas. We explored every corner of the state, leaving the highways behind. Our trips led us to such wonders as the Arikaree Breaks, where the earth falls away into deep loess canyons; Lake Scott, an oasis surrounded by rocky cliffs and buttes; Wyandotte County Lake, where the forest is old and deep;

and the salty waters of the Quivira National Wildlife Refuge, where hundreds of thousands of birds land each year on their migration to summer or winter homes. At each site, John Young hiked with compass and topographic map in hand, committing to paper each bend and rise in the trail. He was unrelenting in his desire for accuracy–at Kanopolis Lake, where high water blocked our passage at many points on the Horsethief Canyon and Prairie Trails, we hiked over 20 miles in the summer heat to make sure he had seen all 11.5 miles of the trail. The topographic maps were then scanned into his computer to begin the long process of translating his field-work into the maps included in this book.

We have strived to portray the trails accurately and objectively. However, we can only see the trails through our own eyes. To us, the sunflower prairies of the Cimarron National Grassland are as beautiful as the verdant Flint Hills in early spring and the wooded hills surrounding Perry Lake in fall. We were delighted to discover so many miles of urban trails; cities such as Wichita, Manhattan, Lawrence, Overland Park, and Leawood and counties such as Johnson and Sedgwick have invested hundreds of thousands of dollars to save, preserve, and even recreate places in the wild, along greenbelts created by creeks, and in parks. In addition, hundreds of miles of non-urban trails, across prairies, sand dunes, wetlands, and hills, along rivers and creeks, and through forests and woodlands, have made even remote wildlife habitats in Kansas accessible to the public. By our count, there are over 450 miles of hiking trails in Kansas. This number is rapidly increasing as more find what we discovered in writing this book–that the diversity, solitude, and beauty of the trails through Kansas offer escape from routine and food for the soul.

This book could not have been written without the love and support of our spouses. David Hauber was a tireless editor and adviser. When he wasn't hiking and traveling with us across Kansas, he stayed with all of the kids, especially on our marathon hiking/driving weekends in western Kansas. Sue Young's unwavering enthusiasm, determination, good judgment, fresh ideas, as well as trailside humor, guided us from start to finish. The children, Erin, Meredith, and Michael Hauber and Bryce Young, led the charge down the trails, ever in search of dead logs over creek beds, rocks to climb, and trees with low branches. We are grateful for the expertise and advice of Rex Buchanan (assistant director for publications and public affairs at the Kansas Geological Survey), who reviewed the manuscript and maps. Rex Buchanan and James McCauley wrote our favorite roadbook and best source of geological history and information, *Roadside Kansas*. Bob Gress, director of Wichita in the Wild in the Wichita Department of Parks and Recreation, also reviewed parts of the manuscript. He and George Potts wrote *Watching Kansas Wildlife: A Guide to 101 Sites*, which opened the door to many wildlife areas and parks that we might have overlooked, as well as offering a site-by-site description of Kansas wildlife. Other books that we frequently carried with us and were helpful resources included H. A. Stephens' *Trees, Shrubs, and Woody Vines in Kansas;* Daniel Fitzgerald's *Ghost Towns of Kansas* and *Faded Dreams: More Ghost Towns of*

Kansas; and Craig C. Freeman and Eileen K. Schofield's *Roadside Wildflowers of the Southern Great Plains.*

We are also indebted to Ken Brunson, wildlife diversity coordinator of the Kansas Department of Wildlife and Parks, as well as all of the state park staff, the U. S. Army Corps of Engineers staff, city parks and recreation staff, and many others who spent hours reviewing and checking our manuscript and maps. Their comments and suggestions were invaluable.

SPECIAL ACKNOWLEDGMENTS

Without the vision, dedication, persistence, and hard work of organizations such as the Kansas Trails Council, the Kansas Sierra Club, Boy Scouts of America, Girl Scouts, rotary clubs, chambers of commerce, and many other groups and individual volunteers, we would not have many of the trails that are described in this book. Park rangers and administrators have dedicated hundreds of hours and stretched limited funds to build and maintain trails. As you hike, you cannot help but be amazed at the miracles that have been worked to design, clear, and maintain these trails. In woodlands, dense understory can take over a trail in a matter of weeks, and trees felled by a storm can take hours to clear. Prairie trails must be mowed frequently, and woody vegetation must be cleared. Bridges, sometimes elaborate and very costly, must be built over streams and low-lying areas, and boardwalks laid over wetlands and other fragile areas. Then there are trail signs, maps, and markers to be posted.

Special mention should be made of the Kansas Trails Council, Inc., a not-for-profit organization of trails enthusiasts, including backpackers, hikers, bicyclists, canoeists, horseback riders, educators, and historians dedicated to the development, support, and maintenance of trails throughout Kansas. Trail coordinators oversee, and have been instrumental in developing and maintaining, trails at Clinton Lake, Elk City Lake, El Dorado State Park and Wildlife Area, Perry Lake, and Tuttle Creek Lake. Members work to maintain trails at many other locations. *Kansas Trails,* a newsletter published four times a year by the Kansas Trails Council, informs members about existing and future trails, events, workdays, meetings, outings, races, and competitive trail rides. More information about the Kansas Trails Council can be obtained by writing to 2760 N.E. Sunbird Lane, Weir, Kansas 66781 (mbarnes @ ckt.net).

Safety and Hiking Tips

In hiking over 450 miles of Kansas trails in all seasons, we gained a full appreciation for the unpredictability of Kansas weather and for the wisdom of planning ahead. It is beyond the scope of this book to cover hiking and safety with any depth. Below are some fundamental tips, including a few that may be unique to Kansas.

WATER AND FOOD: Whether you are hiking in temperatures of 20°F or 90°F, carry water, plenty of it, and stick in one more bottle than you think you might need. Drink frequently before, during, and after your hike; don't wait until you are thirsty. On a 10-mile hike on a summer day, we carried at least four 24-ounce bottles of water per adult. Never drink from streams, springs, or wells—they may contain bacteria, viruses, parasites, fertilizers, pesticides, insecticides, and herbicides. We frequently carry apples, peanut butter sandwiches, granola bars, and protein bars. We were continually amazed at how quickly hunger strikes on a hike.

HIKING ATTIRE: The best investment you can make for hiking is good boots. Find some that are comfortable and, preferably, waterproof, especially for winter hiking. Two layers of socks—a wick-away liner sock and an outer wool hiking sock—are sure to keep your feet from blistering. Layered clothing works best, especially in winter. In cold weather, start with a layer of moisture-absorbing long underwear and layer fleece on top. Avoid cotton as an underlayer. It absorbs and holds moisture, so that if you sweat and later head into a cold wind, you are bound to be chilled. If you are hiking around a lake or in open prairie, dress with extra layers. Always anticipate that the wind chill in Kansas will be much worse than the actual temperature. In summer, we frequently wore loose pants instead of shorts, particularly in the woods, where poison ivy may line the trail.

HUNTING: We have included a hunting reminder in each chapter if the trail passes through an area open to public hunting. It is always a good idea to hike in bright clothing, any time of year, or invest in an orange hunter's vest and hat. During deer season, we tried to avoid wooded trails in public hunting areas. We also learned that trappers may set traps, right on the trail. (One year, a dog was injured on a trail at Hillsdale Lake when its foot was caught in a trap.) Hunting seasons vary from year to year. If you have any concerns about hiking in an area that might be open to hunting, call the park to find out.

WEATHER: In Kansas, it's always unpredictable. We have experienced temperature changes of 20° to 30° while hiking. One November we encountered a thunderstorm, with plenty of lightning, at Perry Lake. At Clinton Lake, we found ourselves in snow up to our knees when snow elsewhere had melted days before. Watch the Kansas skies–a bad storm can move in quickly. Recent studies have shown that if you can see lightning, you can be struck, even if the sky overhead is clear. Know the signs for hyperthermia, dehydration, and heat exhaustion. In summer, start your hike at sunrise to avoid the heat of the day.

SUN: Cover up. The sun over open prairie can be intense in nearly every season. Wear plenty of sunblock, cover your head and neck, and try to avoid hiking in open areas when the sun is high.

FIRST AID KIT: We typically carry a blister kit, bandages, aspirin, antihistamines (for bug bites, stings, etc.), a topical antibiotic, and alcohol wipes.

SNAKES, POISON IVY, AND BUGS: They can't be avoided in Kansas. We went for over a year before we saw our first copperhead, and then we saw two in one hike at Clinton Lake. We never saw a rattlesnake on our hikes, but both prairie and timber rattlesnakes are out there. Watch your step, especially in rocky areas, don't pick up large rocks or logs, and don't sit anywhere without looking first. Poison ivy grows anywhere, even in the sand. Try to avoid contact, but if you can't, wash with an ivy cleanser as soon as possible. In the warm season, you will share the trails with ticks, mosquitoes, spiders, and other bugs. Ticks in the late spring and summer are one of the worst pests. The best defense is covering up and wearing a hat. Always make a full-body tick check at the end of your hike.

KNOW YOUR LIMITS AND DON'T HIKE ALONE: Many of the trails in this book are in remote areas, and frequently we were the only hikers on the trail. Always hike with someone. If your weekly exercise routine is limited to 30-minute workouts, don't set out on a 15-mile hike at Lake Perry. Many of the trails in Kansas are hilly and rocky. A 6-mile hike at the Konza Prairie is much more strenuous, and will take longer, than a 6-mile hike on city sidewalks.

CALL AHEAD: Hike routes change. High waters may make a lake trail impassable. (For example, after the floods of 1995, we found high water at Tuttle Creek Lake, Kanopolis Lake, Council Grove Lake, and John Redmond Reservoir.) Some trails are abandoned when funds or volunteers are not available to maintain them. We have included telephone numbers in each chapter.

NO-TRACE HIKING: Walk out with whatever you carry in and leave the trail as you found it. Be sure to check ahead if you intend to hike with your dog. Some places, such as the Konza Prairie (owned by the Nature Conservancy), prohibit dogs or other animals on the trail because of ongoing research. Wading in the creeks and off-trail hiking are also prohibited on the Konza Prairie. Do not pick or dig wild-flowers or other flora.

STAY ORIENTED: Those who believe that all of Kansas resembles the flat fields in *The Wizard of Oz* are most likely to find themselves lost in the woods. Kansas is not flat, many areas are heavily wooded, and some of the trails in this book are in parks that cover thousands of acres. Follow the maps in the book and keep track of trail markers or blazes. Unofficial foot trails or animal paths may look like branches of the trail if you are not paying attention. On shorter or uncomplicated hikes, for which a map is not included in this book, take time to study any map at the trail-head or park office and get a feel for the hike. If you do find yourself lost, take time to reorient and do not panic. Also, do not separate from your fellow hikers. If you cannot find your way out, stay put and wait for someone to find you. Before you set out, let someone know where you are hiking and when you anticipate finishing.

ESTIMATION OF MILEAGE: The mileages for many of the hikes in this book are based on our pedometer readings and are not exact.

HIKING GUIDE TO

Kansas

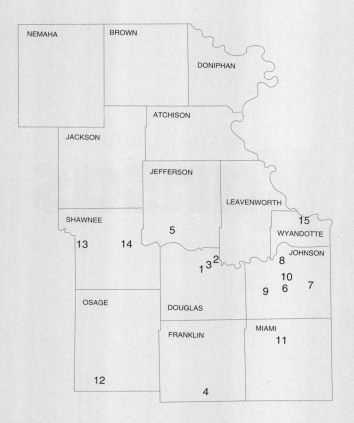

NORTHEAST REGION

1. Clinton Lake
2. Kansas River Trails
3. K-10 Trail
4. Prairie Spirit Trail
5. Perry Lake
6. Ernie Miller Park
7. Indian Creek/Tomahawk Creek Trail
8. Mill Creek Streamway Park
9. The Prairie Center
10. Shawnee Mission Park
11. Hillsdale Lake
12. Melvern Lake
13. Green Memorial Wildlife Area
14. Shunga Trail
15. Wyandotte County Lake Park

NORTH

Northeast

REGION

Clinton Lake

More than 60 miles of hiking trails surround Clinton Lake, more than in any other state or federal park in Kansas. The multitiered trail system on the north and south shores passes through scenic woodlands and patches of prairie on the ridges surrounding the lake. Lower trails parallel the shore, offering spectacular views of the lake and of a variety of water birds. In winter, the wind forms amazing ice sculptures along the shore. Upper trails cut deeper above the coves, providing fewer but more panoramic views of the lake. The state park trails, while not as remote as the others, are nonetheless secluded and in many areas rugged. The trails are well cleared (except for the last 4-mile section of the north shore trail, outside of the state park and the horse trail southwest of Rockhaven Park toward Rock Creek). The George Latham Hiking Trail, which follows the perimeter of the peninsula of the Woodridge Primitive Camping Area, passes through woodlands, scenic valleys, and open fields. Vistas of Clinton Lake can be seen from many sections of the trail. Ownership: USACE (785) 843-7665; KDWP (785) 842-8562.

HUNTING REMINDER: Hunting is not permitted in the state park but is allowed at the northwestern end of the trail, where it crosses into the Corps of Engineers property. Hunting is also permitted outside of the Rockhaven area. No hunting is allowed in the Woodridge Primitive Camping Area. Always wear bright colors—the orange hat and vest worn by hunters—and check with the park office as to hunting seasons.

HIKE LENGTHS
Clinton State Park Trails .... 11 miles one-way blue (14 miles blue & white)
Woodridge Primitive Camping Area
    George Latham Hiking Trail .... 4.5 miles (round-trip)
Rockhaven Park Trails (all one-way)
    Rockbottom Trail .... 7.6 miles
    Benjamin Trail .... 12.6 miles
    Rimrock Trail .... 11.5 miles

Rockhaven Park Trail, Clinton Lake

DIRECTIONS

Clinton Lake is near Lawrence in Douglas County. From I-70, take K-10 from the Lecompton/Lawrence Exit (Exit 197) south to the Clinton Parkway/North 1400 Road exit. Turn right and immediately right again onto old County Route 13/East 900 Road. There are two entrances off of County Route 13 to Clinton Lake on either side of the Corps of Engineers Visitors Center.

TRAIL ACCESS

Clinton State Park Trails

OVERLOOK PARK TRAILHEAD: This trailhead is located to the north of the dam and to the south of the Clinton Lake Visitors Center. From County Route 13/East 900 Road, take the first road entering Clinton State Park, on the east side of the Visitors Center, as shown on the map. This short road leads to, and circles at, Overlook Park. The trailhead is 100 yards west of Overlook Park, marked by a trail sign. Parking is available at this trailhead.

LAKE HENRY TRAILHEAD: Take the park road to the north of the Visitors Center 1.2 miles to the state park office and turn south, toward the marina. Turn right (west) off the park road about .1 mile south of the state park office, and turn left (south) almost immediately on the gravel road leading to the trailhead. There is a trail sign to "Lake Henry Bike Trail Parking Area" just off the park road. A short trail leads downhill from the trailhead to a point at the southeast corner of Lake Henry.

Access points from the picnic/camping areas in Clinton State Park are shown on the map. Note that concrete stairs lead down from picnic areas located off the third park road after the state park office (the second picnic area past the state park office).

Woodridge Primitive Camping Area

GEORGE LATHAM HIKING TRAIL TRAILHEAD: Follow the general directions to Clinton Lake, but exit off of K-10 at U.S. Highway 40. Travel west on U.S. 40 to County Route 442. (County Route 442 continues west, while U.S. 40 turns north.) Continue west on County Route 442 for 4.5 miles to Stull. Turn left (south) on County Route 1023 for 3.6 miles to County Route 2 (a gravel road). Turn left (east) on County Route 2 for 1 mile to East 350 Road and turn left (north) to the entrance to Woodridge (about .5 mile). The trail is circular and the trailheads are marked by signs and blue blazes.

Rockhaven Park

CLINTON PASS TRAILHEAD: This trailhead is located on the south shore of Clinton Lake in the Rockhaven Public Use Area. Follow the general directions to Clinton Lake, but continue on County Route 13 across the dam. From here, the road veers east and intersects with County Route 458. Turn right (south) on County Route 458 and continue for about 5 miles to East 700 Road, a gravel road leading to Rockhaven, and turn right (north). This road is marked by a directional sign to Rockhaven. Travel 1.1 miles on East 700 Road to the parking/camping area at Rockhaven. The trailhead for all three trails noted is well marked by a large sign at Clinton Pass, at the north end of the camping area. As you hike down Clinton Pass, watch for the flags marking each of the trails: Rimrock Trail (upper)–blue, Benjamin Trail (middle)–yellow, and Rockbottom Trail (lower lake shore)–orange.

LAKE DAM ACCESS: There is no parking or trail sign here, but you can park off the road on the shoulder. We had difficulty locating the orange-flagged Rockbottom Trail by the dam, but we were able to locate the yellow-flagged Benjamin Trail and the blue-flagged Rimrock Trail here. The Corps of Engineers map at the Rockhaven trailhead shows all three trails ending at the dam, but when we hiked the trails in January 1996, it appeared that the Rockbottom and the Benjamin Trails run concurrently from the dam for a short distance.

EAST 535 ROAD ACCESS: This road leads north off of County Route 458 to the Wildlife Refuge. Watch for the flags in the trees along the road marking the trails. Parking is available at the end of the road by the Wildlife Refuge.

ⓘ GENERAL INFORMATION

Clinton Lake, created in 1977 by damming the Wakarusa River, was one of the last of many lakes constructed by the Corps of Engineers in northeastern Kansas. Normally the lake covers 7,000 surface acres, making it one of the smaller of the Corps lakes. The area flooded was once farmland. The town sites of Bloomington, Belvoir, and Sigel (which originally may have been called Yates Center), now covered by Clinton Lake, were settled soon after the treaty with the Shawnee Indians in 1854. Originally, Bloomington was located in the center of the peninsula where the town of Clinton (named after a settlement in Indiana) is today, but in 1887 it was relocated about three-quarters of a mile east, to the area now called Bloomington Park, one of the largest Corps parks on the lake. Inhabitants of Bloomington once provided stations on the underground railroad for fugitive slaves. By 1865, however, Bloomington had faded, and it was declared vacant in 1876. The town of Belvoir was originally located south of the Wakarusa River, along a shortcut from Lawrence to the Old Santa Fe Trail. When the St. Louis, Lawrence, and Denver Railroad was constructed in 1872, the post office for Belvoir was moved 2.5 miles north (just south of the present Woodridge Primitive Area) along the rail line. (The original town site of Belvoir was not flooded.) Sigel, located west of the northern end of the lake dam, declined following the abandonment in 1894 of the St. Louis, Lawrence, and Denver Railroad.*

* This and more information can be found in *Soil of Our Souls: Histories of the Clinton Lake Area Communities* by Martha J. Parker and Betty A. Laird (Lawrence: Coronado Press, 1976).

THE HIKES

Clinton State Park

CLINTON STATE PARK TRAILS: The main trunk of the trail system on the north shore of the lake is blazed in blue. White-blazed segments intersect with the main trunk. Typically, the white-blazed segments travel above the blue-blazed trail, cutting higher and deeper into the ridges and above the coves, but occasionally these segments cross below the blue-blazed trail, closer to the lake. Crossover trails, which link the trails, are also flagged in white. We strongly recommend closely following the map. The trails take some unexpected twists, turns, and loops, making it easy to become disoriented, particularly at unmarked forks or between trail flags. If you keep track on the map of where the blue and white trails intersect, where they run together, and where they diverge, you will be able to pinpoint your location with some accuracy. The Clinton State Park Trails, designed by the Kansas Trails Council, are the only trails at Clinton Lake open to mountain bikers. In late spring, when we hiked here, the lush foliage of the trees provided a canopy over the trail, but also obscured some views of the lake. Beware, the lush understory is riddled with a healthy crop of poison ivy. We also encountered two copperheads on our hikes at Clinton.

We entered at the trailhead just west of Overlook Park and traveled west to the end of the trail outside the state park, on the Corps of Engineers property. To vary your return trip, we suggest following the white-blazed segments. For easy reference, the blue-blazed main trunk is referred to as the "Blue Trail" and the white-blazed segments as the "White Trail." From the trailhead, the Blue Trail heads downhill, southwesterly, into the woods. The dense foliage of the hickory, oak, and hackberry trees muffles most of the noise of surrounding park roads. A short distance past the trailhead, the White Trail splits to the right. As the Blue Trail nears the lake shore, it veers north and wraps around the cove, coming within sight of the park road, where it joins the White Trail. The two trails parallel the road for a short distance but do not cross it. (This is a low spot—we were up to our ankles in mud when we hiked this section after some heavy rains.) Soon, the Blue Trail forks to the left, almost directly south, into the woods, while the White Trail forks to the right, southwesterly.

The Blue Trail continues south, crossing the White Trail before reaching the road to the marina. Where the Blue and White Trails cross, the Blue Trail veers to the right (southwesterly and further away from the lake), while the White Trail veers to the left (south and closer to the lake). When you reach the road leading to the marina, cross it. The Blue and White Trails merge on the other side. About .4 mile past the road, watch for an unmarked trail on your right—it leads northeasterly up to the Lake Henry Trailhead.

Just past the trail to the Lake Henry Trailhead, the White Trail splits from the Blue Trail, heading right (north) around Lake Henry (an especially picturesque segment). The Blue Trail continues straight and crosses the Lake Henry dam. Those who lived around Lawrence in the 1960s might remember Lake Henry as the "nudist" swimming hole. Today, its only claim to fame is the trout that enjoy its waters. After crossing the dam, the trail continues west and then veers southeasterly around another cove. At the northern end of the cove, the Blue Trail intersects with another trail on the right. The trail on the right is a .5 mile loop within a loop and is shown on the map. (Follow the map closely here—it's easy to become disoriented.) The Blue Trail then crosses a stream (which we crossed by logs and rocks after recent rains) and heads southeasterly out of the cove area. Watch for a cut-over trail on the right, marked with a white flag. This is one of many cut-over trails that link the Blue and White Trails.

Before the Blue Trail reaches the end of the cove, it crosses and climbs above the White Trail. After a short distance, the Blue Trail descends a hill and again joins the White Trail. They run concurrently west along a ridge above the lake for a little less than a mile. This is one of the few areas where the trails emerge from the woods. Concrete stairs on your right lead north up to picnic/campground facilities—a good place to replenish your water supplies. Side trails on your left lead south down to the lake. A short distance past the third concrete staircase, the White Trail splits off to the right and climbs above the Blue Trail. Shortly after this, the Blue Trail intersects with a trail to the right with a blue flag on it. This is a new link to the White Trail. As the Blue Trail wraps around the cove, there appear to be two Blue Trails—one leads uphill to the right, and another, marked by tire-tracks, leads down to the lake. Both are part of the Blue Trail, but the lower trail may have been abandoned when the area flooded. The two merge after a short distance. Note that after the Blue Trail wraps around the cove and heads south, it again joins the White Trail and parallels the lake shore.

The White Trail splits again from the Blue Trail, which comes to a gravel road leading to the lake and a sandy beach. (On a hot day, this is a good place to stop and put your feet in the water.) Turn left on the road and watch for the blue flag in the tree. Just past the road, there is a concrete staircase leading up to a picnic area, and after about .3 mile the Blue Trail forks. The trail to the right, heading northwest, is a link to the White Trail. As you continue on the Blue Trail, you will come to another fork—the Blue Trail is on the right, and the trail to the left travels down to the lake. About .7 mile past the gravel road noted above, the Blue Trail intersects, and for about 50 yards travels concurrently with, the White Trail, which then descends below the Blue Trail, close to the lakeshore. About .25 mile later, the Blue Trail winds through some interesting rock formations.

Watch for a fork in the Blue Trail—the trail to the right leads up to a campground. Next several trails cross the Blue Trail—leading right, up to the campground/picnic facilities and left, down to the lake. The White Trail rejoins the Blue Trail just past the boat-ramp area but splits away only .2 mile further. Shortly after this, the Blue Trail crosses the park road.

Be warned that when we hiked, the last 4 miles of the Blue Trail were overgrown and nearly impassable at points because of high weeds. Machetes would have been useful. We couldn't locate any part of the last mile of the trail and spent an hour wandering in a field looking for markers. In spite of the ticks, the tall weeds, the high waters, and a persistent fear that a timber rattler or a copperhead lurked beneath the weeds, this portion would be worth the hike if it were maintained. There are some beautiful views of the lake, and at one point the trail comes to the edge of virgin prairie.

About 200 yards after crossing the park road, the Blue Trail is joined by the White Trail. Half a mile further, the trail crosses an old pond dam, in full view of the lake, then travels in and out of the woods through brome fields. At .7 mile past the park road, the trail appears to dead-end at a barbed-wire fence. We climbed the fence, turned right on the adjacent dirt road, and took an immediate left on the intersecting gravel road. (Note that you leave the state park when you cross the fence and enter the Corps of Engineers property across the road.) The trail continues on the left side of the road heading west—watch for the blue ribbon in the tree. Two hundred yards later, the trail reaches an area where it may be obscured by weeds after high waters—the lake had recently receded from this area when we hiked through it. From here the trail veers north/northeasterly. Less than .5 mile later, we reached another high-water area—the weeds towered over our heads, and we had to leave the trail for about 100 yards.

From here the trail travels through scenic woods, with occasional views of the lake. At 1.75 miles from the park road, the trail crosses a clear, limestone-bottomed creek. When the mosquitoes are not looking for a meal, this is a wonderful picnic spot. The trail then veers west and, about .2 mile further, reaches an area of virgin prairie. The sign marking this spot lay on the ground. From here, the trail veers north again, into the woods adjacent to the prairie. About .4 mile past the prairie (2.5 miles past the park road), the trail parallels Coon Creek for a short distance before crossing it at a low spot. Unfortunately, after you cross, there is no indication of which direction the trail leads. Straight ahead, you face a steep, 15-foot dirt bank, which will put your climbing skills to the test. Past the creek bank, the trail travels on an old farm road for about 100 yards before it reenters the woods. Watch for the blue flag at the corner of the woods. The trail comes within view of the creek again at 2.9 miles past the park road, then leaves the woods. From here, we could no longer follow the trail. The Kansas Trails Council map shows that it travels south, parallel to County Road 1029.

Woodridge Primitive Camping Area

GEORGE LATHAM HIKING TRAIL: This scenic trail, which children will enjoy, follows the perimeter of a 500-acre peninsula. Because of its remoteness, you are likely to see a variety of wildlife in any season; one hiker had seen a bobcat. The trail is circular and can be shortened by cutting across on an old farm road a short distance from the trailhead (if you hike the trail clockwise) or past the 1-mile marker (if you hike the trail counter-clockwise). The mile markers measure the distance counter-clockwise. Not knowing this, we hiked (and describe) the trail in the other direction, starting at the trailhead near the bathrooms and traveling north. (The other trailhead is southeast of the parking area, near the woods.) Watch for the blue blazes on trees, and note that a double blaze signifies a sharp turn.

Hiking clockwise, you will see the first of many stone walls, reminders that this area was once farmland. Shortly past the trailhead, the trail intersects an old farm road, which will take you to the northeastern edge of the peninsula, close to the 1-mile marker. About 1.5 miles from the trailhead, you will reach a bench overlooking the lake. It is dedicated to George Latham, who designed the trail. The terrain becomes a little rough from here as the trail travels through woodlands above the lake. Just before the next mile marker (mile 2 if you hike counter-clockwise; 2.5 miles if you hike clockwise), watch for an old hay loader. After this, the trail travels in and out of the woods and sometimes alongside open fields. The two- to three-foot stone walls along this section are remarkable. The trail intersects several paths that lead to campsites or down to the lake. As the trail heads southwest, away from the lake, it passes through a beautiful wooded valley. The trail ends at the edge of the woods, close to the parking area.

Rockhaven Park

Horses are permitted on these trails, though for the most part we observed little erosion, perhaps because access may be blocked by the Corps of Engineers when the trails are muddy. The Rockbottom Trail, flagged with orange ribbons, generally runs close to the shoreline; the Benjamin Trail, flagged with yellow ribbons, travels between the Rockbottom and the Rimrock Trails and is the most difficult. It climbs above and circles many drainage areas around the lake. The Rimrock Trail, flagged with blue ribbons, travels along a ridge above the lake and sometimes emerges from the woods to travel through open meadows. The Rockhaven Park trails do not intersect, but are linked by "passes" and many crossover trails, flagged with white ribbons (shown on the map). In the winter of 1996, we were surprised to find that while recent snows had melted elsewhere, we were up to our knees in snow on parts of the Rockbottom Trail. Northern winds off the lake can be bitter in exposed areas, especially along the Rockbottom Trail. Notwithstanding the cold winds and the snow, we enjoyed hiking these trails in the winter, when they were clear of undergrowth, and no foliage obstructed the views of the lake.

The area outside of the Rockhaven public use area is open to hunting. Since Rockhaven Park is, at its widest, less than a mile across, significant portions of these trails are in public hunting areas. Unfortunately, there is no sign on the trail to indicate where the hunting area begins. Note that while the trails continue west, then southwest across East 535 Road and along Rock Creek, parts were completely overgrown and seemed better suited for horse travel.

ROCKBOTTOM TRAIL: From the trailhead, descend steep and rocky Clinton Pass and watch for the orange flags at the bottom, close to the shore. Turn right (east) to travel to the dam (about 4.4 miles). The trail parallels the shore and then veers south around an inlet. Watch for the "Downing Pass" sign on your right—the trail veers left, away from the sign. As with other passes shown on the map, this pass and Callie

Pass—less than .5 mile further east—will take you up to both the Benjamin and the Rimrock Trails. The trail along this stretch is somewhat hilly and rocky. After about 1.8 miles, it climbs and follows a ridge above the lake. Before you reach Punches Pass West, you will see a crossover trail flagged with white ribbons. Note that Trolla Pass (which on the Benjamin and Rimrock Trails is marked by a sign about .5 mile before Punches Pass West) is not marked on the Rockbottom Trail.

Once you pass the sign for Punches Pass East, the trail becomes somewhat difficult to follow as it crosses a once-flooded area. Watch closely for the orange blazes. When we came to Rock Crusher Road, less than .5 mile from Punches Pass East, we traveled up the road to the right for about 50 feet and then left to continue on the trail. We lost the trail after about another .2 mile. Most of this area is open meadow, and it may be that the trail had not been mowed. While we saw a few orange ribbons closer to the shore as we neared the dam, we were not certain that we were following the trail. As long as you continue to parallel the lakeshore, you will eventually reach the lake dam.

Returning to Clinton Pass, turn left (west/southwest) to travel to East 535 Road. This section of the Rockbottom Trail is about a mile shorter than the east section, but the terrain is similar, close to the shore and fairly flat. Parts are rocky, and the sections of trail that wrap around the coves are especially scenic. In winter, the wind sculpts the ice around the trees that stand in the coves. The trail is well defined, and you should not have difficulty following it unless there have been recent high waters.

About 2 miles from the start, watch for the bald eagle nesting area in the trees standing in the lake. About .25 mile further, the trail intersects with a white-flagged crossover trail. (We missed the orange flag and were some distance down the crossover path before we discovered our error.) About 2.5 miles from the start, you should see a yellow Corps of Engineers boundary marker. (The Corps of Engineers map of these trails shows three passes between Burns Pass—about .4 mile from Clinton Pass—and the end of the trail. None of these, however, was marked by a sign on the Rockbottom Trail. It is likely that these were white-ribboned crossover trails.) After passing the Corps of Engineers boundary, the trail travels through an area littered with dead wood and trash from high waters. Toward the end of the trail, it veers away from the lake and follows a creek. The trail ends at East 535 Road.

BENJAMIN TRAIL: You should have no difficulty following the Benjamin Trail from Clinton Pass east 8.38 miles to the lake dam. Unlike the Rockbottom Trail, this trail has not been damaged by floods. We found many sections to be strenuous—the trail climbs up and around numerous drainage areas, only to descend again toward the lake. Snow accumulates on this ridge and can compound the difficulty of these hills. About a mile past Downing Pass, just before Callie Pass, watch for an old farm road on your right—you will need to take this up a short distance until you see the yellow ribbon marking the trail. Just after Callie Pass, the trail comes closer to the shore before it makes a sharp turn south to climb above a drainage area. You are zigzagging here and on other parts of this trail, as it travels half a mile up one side of a drainage area only to return on the other side, sometimes within view of the path you just walked.

Between Punches Pass West and Punches Pass East, there are two long loops above drainage areas. This section is more than twice as long as the Rockbottom Trail between the same two passes. Between the two loops, the trail comes within view of the lake for some scenic vistas. After Punches Pass East, the trail intersects with several crossover trails and makes a few short zigzags that may appear confusing, only because you may sense, correctly, that you are backtracking. About halfway between Punches Pass East and the lake dam, the trail reaches a rocky ledge overlooking the lake. The view, at least when there is no foliage on the trees, is spectacular. To the west, the hills rise in succession above the coves. This is one of the most picturesque spots on the south shore of the lake. After descending from this ridge, the trail crosses Rock Crusher Road, eventually leaves the woods, and travels to the dam through open fields dotted with small trees and woody vegetation.

The trail from Clinton Pass west/southwest to East 535 Road is only about 4.25 miles and travels about midway between the Rockbottom and Rimrock Trails. Most of the trail runs through woods, but occasionally it crosses fields with scattered cedars and young timber. The trail reaches Burns Pass at .2 mile, then crosses a wooded plateau before crossing a rocky streambed and zigzagging up around an inlet. About 1.2 miles from the start, the trail passes through a field in full view of the lake. Shortly thereafter, you will see the remains of an abandoned farm.

When we traveled this trail going from west to east, we missed a switchback 2.75 miles from Clinton Pass. We went straight to a point overlooking the lake before we realized that the trail backtracked to a ridge before descending to the overlook. Traveling from east to west, the switchback should not be as easy to miss. The woods and views of the lake from this section of the trail are especially scenic.

At 3.5 miles from Clinton Pass, the trail comes to a clearing by a bluff and an old quarried area. The trash dumped here mars an otherwise pretty spot. Watch closely for the trail markers and follow the map—the Benjamin and Rimrock Trails converge here, and there is a connecting white-blazed trail that also passes through. As the trail nears the wildlife area close to East 535 Road, it follows and then crosses a creek, and as it nears County Road 458, it intersects with the Rimrock Trail (flagged in blue). Turn right (west) to continue toward East 535 Road.

RIMROCK TRAIL: Like the Benjamin Trail, the Rimrock Trail has not been affected by flood waters. Of the three trails, this showed the most equestrian use. Unlike the others, which only emerge from the woods at the eastern end, the Rimrock Trail leaves the woods on several occasions. East from Clinton Pass to the dam is about 6 miles. At times the trail travels along or through the fields that border the woods surrounding the lake. Watch closely for the blue ribbons in these areas—some are tied on cedar branches and hard to see. Sometimes we had some difficulty finding where the trail reentered the woods. About 200 yards past Callie Pass, a white-flagged crossover trail veers left back into the woods. Watch the color of the ribbons or you'll find yourself heading down to one of the lower trails.

The Rimrock Trail travels well above the lake, and the views of it are distant. Be aware that there are several unmarked shortcuts or side trails created by horses. About 2.25 miles from Clinton Pass, the trail reaches a rock ledge and overlook. In another mile, the trail crosses Trolla Pass, then climbs and runs through a tree-dotted field for about 1.5 miles to Punches Pass East. As you near the pass, you will see a gravel road and some houses. After the pass, watch for a sign marking Hangman's Cliff (there must be a story here!). For the next .3 mile, the trail passes through a corridor of trees bordered on either side by fields. At the end, there is a tall cellular-phone tower. Follow the old road to the left and watch for the Laddie Pass sign—if you veer left down this pass, it will take you onto the Benjamin Trail but not the Rockbottom Trail. (There is no sign for Laddie Pass on the Benjamin Trail.) When you reach Rock Crusher Road, follow it until you see the blue-flagged trail on your right (a white ribbon marks a trail going straight). From here the trail leads to a field, then reaches the road by the dam. There is a beautiful view of the lake to the west—a nice spot to watch the sunset, yet close enough to the road to get off the trail before dark.

From Clinton Pass west/southwest to East 535 Road is about 5.5 miles. We saw a lot of wildlife on this section of Rimrock Trail and became convinced there was a mass exodus from the public hunting area. We startled many wild turkeys, whose noisy flight to safety can be somewhat unnerving, and deer. Burns Pass is about .5 mile from the trailhead. At .75 mile, when the trail descends, watch closely for the blue ribbon in the tree. Several unmarked trails on your left lead up to a field. The woods here are more mature; note the larger oaks and sycamores. The views of the lake are brief and less frequent than on the lower trails. At 2.2 miles, the trail reaches another clearing with a scenic vista.

Bradley Pass, which is not marked on the lower trails, intersects the Rimrock Trail 2.9 miles from the trailhead. Less than .5 mile further, the trail descends, then takes a sharp left turn uphill. (Watch for the white-flagged crossover trail straight ahead.) The trail soon reaches a field, then returns to the woods and a view of the lake, and at 3.7 miles reaches an old quarry. (The Benjamin Trail also passes by this site.) Watch for the white-flagged crossover trail. As the Rimrock Trail nears East 535 Road, it crosses the same creek that the Benjamin and Rockbottom Trails cross.

After crossing the creek, the Rimrock Trail branches. We took the south branch, which travels up to and parallels County Route 458 for a short distance, then descends into the woods, where it meets the north branch. We veered left to continue to the end of the trail.

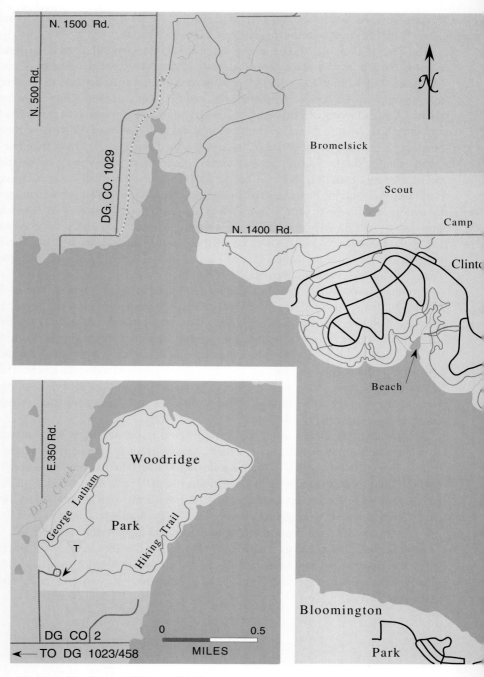

George Latham Hiking Trail

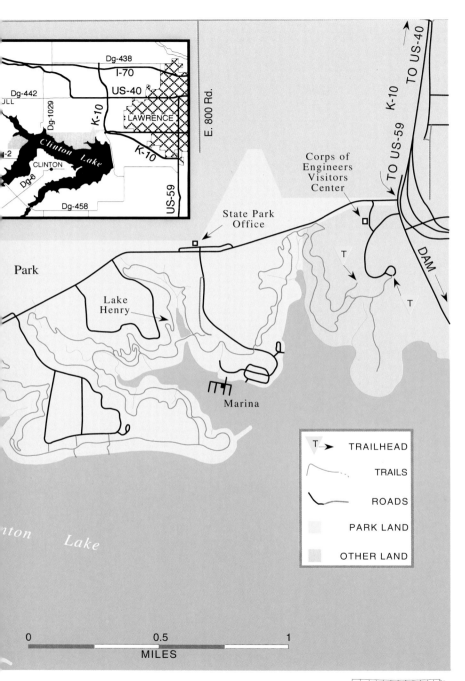

Clinton State Park Trails

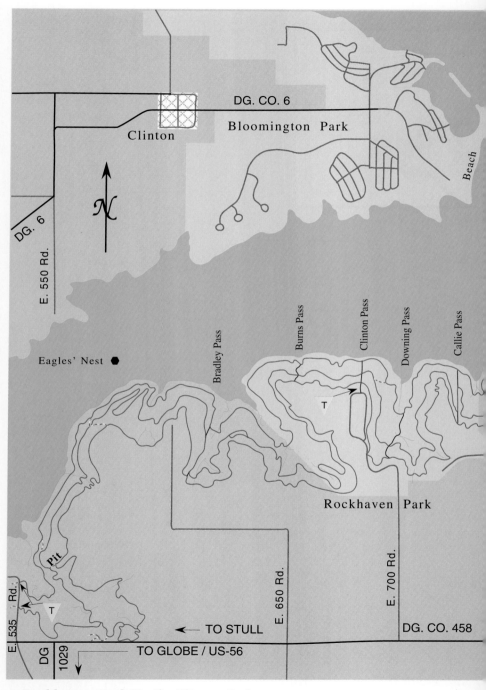

Rockhaven Park Trails, Clinton Lake

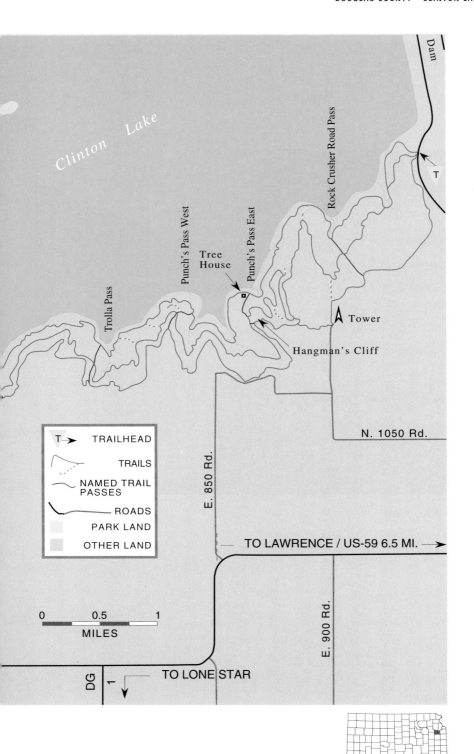

Clinton Lake

Dam

Rock Crusher Road Pass

Punch's Pass West

Punch's Pass East

Tree
House

Trolla Pass

Tower

Hangman's Cliff

N. 1050 Rd.

E. 850 Rd.

T → TRAILHEAD
TRAILS
NAMED TRAIL
PASSES
ROADS
PARK LAND
OTHER LAND

TO LAWRENCE / US-59 6.5 MI. →

E. 900 Rd.

0   0.5   1
MILES

TO LONE STAR

DG
1

Kansas River Trail

Kansas River Trails

More than 15 miles of trail follow the flood-control levee and wind through woodlands along the Kansas (Kaw) River, in northeast Lawrence. While the levee trails are flat and unshaded, they offer several vistas of the river and a pleasant hike through a mixed urban and rural landscape. We preferred the sand-packed mountain-bike trail that follows the river's edge east from the Massachusetts Street bridge, winding between floodplain terraces and descending into quiet, wooded ravines. Most of the sand-packed trail travels through scenic woodlands that flourish in the rich soils of the Kansas River floodplain. This trail is primarily a haunt of mountain bikers, who can zip around bends so quickly that you may find yourself scrambling to get out of their way. The views of the river from the east trail are spectacular. Ownership: Lawrence Parks & Recreation (785) 832-3450.

HIKE LENGTHS

East River Mountain Bike Trail .... 5 miles (one-way)
East Levee Trail .... 5 miles (one-way)
North Levee Trail .... 5.5 miles (one-way)

DIRECTIONS AND TRAIL ACCESS

Three trails start near the Massachusetts Street bridge in North Lawrence: the North Levee Trail, the East Levee Trail, and the East River Mountain Bike Trail. From the Kansas Turnpike, take the East Lawrence Exit and travel south on U.S. 59, which becomes 2nd Street. Before 2nd Street crosses the Massachusetts Street bridge, watch for Elm Street (on your left), and turn east. Street parking is available on Elm Street at the north end of the bridge. There is also a parking lot and access at North 4th Street and Walnut Street (2 blocks east and 1 block south of the north end of the bridge). To hike the North Levee Trail, follow the trail beneath the Massachusetts Street bridge and continue north on the levee. The East Levee Trail also begins on

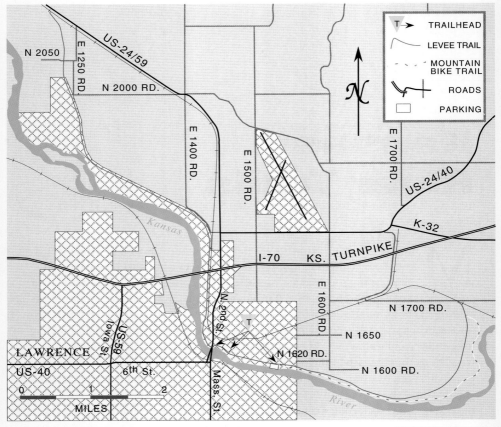

Kansas River Trails, Lawrence

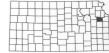

the levee by the bridge but travels east. The trailhead for the East River Mountain Bike Trail is located at the south end of North 8th Street (the road to the parking lot crosses the levee trail).

ℹ GENERAL INFORMATION

Had you walked these river trails one hundred thirty-five years ago, you would have seen the city of North Lawrence in the early stages of development. Then, this community was within Jefferson, not Douglas, County. Dense stands of trees covered the north bank of the river, while the south bank was relatively bare. Settlers on the south side were forced to cross the river to cut and carry back lumber. From the levee trails, you might have seen the long log cabin that John Baldwin built on the north riverbank at the foot of what is now 3rd Street. From this cabin, Baldwin operated a rope-drawn, flat-boat ferry. You also might have seen the Bowersock Building, built in 1865 or 1866 on the northwest corner of Locust and North 2nd Streets; the original post office at the north end of the bridge on the east side of 2nd Street (this site is now in the river); a general store, located near the intersection of Elm and North 4th Streets; a bakery on the southeast corner of Locust and North 2nd Streets; and a lumber yard on the northeast corner of North 3rd and Locust Streets. The first bridge across the river here was completed in 1863 by the Lawrence Bridge Company, despite the deaths of a bridge subcontractor and seven laborers, killed in Quantrill's August 1863 raid. Many of the bridge company's stock-holders lost most or all of their property in the raid. Construction, however, was not materially delayed, and the bridge was completed by December 1863. A 25¢ toll was charged for each crossing.*

THE HIKES

EAST RIVER MOUNTAIN BIKE TRAIL: This trail offers a great retreat from the city, as well as a unique opportunity to see beautiful sections of the Kansas River that can't be seen from any road. We enjoyed the many twists, turns, and climbs taken by this sand-packed and sometimes muddy trail through the wooded floodplain of the Kansas River. For the first 2 miles, the trail closely parallels the river, offering many scenic views. You may see great blue herons, ducks, bald eagles, and geese, as well as other water birds. Be prepared to climb over fallen trees and across several drainage areas and creekbeds. In some areas, bikes have cut deep gullies in the trail. As the map shows, the last 2 miles of the trail do not follow the river as closely. The trail eventually connects to the East Levee Trail before crossing the railroad tracks shown on the map. The sand makes this hike a good aerobic workout.

EAST LEVEE TRAIL: We returned on the East Levee Trail, which parallels the Kansas River east, then north, to N. 1700 Road, outside of the city limits. The flat, hard-packed levee trail is surfaced with limestone screenings. From the trailhead, the first mile east edges the backyards of several North Lawrence residents. The large, well-tended vegetable and flower gardens are testament to the rich soils that cover this river valley. We left the city limits behind about 1.5 miles from the trailhead, and the landscape to the end of the trail at N. 1700 Road is predominantly agricultural. Cultivated fields and pastures border the levee, and several farms can be seen from the trail. The unshaded levee offers a great vantage point for enjoying the endless, and often beautiful, Kansas skies.

* These and many other fascinating stories about the area are found in *Lawrence, Douglas County, Kansas: An Informal History* by David Dary (Lawrence: Allen Books, 1982) and *Early History of North Lawrence* (Lawrence: North Lawrence Civic Association, 1930).

NORTH LEVEE TRAIL: We followed the levee under the Massachusetts Street bridge and north past I-70 with the intent of connecting to the Kaw River Trail. A brochure prepared by the Lawrence Parks and Recreation Department describes a 4-mile trail that begins at the Riverfront Park, just west of the junction of U.S. 24/40 and 24/59. According to the brochure, the trail was completed in 1981 and follows the Kansas River to the old city landfill, now a wildlife area. Unfortunately, in May 1996 we found only short segments of the trail, and the remainder was completely overgrown. Several segments that we were able to follow were beneath a canopy of trees within view of the river. We found ourselves on the bank, just past Riverfront Park, where the river mirrored the spectacular clouds overhead. At another point, a piece of the trail led to a sandbar. Eventually, we gave up on trying to follow the Kaw River Trail through the underbrush, and ended up back on the North Levee Trail, which we followed to its end. Like the East Levee Trail, much of it passes through agricultural areas. We enjoyed the distant views of the tree-covered hills, and lingered for a spectacular sunset on our return trip.

K-10 Trail

The 5-mile K-10 Trail is the most recent addition to the network of biking/hiking trails in Lawrence. An additional 4.5 miles, from Clinton Parkway north to N. 1750 Road, were completed in spring 1998, after the fieldwork for this book was completed. While parts of the trail are definitely urban (sidewalks parallel to city streets), other parts leave the city boundaries altogether and travel through a more rural landscape. Our favorite section is the westernmost mile, which travels through the emergency spillway for Clinton Lake, a manmade channel where beautiful stratification of rock has been exposed on the north side of the trail. The views of Clinton Lake to the west and surrounding hills to the south and east make this a popular area to stop and enjoy the scenery. Ownership: Lawrence Parks & Recreation (785) 832-3450.

HIKE LENGTH

K-10 Trail ....9.5 miles (one-way)

DIRECTIONS AND TRAIL ACCESS

In the summer of 1997, only the first 5 miles of the trail had been completed, from 34th Street and U.S. 59, in Lawrence, to the west end of Clinton Parkway (23rd Street). An additional section of trail now travels north from Clinton Parkway along K-10, to N. 1750 Road, where parking is available. To reach the east end of the trail from I-70 (the Kansas Turnpike), take the West Lawrence Exit (Exit 202) and travel south on Iowa Street (U.S. 59). The trail begins at 34th Street, on the south side of Lawrence. Be aware, however, that the parking area near the trailhead is private parking for movie theater patrons.

To reach the west end of the trail from I-70, take the Lecompton/Lawrence Exit (Exit 197) and follow K-10 south to Clinton Parkway/N. 1400 Road Exit. Turn right, then immediately left onto old County Route 13/E. 900 Road to reach the dam. The

K-10 Trail

west end of the trail is just north of the dam on the east side of the road. You should have no trouble spotting the concrete trail, which snakes through the emergency spillway. Only roadside parking is available. Parking is also available at Wakarusa Drive, as shown on the map.

ℹ️ GENERAL INFORMATION

The K-10 Trail, uniquely paved in concrete, was funded under the federal ISTEA Program, which offers grants to the states to develop alternative transportation programs. The trail was designed to be accessible from many schools, parks, and neighborhoods in south Lawrence. The K-10 Trail generally parallels the Wakarusa River, about a quarter to three-quarters of a mile to the south. At the west end of the trail, and about a half mile south, the Wakarusa River is impounded to form Clinton Lake, which normally covers about 7,000 acres of land. Parts of the K-10 Trail also follow Yankee Tank Creek. I wrongly assumed that the name related to the "Yankee" orientation of nearby Lawrence, the Free-State stronghold during the "Bleeding Kansas" era. The name comes, however, from a story about neighboring farmers on the creek—Ezekiel Colman, an "outspoken abolitionist" from Boston, and Judge John Wakefield, a justice of a squatters' court in the Kansas Territory. Colman

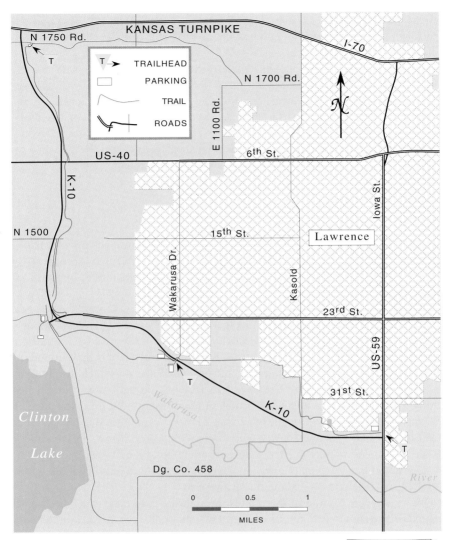

KANSAS TURNPIKE

N 1750 Rd.

I-70

T

T→ TRAILHEAD

PARKING

TRAIL

ROADS

N 1700 Rd.

E 1100 Rd.

N

US-40

6th St.

K-10

Iowa St.

N 1500

15th St.

Lawrence

Wakarusa Dr.

Kasold

23rd St.

US-59

T

31st St.

Wakarusa

K-10

T

Clinton

Lake

Dg. Co. 458

River

0   0.5   1

MILES

K-10 Trail, Lawrence

bought a quit claim, in 1858, to a farm just south of the Wakefield farm, and the relationship between the two men was not an amicable one:

> The judge and his Yankee neighbor were never good friends. Each set a row of hedge trees along the mutual boundary line—a no man's land—still visible today between the two farms. To water his livestock, Colman placed a tank along the stream that rose from Wakefield's spring. After a heavy rain when the stream ran full, the neighbors would say, "The Yankee's tank is running over." Consequently, the stream that meanders southeast to meet the Wakarusa near Brown's Grove is known as the Yankee Tank.*

🏃 THE HIKE

We started the trail at the east trailhead, by the movie theaters. If you are hiking or biking with children, you should be aware that the trail crosses several streets, including Kasold and Wakarusa Drive. There is a crossing light at Kasold, a four-lane street, and a warning sign at Wakarusa Drive.

For a short distance from the east trailhead, the landscape is rural. The trail edges a corn field and an old farm pond, now fenced, and follows the tree-lined border of Yankee Tank Creek. Before the trail crosses Kasold, it travels through a residential area. Between Kasold and Wakarusa Drive, the trail passes in and out of neighborhoods and undeveloped areas. Most of the trail is flat and unshaded. The most picturesque section lies west of Wakarusa Drive. When we hiked here, I thought the beautiful basin through which the trail winds was natural, but later found that it is the emergency spillway for Clinton Lake. Directly ahead lies Clinton Lake. Bordering the trail to the north are rock bluffs cut away by the Army Corps of Engineers during the construction of the emergency spillway. The exposed rockbeds, a geologist's delight, are Pennsylvanian in age, roughly 330 million years old, and are interbedded limestone and shales, deposited by a shallow, fluctuating sea.

One convenient feature of this trail is the mileage markings, which are actually painted on the concrete. In the summer of 1997, the trail ended at the 5-mile marker, at E. 900 Road, which runs parallel to the Clinton Lake dam. Since then, the trail was expanded to follow K-10 north for another 4.5 miles, to N. 1750 Road.

* From *Soil of Our Souls: Histories of the Clinton Lake Area Communities* by Martha J. Parker and Betty A. Laird (Lawrence: Coronado Press, 1976).

Prairie Spirit Trail

I f I could paint my mind's-eye picture of a Kansas landscape, it would look much like the farmland that borders the Prairie Spirit Rail-Trail: fields of ruler-straight crop rows, weathered barns, silos, big skies, cattle standing in farm ponds, and wildflowers growing among the prairie grasses. Once the Leavenworth, Lawrence, and Galveston Railroad ran along this trail, traveling from Leavenworth, Kansas, south to Galveston, Texas. The narrow railroad bridges have been resurfaced. Though now covered by vegetation, the remains of loading docks and pallets can still be seen next to the railbed. Phase 2 of the trail, 15 miles from Richmond to Ottawa, was opened on September 1, 1998, after we'd finished our fieldwork. Ownership: Kansas Department of Wildlife and Parks (785) 296-2281 and (785) 448-6767 (Garnett Chamber of Commerce).

NOTE: The Kansas Department of Wildlife and Parks requires trail users 16 and older to purchase permits. As of September 1998, a day pass cost $2.50 per person, and an annual permit cost $10.50 per person. Annual permits are good for the calendar year in which they are purchased. The same permit can be used on trails at Sand Hills State Park, near Hutchinson. Day passes may be purchased at the trailheads in Richmond, Garnett, and Welda (deposited in a self-pay box). Annual permits may also be purchased at the Garnett Chamber of Commerce office, Kansas Wildlife and Parks offices, Garnett City Hall, the County Clerk's office in Ottawa, or the Country Mart (23rd and Main Streets) in Ottawa. No permit is required to use the section of trail inside the city limits of Garnett.

HIKE LENGTHS
Ottawa to Richmond .... 15 miles
Richmond to Welda .... 18 miles

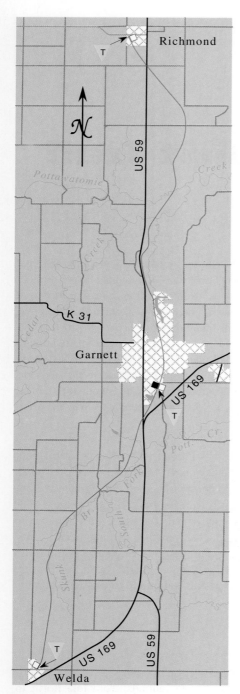

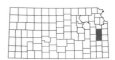

Prairie Spirit Trail

Prairie Spirit Trail

DIRECTIONS AND TRAIL ACCESS

From I-35, exit at Ottawa onto U.S. 59. To reach the access point at Richmond, travel south approximately 12 miles to Richmond and turn right (west) on Central Avenue for .5 mile. The trailhead is just west of the grain elevators. To reach the south access point at Welda, continue on U.S. 59 for another 18 miles to Welda. Take the only street through Welda west .4 mile to the trailhead. The trail can also be accessed at Garnett, the halfway point on the trail, by turning east off of U.S. 59 onto W. 7th Avenue. The trailhead is at the old train depot. The trailhead in Ottawa is at 17th Street and U.S. 59. From I-35, take the 15th Street Exit (Exit 185) and travel west to Main Street (U.S. 59). Turn left (south) to 17th Street. The trailhead is on the west side of 17th Street in the old KDOT rest stop.

GENERAL INFORMATION

The Prairie Spirit Trail is the longest rail-trail to be developed in Kansas. When completed, the trail will follow 50 miles of abandoned railbeds, from Iola north to Ottawa, part of a national movement to convert the thousands of miles of railroad lines abandoned each year into recreational trails. The railroad right-of-way that is now the Prairie Spirit Trail was "railbanked" pursuant to the National Trails System Act after the owner, KCT Railway, filed for abandonment of the line in May 1990. (Railbanking is an agreement between a railroad company, seeking to take a rail line out of service, and a private or government entity, for the use of the abandoned line as a recreational trail. The railroad corridor is thus preserved for future rail transportation.) Two years later, the ownership of the right-of-way was transferred to the Kansas Department of Wildlife and Parks for development of a rail-trail.

The first two phases of development of the Prairie Spirit Trail have been completed. The first phase was the 18-mile section from Richmond to Welda (opened in March 1996), the second was the 15-mile section from Ottawa to Richmond (opened in September 1998), and the last phase will be the 17-mile section from Welda south to Iola.

🚶 THE HIKE

Prairie Spirit Trail
....

We traveled the trail from north to south—from Richmond to Welda. Garnett, a picturesque town of 3,240, lies at the halfway point. The trail is 12 feet wide and is surfaced with compacted, crushed limestone, suitable for wheelchairs and bicycles as well as walking. "Squeeze gates" have been built where the trail intersects roads or streets to slow or stop travelers on the trail. Be sure to observe the stop signs on the trail—road traffic does not slow or stop for trail traffic. There are no guardrails along the trail, and at many points the drop-off on either side is steep and deep. At times, the trail is level with the tops of trees that border it. As we left Richmond, we traveled through scenic farmland. Few trails in Kansas can match the variety and profusion of wildflowers found along the Prairie Spirit Trail.

The trail from Richmond to Garnett is flat and crosses several creeks. The bridges themselves are works of art. Although parts of this section are lined by trees, they provide little shade because they grow at the base of the high railbed. Three miles from Garnett, the trail crosses Pottawatomie Creek, a popular habitat of deer and a variety of birds, including blue and green herons, kingfishers, and wood ducks, as well as other wildlife. As the trail nears Garnett, it passes North Lake Park, a beautiful 255-acre city park, including a 55-acre lake. The striking limestone walls and other improvements were constructed by the Civilian Conservation Corps in the 1930s. In Garnett, the surface of the trail changes to asphalt, and the trail is lit by decorative street lights. The trailhead at Garnett is located in the old brick Santa Fe Depot, originally constructed in 1870 but rebuilt in 1931 after the original depot was destroyed by fire. The depot closed in 1974 and was purchased in 1987 by the City of Garnett, which restored it in 1995 in conjunction with the opening of the Prairie Spirit Trail.

As the trail leaves Garnett, it passes Crystal Lake, the location of the city's water and electric plants. This fishing lake is another area where you may view a variety of wildlife. The trail from Garnett to Welda travels slightly uphill, but this change in grade is nearly imperceptible. Overall, we did not find the second half of the trail as scenic as the first, although sections of rolling hills and open prairie are very picturesque. While the trail is bordered with some trees, it seems more exposed. We found a large stand of purple coneflowers at one rocky section. Perhaps the designers of this trail realized that it was a perfect resting spot, because benches have been placed just off the trail.

Perry Lake Trail

Perry Lake

The 30-mile Perry Lake Trail is one of the gems of northeast Kansas, following the east shore of Perry Lake, located in the Delaware River Valley of the Glaciated Region. The views from the bluffs overlooking the lake are spectacular. Equally scenic are the wooded valleys, littered with limestone and rocks left by retreating glaciers. The trail is rugged and primitive in parts, and the switchbacks on the northern segments are challenging to even an experienced hiker. A new hiking/bicycle trail was completed in late spring 1996 in the Delaware Area of Perry State Park. The terrain on this trail is rocky and rugged, with switchbacks on the steeper hills. In summer, the dense cover of oaks and hickories on this secluded trail, coupled with the steam that seemed to rise from the damp ground and the many winding streams, made us feel as though we were walking through a tropical rainforest. As we finalized this book, an extension to Grasshopper Point was under construction.

The Thunder Ridge Nature Trail in the Slough Creek Public Use Area was recently expanded to create a 3-mile loop, with 30 interpretive stations. The trail is predominantly in oak-hickory forest habitat, with rolling hills and occasional prairie vistas. The brochure available in the Corps office includes a description of each point of interest corresponding to the numbered posts along the trail. The 2.4-mile nature trail in Perry State Park (not to be confused with Perry Park on the east side of the lake) meanders through wooded hills northwest of the dam. While sections of the trail are scenic, we did not find it as interesting as the Perry Lake Trail or the Delaware Area trail. Ownership: USACE (785) 597-5144; KDWP (785) 246-3449.

HUNTING REMINDER: Much of the Perry Lake Trail travels through the public hunting area that surrounds Perry Lake. We recommend that you wear bright colors—preferably an orange hunting vest and hat worn by hunters—and check with the park office as to hunting seasons.

HIKE LENGTHS

Perry Lake Trail .... 30-mile loop

    Estimated distance between access points:

        Kiowa Road access point to Old Military Trail trailhead .... 3.65 miles

        Old Military Trail trailhead to Lakewood Hills access .... 7.3 miles

        Lakewood Hills access point to Longview Park .... 1.75 miles

        Longview Park to Lakeside Village .... 2.75 miles

        Lakeside Village to Slough Creek trailhead...................................... 3.4 miles

        Slough Creek trailhead to Audubon Sanctuary Road .... 5.1 miles

        Audubon Sanctuary Road to 82nd Road... 2.6 miles

        82nd Road to Kiowa Road access point .... 3.68 miles

Delaware Area Trail

    Blue Loop.. 2 miles

    Blue/White Loop... 4 miles (to be extended)

Perry State Park Nature Trail .... 2.4-mile loop

Thunder Ridge Nature Trail .... 3-mile loop

 ## DIRECTIONS AND TRAIL ACCESS

Perry Lake Trail

Following are directions to eight access points on the Perry Lake Trail, from north to south/southwest:

KIOWA ROAD ACCESS: From U.S. 59 at Oskaloosa, travel west on K-92 for 5.15 miles to Kiowa Road and turn south. Note: Kiowa Road to the north is marked. Kiowa Road to the south (a dirt road) is not, but is just west of Kiowa Road north. (Coming from Perry, Kiowa Road is approximately 1.5 mile east of the intersection of Ferguson Road and K-92.) Travel .15 mile on Kiowa Road to the access point, which is immediately south of the concrete bridge over the Little Slough Creek. There is no designated parking area. Look for the trail by the "U.S. Reservation Boundary" mark, which is yellow. The blue blaze on the tree marking the trail is not easily seen from the road.

MILITARY TRAIL PARK TRAILHEAD: Turn south on Ferguson Road off of K-92 and look for the "Old Military Trail" sign. Turn west off of Ferguson Road into the Military Trail Park. There is parking at the trailhead, and the trail is marked as the "Perry Lake Trail."

LAKEWOOD HILLS ACCESS: From Ferguson Road, turn west onto 86th Road. This is a paved road, 2.2 miles south of the intersection of K-92 and Ferguson Road. Look for the "Slough Creek/Longview" sign, just before 86th Road. Travel 1.5 miles west on 86th Road to the Lakewood Hills subdivision and turn north to follow the road through the subdivision down to the lake and the boat ramp. The trail crosses this road just before the boat ramp.

LONGVIEW PARK ACCESS: Follow the directions to Lakewood Hills above, but continue on 86th Road as it turns south, past the Lakewood Hills entrance (this becomes Hamilton Road), toward Longview Park. Turn right (west) off of Hamilton Road at the first park road leading to Longview Park. There is a National Recreation Trail sign where the trail crosses this road and a small parking area approximately fifty feet south.

LAKESIDE VILLAGE ACCESS: From the intersection of K-92 and Ferguson Road, travel 4.1 miles south to the Lakeside Village entrance. The road entering Lakeside Village is Main Street. At the first juncture on Main Street, veer left to stay on Main Street. At the next juncture, veer right, again staying on Main Street, which leads to a boat ramp. Look for the blue blazes on the trees as you come in sight of the lake. Hikers can park at the ramp and walk back east to the trail.

SLOUGH CREEK PARK TRAILHEAD: This trailhead is in Slough Creek Public Use Area, west off of Slough Creek Road (which runs south from Ferguson Road). Look for the Slough Creek sign and the entrance, which is 5.1 miles south of the intersection of K-92 and Ferguson Road. Follow the "Slough Creek Day Use Area" signs, then proceed to the shower building and look for the trail-access parking area across from the shower building. Note: this trailhead is a stub off of the main trail.

AUDUBON SANCTUARY ACCESS: Take 74th Road east off of Ferguson Road and veer right (south) as the road travels through Tammy Heights subdivision. The trail crosses this road next to the gate to the sanctuary. Be sure to park as far off the side of the road as possible.

82ND ROAD ACCESS: 82nd Road intersects Ferguson Road approximately 2.7 miles south of the intersection of K-92 and Ferguson Road and approximately .5 mile south of 86th Road. Turn east onto 82nd Road and travel approximately .6 mile to an old farm road leading right (south). The trail is marked at the old farm road.

NOTE: The Corps of Engineers strongly encourages hikers to park at either the Old Military Trail access point or the Slough Creek Day Use Area, where parking is available and routine patrols are made. Trail maps and information are also available at these trailheads.

Access to Other Trails at Perry Lake

DELAWARE AREA TRAIL TRAILHEAD: From U.S. 24, take K-237 north 4.4 miles to Perry State Park. Continue northeast 1.1 miles past the state park office, across the

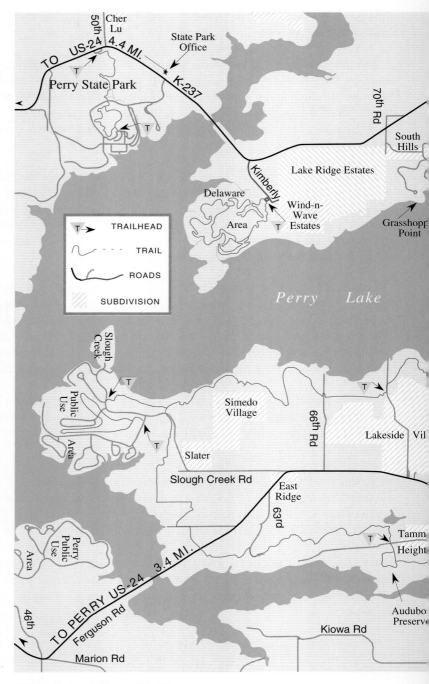

Perry Lake Hiking Trails

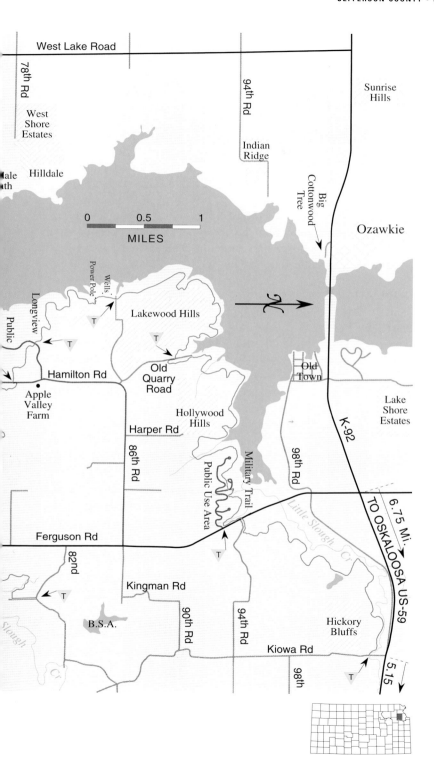

West Lake Road

78th Rd

94th Rd

West
Shore
Estates

Sunrise
Hills

Indian
Ridge

ale
th

Hilldale

Big
Cottonwood
Tree

Ozawkie

0   0.5   1

MILES

Power Pole

Wells

Longview

Lakewood Hills

T

Public

T

T

Hamilton Rd

Old
Quarry
Road

Old
Town

Lake
Shore
Estates

Apple
Valley
Farm

Hollywood
Hills

Harper Rd

86th Rd

98th Rd

K-92

Public Use Area

Military Trail

Little Slough Cr.

6.75 Mi.

Ferguson Rd

T

TO OSKALOOSA US-59

82nd

Kingman Rd

T

90th Rd

94th Rd

Slough

B.S.A.

Hickory
Bluffs

5.15

Cr.

Kiowa Rd

98th

T

lake to Kimberly Drive (the first fork in the road past the bridge). Turn east onto Kimberly Drive and travel .4 mile to the trailhead, where parking is available. There is a self-pay station (Kansas Department of Wildlife and Parks), as well as a bulletin board.

PERRY STATE PARK NATURE TRAIL TRAILHEAD: Follow the directions to the Delaware Area Trail, but turn east at the park road across from the state park office. Continue on this road .5 mile and turn left (east) at the road leading to the boat ramp. Continue .4 mile to the parking area near the showers and trailer dump station. Follow the gravel road behind the camping area to the trailhead, marked by a large sign.

THUNDER RIDGE NATURE TRAIL TRAILHEAD: This trail is in the Slough Creek Public Use Area, which is west off of Slough Creek Road. See the directions to the Slough Creek Public Use Area above. After you enter Slough Creek, watch for the campground entrance. The trailhead is adjacent.

ⓘ GENERAL INFORMATION

The land covered by Perry Lake was once part of the Delaware Reserve, a Delaware Indian reservation created by treaty in 1829 and ceded to the United States just weeks before Kansas was admitted as a territory in 1854. Shortly after, Congress established mail routes across Jefferson County, including one along the old military and freight road from Fort Leavenworth to Fort Riley. This road followed the Little Slough Creek Valley and can be seen from the segment of trail between the Old Quarry Road and the Old Military Trail trailhead. The military road crossed the Grasshopper River (renamed the Delaware River in 1875) at Ozawkie (then spelled "Osawkee"). At that time Ozawkie was on the east side of the Delaware River, about one mile north of the mouth of Little Slough Creek. The oldest town in Jefferson County, Ozawkie was named the county seat in 1855 but lost that status to Oskaloosa three years later as a result of political battles between proslavery and Free-State groups. (The majority of the early settlers of Ozawkie were proslavery.) The Free Staters settled on the west bank of the Delaware, in Pleasant Hill, where Ozawkie was relocated in 1960, in preparation for the construction of Perry Reservoir.

🚶🚶 THE HIKES

PERRY LAKE TRAIL: The trail can be hiked in either direction because it is blazed (in blue) both ways. The trail is predominantly wooded and may be challenging in the late spring and summer because of the thick undergrowth of encroaching poison ivy, nettles, briars, and other woody vegetation. Be prepared for ticks and mosquitoes in the warm seasons. We hiked this trail in its entirety in the winter, after the deer-hunting season. Starting at the Kiowa Road access point, we hiked southwest toward the Old

Military Park and proceeded counterclockwise. The first section of the trail, from Kiowa Road to 94th Road, is called the Little Slough Creek segment. It follows the creek along the creek bottoms at the eastern end and then along the bluffs overlooking the creek. The lake can be seen only briefly from this section of the trail.

Just before the trail reaches 94th Road, as shown on the map, it ascends to a once-cultivated field. Immediately past two rock-strewn washes, the trail branches right, at a pole, with the right branch circling a field and eventually rejoining the main trail, which descends to 94th Road. The trail follows 94th Road (gravel) west for a short distance before it crosses Ferguson Road and heads left (southeast) parallel to Ferguson Road. Look for the blue-tipped trail marker just outside the woods. Shortly after entering the woods, watch for the double blaze, indicating a sharp turn to the right. (If you miss the turn, the trail ahead leads to the parking area and trailhead in the Old Military Trail Park.) After turning, the trail climbs sharply and is blocked at times by fallen trees. This segment, between the Old Military Park trailhead and the Old Quarry Road (shown on the map), is the most rugged and perhaps the most scenic. The views of the lake from the bluffs are spectacular. Just before reaching the Old Quarry Road, the trail crosses an old field road. At the Old Quarry Road, turn right (north), and follow the road for approximately 350 feet to the two tall steel posts marking the trail.

From the Old Quarry Road, the trail climbs a ridge in full view of the lake. In January we saw several eagles soaring over the frozen lake. When the trail reaches a pond, veer right and up the hill. Eventually, the trail heads south through several cultivated fields, with houses to the east (your left). At the end of the field, watch for a stand of trees marked by a blue blaze. The trail passes through the trees to another field; it then crosses a paved road leading to the boat ramp of the Lakewood Hills subdivision. After traveling through a ravine and back up to a field, the trail becomes difficult to follow. It reenters the woods across the field, east of the second wellhead (shown on the map) and the light pole. After crossing the road in Longview Park, the trail intersects another trail marked by white blazes, leading to a hiker's campground. After passing the camping area, the Perry Lake Trail crosses Hamilton Road just south of Apple Valley Farms.

The trail continues on the other side of Hamilton Road next to the hedgerow and follows, and eventually crosses, Hoover Creek. (With no bridge, this creek may be hard to cross after rains.) The trail becomes difficult to follow after passing through an area littered with large boulders and follows an abandoned road for a short distance. When the trail reaches the road leading from Lakeside Village down to the lake, travel left (east) on the road for approximately 150 yards, then south, just beyond a small drainage ditch. The trail flattens as it travels along the lakeshore but eventually reenters the woods and descends into scenic valleys and streambeds. Look for the limestone foundation of an old homestead. When you reach a juncture on the trail, shortly before Slough Creek Public Use Area, take the trail to the left (east) to remain on the Perry Lake Trail loop. The trail to the right leads to the trailhead in Slough Creek Park.

The segment between Slough Creek Public Use Area and Ferguson Road is not as scenic as the northern part of the trail. After the trail crosses a paved park road, it again becomes difficult to follow, passing through tall weeds and woody vegetation and briefly following another abandoned road. After crossing Ferguson Road, the trail heads north along the Slough Creek arm of the lake and winds along a tree-canopied creekbed before reaching an old dirt road. Turn right (east). The trail veers left off the road, into the woods. Eventually the trail crosses the road leading to the sanctuary managed by the Topeka Audubon Society. Follow the road, entering the sanctuary. At the picnic area, a side trail to the right (south) leads to the Prairie Grass and Wildlife Preservation Area and to the bald eagle nesting area. This trail rejoins the main trail (which continues straight), unless you take the detour down to the lake.

After rejoining the main trail, be prepared for a climb. Watch for the Meditation Point spur, at the north end of the Audubon area, where members have placed a bench overlooking the Slough Creek arm of the lake. The trail continues north, then west across an intermittent stream, then north around the edge of a cultivated field to an old farm road. The trail follows the farm road about .25 mile before it intersects with 74th Road. The remainder of the trail follows county roads back to the starting point. Go right (east) on 82nd Road 1.2 miles to Kiowa Road. Turn left (north) and travel 2.5 miles to the access point.

Be sure to check in the Corps of Engineers office for locations of water sources along the trail and camping facilities.

DELAWARE AREA TRAIL: The trail is well marked and consists of an inner loop, blazed in blue, which connects to an outer loop, blazed in white. The western branch of the blue loop intersects the northwestern end of the white loop 1 mile from the trailhead, and the eastern branch of the blue loop intersects the north-eastern end of the white loop .3 mile from the trailhead. The inner blue loop is about 2 miles. The white-blazed trail covers about 2.5 miles, making the entire loop, excluding the inner section of blue trail, about a 4-mile hike. After we completed our fieldwork, the trail was expanded to include a loop up to Grasshopper Point, which is marked on the map. Like many other trails designed for bicycling, this trail packs a lot of mileage into a relatively small area by zigzagging—you may see another section of trail only a short distance away, as shown on the map.

At the trailhead, we veered right to cover the western half of the blue loop first. The trail descends to a rocky stream, then travels above a deep ravine. At .6 mile, the trail leaves the woods for a short distance. At .9 mile, the trail climbs a hill for a view of the lake, then intersects the white-blazed outer loop (to the right) which continues south. We followed the white-blazed loop. Double, or stacked, blazes indicate a sharp turn on the trail. Much of the outer loop winds along a ridge, providing a great view of the lake, even through summer's foliage. Frequently the trail descends toward the lake, only to climb immediately back up the ridge, which is rocky in places. Sections of the trail pass through woodlands so dense that the light is dim, even at midday.

At 2.6 miles from the trailhead, the white trail intersects with the eastern branch of the blue trail. (We backtracked west along the inner section of the blue trail to see what we had missed. This is only a .5 mile section through woods and, briefly, an open meadow. We returned to the intersection of the blue and white trails.) The trails join for about 50 yards, then the white trail branches to the right (southwest) and travels down the ridge toward a peninsula, then back up along a ledge over-looking the lake. The white trail reconnects to the blue trail only 150 yards further north on the blue trail. The last .4 mile of the trail travels through less mature tim-ber and woodlands. The Delaware Area is an isolated area, with no roads, picnic areas, or other improvements on this peninsula, other than the road leading to the trailhead. The terrain is challenging and resembles the northern sections of the Perry Lake Trail. All hikers and bikers are reminded to remain on the blue- or white-blazed trails and not to venture off on paths leading to adjacent private property.

PERRY STATE PARK NATURE TRAIL: The nature trail begins off of a gravel road behind the camping area, traveling uphill through young timber, and soon branches at the loop shown on the map. We followed the shorter branch to the right first, although the branch to the left (southeast) is more scenic. At less than .5 mile, the branches of the loop join and cross the park road. (Caution children to wait at the road.) Just past the road, the trail is rocky but it soon evens out, as it travels through an area dominated by dogwood, cedar, locust, and osage orange trees. At 1 mile, the trail leaves the woods and tunnels through a field of native tallgrass to a park shelter near the road to the state park office. The trail was originally designed to include an additional 3 miles through a wetlands area, but lack of funds prevented the comple-tion of this segment. On our return trip, we followed the southern branch of the loop, which travels through older, more scenic woodlands. Near the end of the loop, the trail travels along a ridge overlooking an especially picturesque valley.

THUNDER RIDGE NATURE TRAIL: After we completed the fieldwork for this book, the nature trail in the Slough Creek Public Use Area was expanded to create a 3-mile loop with 30 interpretative stations, referenced in the trail brochure. While we have not hiked this trail, the description provided by the natural resource management specialist for the Corps of Engineers sounds inviting. The Corps has recently con-structed new rock and bridge crossings on the trail and added benches for rest stops. The trail travels through an area forested predominantly in oaks and hickories, with rolling hills and prairie vistas. The Corps notes that the trail is well maintained and can be hiked at any time of the year, including summer, when the trail is mowed, weed-whipped, and cleared. The trail includes "spur" access to each campground, which allows hikers to leave the trail for water or restroom needs.

Ernie Miller Park

Ernie Miller Park

M y children hiked the trails in Ernie Miller Park on school field trips long before I visited it. As urban development in Johnson County has pushed south and west, Ernie Miller Park has become an island of woodlands and prairie and a refuge for a variety of wildlife. The park is secluded and even primitive in some areas, although you may hear traffic sounds at certain points along the trail. The southern entry to the Ridge Trail, which crosses a footbridge and climbs through a canopy of trees, is especially picturesque. The trails also pass through prairie, where colorful wildflowers are prolific in spring, summer, and fall. Ownership: Johnson County Parks & Recreation (913) 764-7759.

HIKE LENGTHS

Old South Trail .... 1.75 miles
Ridge Trail .... .75 mile
Bittersweet Nature Trail .... .33 mile

DIRECTIONS AND TRAIL ACCESS

The Ernie Miller Park is off K-7, 3.1 miles south of K-10 and 7.5 miles south of Shawnee Mission Parkway, on the west side of K-7. The trailhead to the Old South Trail starts just inside the park's entrance, by the picnic shelter. The Bittersweet Nature Trail starts by the Information Shelter/Nature Center. The Ridge Trail is accessed from either the Bittersweet Trail or the Old South Trail.

GENERAL INFORMATION

The 113 acres of Ernie Miller Park were purchased by the Johnson County Park and Recreation District from the City of Olathe in 1972. The land had had only two prior owners—the Josiah Hayes family, from 1861 to 1964, and John W. Breyfogle, who owned the land until it was purchased in 1966 by the City of Olathe. The park is named after Ernie Miller, sometimes called "Mr. Olathe," who died in 1966. A ranger and a park naturalist staff the park and offer many educational programs and interpretive activities designed to stimulate interest in the environment and a variety of ecological habitats. The predominant feature of the park's trails is the woodlands. Bur oaks, black walnuts, and hickories tower overhead. More unusual trees include shingle oak (not common in Kansas and easily identified by its elliptic leaves, with no teeth or lobes), western buckeye (its palmate leaves have 7 leaflets, and its shiny red-brown seeds are slightly poisonous), and the pawpaw tree (a small tree with banana-like fruit).

🏃 THE HIKES

Before starting your hike, stop at the Nature Center for a map of all of the trails and facilities. Signs at the Nature Center also include maps of the trails. The more rugged of the trails are the Old South Trail and the Ridge Trail. A description of the Ridge Trail is included in the description of the Old South Trail.

OLD SOUTH TRAIL: The Old South Trail can be accessed by a paved path leading from the Nature Center. The trail is a loop that travels primarily through scenic woods and along steams, although it also skirts two native grass restoration areas, where you will see a wide variety of prairie wildflowers. The terrain is relatively flat and even, although the trail crosses several dry creekbeds and climbs in and out of a valley. From the trailhead, the trail winds south through the woods for about .4 mile, then heads west through a valley for about .2 mile, before traveling north for another .2 mile to a fork. This is the only confusing point on the trail. At first glance, there appear to be four options—two paved trails and two wood-chipped trails. Ignore the wood-chipped paths that wrap to your left and to your right. The paved trail that continues north (slightly to your right) leads to the amphitheater. The trail that turns west to cross the pedestrian bridge leads to the Ridge Trail described in the next paragraph. If you opt for the amphitheater, the trail intersects another paved trail leading right (northeast). This trail returns to the trailhead, if you turn right (east) at the next intersecting paved trail, or to the Nature Center, if you turn left (northwest). Another option at the amphitheater is to continue straight ahead, passing the pond on your right, to connect to the Bittersweet Nature Trail, a short distance past the pond. When you intersect the Bittersweet Nature Trail, you can turn right (east), which is the shortest route to the Nature Center, or continue northwest to travel the remainder of the Bittersweet Nature Trail.

RIDGE TRAIL: If you opt for this trail, turn left and cross the pedestrian bridge over Little Cedar Creek. Lush woods line the creek and cover the ridge. After crossing the bridge, you can follow the Upper Ridge Trail straight ahead (a steep and sometimes slippery climb to the top of the ridge), or follow the Lower Ridge Trail to the right (which travels along Little Cedar Creek). Both are wooded and scenic. The Upper Ridge Trail and the Lower Ridge Trail eventually merge, then cross the rocky Little Cedar Creek before intersecting with the paved Bittersweet Nature Trail. You can take the paved trail either direction to return to the Nature Center.

BITTERSWEET NATURE TRAIL: This is a short, paved nature trail that is accessed from the Nature Center and is handicapped-accessible. The focus of the trail is the deciduous forest through which it travels. Watch for woodland wildflowers, such as Dutchman's britches, woodland phlox, jack-in-the-pulpit, and rose verbena. Trails leading off of the Bittersweet Nature Trail connect to the Ridge Trail and the Old South Trail.

Indian Creek/Tomahawk Creek Trail

Indian Creek/ Tomahawk Creek Trail

M ore than 12 miles of paved trail follow a greenbelt along Indian Creek, through Overland Park, and along Tomahawk Creek, through Leawood. This urban trail weaves through a well-landscaped business park, where office buildings rise above the surrounding trees, residential areas, and thirteen park areas in Overland Park. Much of the trail is surprisingly quiet, and parts are even secluded, despite the fact that it travels within close proximity of several major highways and busy city streets. This trail is well-traveled by walkers, bikers, roller-bladers, and runners; on a sunny day in spring or fall, you may even encounter a traffic jam on the trail. Designed to accommodate two-way bike passage, the 10-foot wide asphalt trail showcases the natural beauty of the creeks and the gallery forest that borders the creeks. Eventually, it will connect to an even larger network of trails. Ownership: City of Overland Park (913) 451-9165.

HIKE LENGTH
Indian Creek/Tomahawk Creek Trail................ approximately 12 miles one-way

DIRECTIONS AND TRAIL ACCESS

The Indian Creek/Tomahawk Creek Trail spans Overland Park and Leawood, in Johnson County. Most of the trail is east of U.S. 69 and south of 103rd Street (which is north of I-435). As the map indicates, the trail can be accessed at many points:

WEST TRAILHEAD: This is in Overland Park, at the intersection of 119th Street and Quivira.

CORPORATE WOODS ACCESS: From College Boulevard (east of U.S. 69 and west of Antioch) turn north at Indian Creek Parkway and continue past 109th Street (watch for a small park area, with a shelter and trail sign, where parking is available).

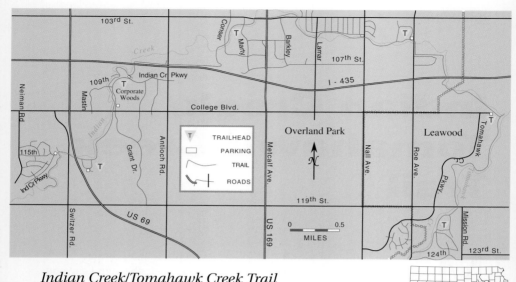

Indian Creek/Tomahawk Creek Trail

NALL HILLS PARK ACCESS: This is in Overland Park, south of 103rd Street, north of I-435, and east of Lamar Avenue.

LEAWOOD CITY PARK ACCESS: The eastern-most point on the trail is a loop into Leawood City Park, bordered on the north by I-435. College Boulevard lies to the south, but the park cannot be accessed from it. From the intersection of 103rd Street and Mission Road, continue east on 103rd Street to Lee Boulevard; turn south on Lee and follow it under I-435 to the park.

[i] GENERAL INFORMATION

The City of Overland Park, named after the historical Overland Trail, began accumulating land for the Indian Creek Trail in the late 1960s, long before the exercise craze hit, and not many years after the city was incorporated in 1960. Planners designed the trail to stimulate people to exercise, and two exercise stretches were built, one with 20 stations and the other with 16. Most of the land along Indian Creek is in the floodplain and was donated to the city because it was undesirable for commercial development. Construction on the trail began in 1977. Overland Park's 8.16 miles of trail and Leawood's 4.3 miles were completed in 1984. As you hike some of the more secluded sections, you may find it hard to believe you're in one of the most populated counties in Kansas. Overland Park, the largest city in Johnson County, has been one of the fastest-growing cities in the state, with a population of 572 in 1940, 82,000 in 1980, 111,790 in 1990, and 135,000 in 1997. It is now the fourth largest city in Kansas, just behind Topeka.

THE HIKE

We began the trail at the Cross Creek Park, shown on the map, and headed northeast, following Indian Creek through the park. The trail crosses under U.S. 69 and loops around Indian Valley Park, where you may see soccer games in progress in spring and fall. The trail then heads north through Shannon Valley Park for .6 mile, edging tree-lined Indian Creek. The next segment of trail spans a portion of Corporate Woods Park, where office buildings stand among trees in a "naturally" landscaped setting. At 109th Street, a spur trail to Mastin Street branches left (west). Continue north across 109th Street, but watch for the trail to branch again toward the west, a scenic spur through the woods, across a bridge and over to Farley Street. The next half mile to I-435 is one of the prettiest segments of the trail, which tunnels under a lush canopy of mature hardwoods. Watch for the trail to branch near a large trail sign. To remain on the trail, follow the left branch, which travels north under I-435. The other branch continues east for .5 mile to an access point on Antioch Road.

The next mile, which runs adjacent to, and in full view of, I-435, was our least favorite. At the east end of the Brookridge Country Club, the trail turns north, away from the highway, around an apartment complex, and toward the Indian Creek Recreation Center and Pinehurst West Park. From here, the trail crosses under Metcalf Avenue, just north of 103rd Street. East of Metcalf, the trail climbs a picturesque, wooded hill overlooking Indian Creek, another quiet area on the trail, then travels through James Place Park. The next park on the trail is Nall Hills Park. To the east of Nall, the trail loops around Roe Park, then crosses under Roe Avenue. Here, the trail climbs up to, and follows, the sidewalk on the east side of, and adjacent to, Roe in a commercially-developed area of Overland Park. Past the garden center, the trail turns east towards Foxhill North Park, a scenic segment.

Just west of Mission Road, at the south end of Foxhill North Park, the trail crosses under I-435, travels through Foxhill South Park, and heads toward the confluence of Indian Creek and Tomahawk Creek. Watch for the trail to branch before it reaches Leawood City Park, where it loops around the park. The branch to the right (south) follows Tomahawk Creek through the Tomahawk Creek Greenway, ending at Hawthorne Valley Park. The next 4 miles of trail pass in and out of scenic woodlands along Tomahawk Creek, through residential areas, and within view of some commercial developments near 119th Street. As the trail nears Hawthorne Valley Park, south of 119th Street, it dips into a quiet wooded valley.

Mill Creek Streamway Park Trail

Mill Creek Streamway Park

The Mill Creek Streamway Park Trail, which ties into Shawnee Mission Park, is an asphalt trail that follows Mill Creek over widely-varied terrain. The hilly 2-mile section through woodlands between the Midland Drive access point and the loop by the lake dam is especially picturesque. Benches set off from the trail along the ridge overlook pastures in the valley below. Bluebird houses line the trail. After descending the ridge, the trail passes through meadows and, at the lake dam access point, through wetlands, a prime location for bird watching. At the north end, the trail crosses a bridge to Nelson's Island in the Kansas River. The 1-mile loop on the island is heavily wooded and rich in wildlife. In spring and summer, when the dense foliage of the towering, vine-covered cottonwood, hackberry, and hickory trees blocks the sun, the forest on the island seems almost primeval. In the summer of 1997, a 3-mile extension was added at the south end of the trail, linking it to 95th Street; eventually the trail will connect to Ernie Miller Park in Olathe. (Note: for a map of the trail south of Shawnee Mission Parkway, see Shawnee Mission Park Trail map.) Ownership: Johnson County Parks & Recreation (913) 831-3355.

HIKE LENGTH

Approximately 11.16 miles one-way, from the end of Nelson's Island to 95th Street. The hike can be broken into the following segments. (Distances shown are one-way, except for the dam loop and the Nelson Island loop.)

Shelter 8 access point to 87th Lane access point .... 1.57 miles

87th Lane access point to 95th Street .... 1.25 miles

Shelter 8 access point to the Midland Drive access point............... 3.43 miles

Dam loop, starting at the Shelter 8 access point.............................. 1.66 miles

Midland Drive access point to Barker Road access point .... 1.16 miles

Barker Road access point to the Wilder Road access point .... 2.95 miles

Wilder Road access point to Nelson Island pedestrian bridge.......... .43 mile

Nelson Island Loop.. 1 mile

⌐⊕ DIRECTIONS AND TRAIL ACCESS

The Mill Creek Streamway Park Trail can be accessed at the following points:

SHAWNEE MISSION PARK, SHELTER 8 ACCESS: Shawnee Mission Park is generally located north of K-10, south of Shawnee Mission Parkway, east of K-7, and west of I-435. From Shawnee Mission Parkway, exit south onto I-435. Take the Midland Drive Exit (watch for the Shawnee Mission Park sign just before the exit). Turn left (east) onto Midland Drive, passing under the overpass. At the four-way stop (Renner Road) turn right (south) onto Renner. Continue on Renner to the main entrance to Shawnee Mission Park on the right (west). The entrance is just south of the Theater in the Park entrance. After entering the park, veer right past the Visitors Center. Remain on this road until it ends at the intersection with Barkley Road (marked by a stop sign). Turn right and continue on Barkley Road past the marina and across the dam. The access point is on the right side of the road (opposite the parking area for shelter 8), just past the dam, at the crest of the hill. Parking is available. A large park sign with a map marks the trailhead.

MIDLAND DRIVE ACCESS: Turn south onto Midland Drive off of Shawnee Mission Parkway. Midland Drive is approximately 1 mile west of I-435 and on the south side of Shawnee Mission Parkway. You will immediately see a sign for the Mill Creek Streamway Park Trail. There is a parking lot.

BARKER ROAD ACCESS: Turn north onto Barker Road off of Shawnee Mission Parkway. (This is just across from Midland Drive, but the road to the north is Barker.) Continue on Barker until you see the well-marked entrance to the trail on the left (west) side. There are a large parking area, restroom facilities, and a playground.

WILDER ROAD ACCESS: Take the Holliday Drive Exit off of I-435 (this exit is south of I-70, just past the bridge over the Kansas River, and 1 mile north of the Johnson Drive exit.) Travel southwest on Holliday Drive for approximately 1 mile to the four-way stop in the community of Holliday. Turn right (north) at the stop sign, cross the railroad tracks, and watch for the sign marking the entrance. There are parking and restroom facilities.

87TH LANE ACCESS: From I-435, exit west at 87th Street. Follow 87th Street to 87th Lane and take it south to the trailhead. There is a parking area and shelter.

ⓘ GENERAL INFORMATION

The Mill Creek Streamway Park Trail, which ties into Shawnee Mission Park on the west boundary, is part of a unique concept commonly called the Streamway Park System. Johnson County's goal is to acquire and develop over the next 20–30 years a linear park system, "greenways" covering over 100 miles along eight of the major streamways. Where possible, the greenways are to be linked to existing parks. Much of the land for the streamway parks lies within the 100-year floodplain and is being acquired by easements, donations, and purchases. The width of the greenway may range from 200 feet to .125-mile on one or both sides of the stream. When completed, the Mill Creek Streamway Park, the pilot development, will include over 15 miles of pedestrian/biking trails, reaching from Nelson's Island in the Kansas River on the north end to Olathe on the south, with offshoots to Ernie Miller Park, Prairie Center Park, Lake Olathe, and Cedar Lake.

Nelson's Island is a 15-acre island donated in 1992 to the Parks and Recreation Foundation of Johnson County. It is named after Frank Nelson, who is said to have lived on the island in the late 1920s and 1930s. Although the island was used for a sand plant at one point, the only other visitors have been occasional fishermen able to reach the island when water was low. In May of 1996, a state archaeologist confirmed the discovery of remnants of a 120-foot dam across Mill Creek, about .5 mile southwest of the Wilder Road access point. The dam provided power for a Shawnee Indian saw- and grist-mill built in 1837 to induce the Shawnee Indians to leave Ohio. A flood destroyed the mill in 1844, and it was never rebuilt.

THE HIKE

Little guidance, other than the map included in this chapter, is needed to hike this trail. The entire trail is asphalt and large signs with maps are at each of the access points, as well as at several points along the trail. Beginning at the trailhead south of the dam, a 1.6-mile loop travels through the meadows and by the wetlands. At the north end of the loop, you can continue across the pedestrian bridge, after which the trail runs north through meadows, then climbs and winds along a ridge through woods, one of our favorite sections of the trail, as well as one of the most strenuous. After the trail descends from the ridge and crosses the bridge over Mill Creek, veer right (east) to reach the Midland Drive access point or left (northwest) to continue.

The remainder of the trail north of Shawnee Mission Parkway is less wild, with few changes in elevation. Near the Barker Road access point, the trail borders a subdivision and a sports complex. You may have some difficulty following the trail once it reaches Johnson Drive (55th Street). When the trail intersects the sidewalk on Johnson Drive, turn right (west) and walk across the Johnson Drive (55th Street) bridge. Once over the bridge, the trail heads back east around the ball diamonds and follows Mill Creek, crossing it twice before reaching the Wilder Road parking area. The trail passes through prairie areas and along the corridor of trees bordering Mill Creek. Wildlife is abundant. After crossing the first bridge over Mill Creek, the trail loops around an island of trees before it reaches the second bridge. The trail on Nelson's Island consists of two loops connected by a short segment of trail. The towering woods and dense understory that cover the island virtually envelop you. At several points on the north side of the island, the trail provides beautiful vistas of the Kansas River.

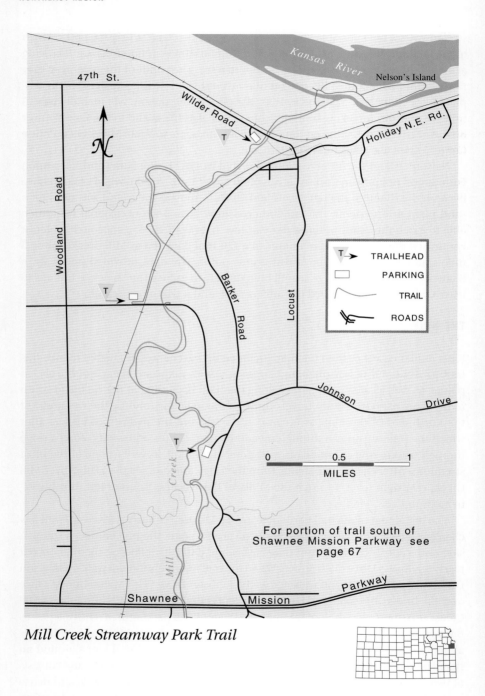

Mill Creek Streamway Park Trail

Within the map:

Kansas River

Nelson's Island

47th St.

Wilder Road

Holiday N.E. Rd.

Woodland Road

Barker Road

Locust

T

TRAILHEAD

PARKING

TRAIL

ROADS

Johnson Drive

Creek

Mill

0   0.5   1
MILES

For portion of trail south of Shawnee Mission Parkway see page 67

Shawnee Mission Parkway

The newest addition to the trail is a 2.82-mile segment leading south to 95th Street from the 2-mile dam loop just south of the dam. If you access the dam loop from the shelter 8 access point, take the loop left (south) and then west. You should have no trouble spotting the intersecting trail on your left at the bottom of the hill. The first section of the trail skirts the gallery forest and large power lines along Mill Creek. Much of the trail to the 87th Lane access point is exposed and flat and parallels the railroad tracks. Sections of the trail pass through scenic wooded areas along the creek.

The Prairie Center

The Prairie Center

T he Prairie Center is a 293-acre preserve just west of downtown Olathe, in Johnson County. Six miles of trails wind through it, across hills of native tall-grass into timbered stretches of oak, hickory, locust, and hackberry, and crossing tree-lined creekbeds, at times impassable because of high water. The Osborne East Trail and the Wagner West Trail are self-guided circular trails. A trail guide to the Osborne East Trail is available at the Cedar Niles entrance, explaining the natural history of the area and certain features marked by signposts. When we hiked, no trail guide was available for the Wagner West Trail, and we were unable to precisely determine its route. However, all trails on the west side of the preserve were mapped. Ownership: KDWP (913) 894-9113.

HIKE LENGTHS

Osborne East Trail .... 1.6 miles
Wagner West Trail .... 1.2 miles

Combined with the back trails, the total is approximately 6 miles.

DIRECTIONS

Exit west off of I-35 onto K-150 (135th Street), or take K-7 until it intersects with K-150. Travel west on this highway for approximately 6 miles (from I-35) or 3 miles (from K-7) to Cedar Niles Road. The Prairie Center is marked by a large sign and a stone house. Turn south onto Cedar Niles Road to the parking area behind the homestead. The Prairie Center trails also can be accessed from the western boundary of the Prairie Center by continuing on K-150 (135th Street) to Moonlight Road. Travel south on Moonlight Road for approximately .3 mile to the parking area. When Cedar Creek is impassable, the Moonlight Road trailhead provides access to the trails on the western half.

[i] GENERAL INFORMATION

The Prairie Center was once the homestead of George W. and Frieda Algire, who settled at the site in 1913. Using limestone taken from this land, George Algire, a mason, hand-built the stone house, a brooder house, a chicken house, a garage, stone walls, and lamp posts. Near the roof of the house, hidden behind a stone slab on which he carved the letter "A," Algire kept a handwritten history of the times in a fruit jar. Pioneers passing through this area in covered wagons often camped in the pastures. The origins of the Prairie Center can be traced to R. C. Wagner and Larry Wagner, his son, who bought the land in 1963. The Wagners preserved the original prairie that remained on the land; replanted native tallgrasses, such as little and big bluestem, Indian grass, and switchgrass; and built trails. In 1983, the Grassland Heritage Foundation acquired the property and continued the restoration efforts begun by the Wagners. Seven years later, ownership was transferred to the State of Kansas, although the Grassland Heritage Foundation continues to operate the Prairie Center.*

𝕏 THE HIKE

The Osborne East Trail begins immediately west of the parking area off of Cedar Niles Road. About two-thirds of the East Trail passes through native tallgrass, including both virgin and reseeded prairie. A wide variety of wildflowers is interspersed with the grasses, and Mead's milkweed deserves special mention. One of the rarest plants of the tallgrass prairie, it is one of only two globally threatened plants to occur in Kansas. This modest plant, with its single cluster of individually stalked white flowers, often goes unnoticed in a field of showier wildflowers. To follow the East Trail markers in order, head left (south) from the nature trail sign. The first third of the trail parallels Cedar Niles Road. A tract of virgin prairie appears at markers 8 and 9. As the trail travels south, it intersects several other unmarked trails as shown on the map. To follow the self-guided trail, continue south to the hedgerow of osage orange trees at marker 16, where the trail turns right (west). This portion, running along the southeastern part of the Prairie Center, presents striking views of the tallgrass. The trail follows the hedgerow for a short distance, then veers northwest, toward a large pond and picnic area (including a restroom).

At the southern edge of the picnic area, the trail splits in three. The left fork turns back south into the woods and travels through the western half of the Center. The other two forks skirt opposite sides of the picnic area, joining at the north by a grove of cedar trees marking the homestead of James Lawrence, who acquired the property in 1860. Here, the self-guided trail continues straight (northeast) along the pond dam and returns to the parking area. The left trail travels northwest down the hill to Cedar

* This and other information about the Prairie Center can found in "A Piece of History Saved: The Prairie Center" by Steven B. Case in *Kansas Wildlife and Parks,* September/October 1994.

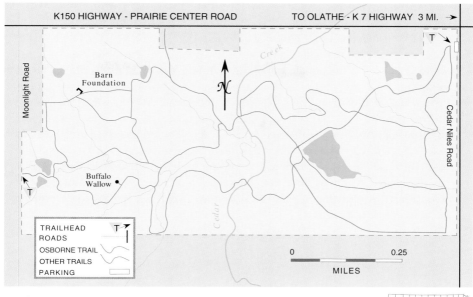

The Prairie Center Trails

Creek and through the western half of the Prairie Center. Shortly before the creek, the trail intersects two trails on the right (north) side. The second trail of these parallels the creek for a short distance before rejoining the first. After converging, these trails eventually head east back to the Osborne East Trail.

If you continue across Cedar Creek, you may have difficulty if there have been recent rains. (If the water is high or swift, turn back.) After crossing, look for the stone wall on your left. The trail soon intersects another trail to the left. The left trail proceeds south and then west, bypassing the northwestern portion of the Prairie Center. If you go straight, the trail continues northwest through a wooded area and then through a field once planted in brome. Much of this portion is mowed grass and at times may be difficult to follow. When you reach the next fork in the trail, do not veer right—that trail dead-ends at 135th Street. Continue straight (northwest) and then veer left (southwest) at the pond dam. The trail continues south past the dam and travels gradually uphill through pastures, eventually becoming part of the Wagner West Trail. Look for the markers.

There are several trail loops off of the Wagner Trail. The first two, on the right, lead westerly and eventually intersect near the foundation of an old barn. Continue west after the intersection until you are in view of the houses along Moonlight Road. Take the left trail (south), paralleling Moonlight Road, toward the woods. When you come to the fork in the woods, go right, toward the pond. This part can be very muddy after a rain. At the southern tip of the pond, the trail forks again. Going right (west) leads to the parking area on Moonlight Road. Veer left. Here you pick up the beginning of the Wagner Trail near the Moonlight Road trailhead. Much of this portion of the trail is wooded. Watch for the buffalo wallow on your left. Shortly after this you will reach another juncture. The left trail crosses a creek and travels northeast before it intersects the trail leading from the cedar groves and picnic area described above. The right trail travels south across a small creek, through dogwood and sumac, before turning back north, crossing the creek again. It then continues east before it crosses Cedar Creek, south of the first crossing. Water often flows over the concrete road that crosses the creek—exercise caution. The trail continues east until it reaches the picnic area. Here you can pick up the rest of the Osborne East Trail at the north end of the picnic area by crossing the pond dam. This trail will take you back to the parking area on Cedar Niles Road.

Shawnee Mission Park

T he network of trails surrounding Shawnee Mission Lake provides a scenic retreat from nearby suburban areas. The South Shore Trail (hiking and equestrian use only) travels along a secluded, wooded ridge above the lake, skirting each cove. In winter, there are many excellent vantage points for observing the geese, ducks, and herons that frequent the lake. At times the trail descends to cross rocky, and sometimes flooded, streambeds, only to ascend water-carved limestone steps. Well-worn foot paths lead down to the lake. The North Shore Trail (hiking and biking) takes you uphill north of the lake and meanders through quiet woodlands. At times, this trail is difficult to follow because of numerous side-trails. Ownership: Johnson County Parks & Recreation (913) 438-7275.

HIKE LENGTHS

South Shore Trail .... 3 miles (one-way)
North Shore Trail .... .6 mile one-way (can be extended by hiking the
                                        numerous foot/bike trails leading from the trail)
Sertoma Woodland Trail .... .4 mile

The 11-mile Mill Creek Streamway Park Trail (see p. 53) can also be accessed from Shawnee Mission Park.

DIRECTIONS AND TRAIL ACCESS

Shawnee Mission Park is generally located north of K-10, south of Shawnee Mission Parkway, east of K-7, and west of I-435.

SOUTH SHORE TRAIL: From Shawnee Mission Parkway, exit south onto I-435. Take the Midland Drive exit off of I-435 (watch for the Shawnee Mission Park sign just before the exit). Turn left (east) onto Midland Drive, passing under the overpass. At

South Shore Trail, Shawnee Mission Park

the four-way stop (Renner Road) turn right (south) onto Renner. Continue on Renner to the main entrance to Shawnee Mission Park on the right (west) side. Veer left at the Visitors Center. When the road divides, take the right branch (Barkley Circle—the branch to the left is Barkley Drive). Continue on Barkley Circle for .25 mile to the Walnut Grove parking area. The trail also can be accessed by taking the left branch past the Visitor's Center for about .5 mile to the shelter 10 parking area, on the north side of the road. Alternatively, continue past shelter 10 on Barkley Drive to shelter 8 near the dam. Parking is available. Note: to avoid hiking this trail out and back, you can take two cars and park one at the end of the trail in the parking area for shelter 8.

NORTH SHORE TRAIL: Follow the directions to the South Shore Trail, but veer right at the Visitors Center. Remain on Barkley Drive until it reaches a T intersection. Turn right and continue on Barkley Drive past the marina. Parallel parking is available just before the dam, and the trailhead is marked by a large sign on the right side of the road. Note: this trail appears only as a dashed line on the map because bike use is constantly creating new side-trails too numerous to map.

SERTOMA WOODLAND TRAIL: Follow the directions to the North Shore Trail. After turning right onto Barkley Drive, watch for Small Lakes Road on your right. The trail may be accessed either at the shelter 2 parking lot or at the Theater in the Park concession stand.

GENERAL INFORMATION

Shawnee Mission Park is the largest park in Johnson County, covering 1,250 acres, and includes a 150-acre lake, which opened in May 1964. The land was acquired from ten farms. The trails in Shawnee Mission Park cross a number of streams and rivulets, which eventually feed into Mill Creek. Mill Creek then enters the Kansas River close to Nelson Island, at the north end of the Mill Creek Streamway Park. Even in the driest weather, areas along the trails close to the watercourses are cool and moist, as evidenced by the dense understory of grasses and herbaceous plants. The area is rich in wildlife: watch for fox, deer, raccoon, coyote, and opossum tracks. In spring and early summer, woodland wildflowers, such as blue phlox, and flowering trees, such as rough-leaved dogwood and redbud, can be seen along the trail.

THE HIKES

SOUTH SHORE TRAIL: To reach the trail from Walnut Grove, follow the asphalt walk from the south end of the parking lot; veer right over the creek and then right to the trail. Alternatively, park at the west end of the lot and walk past the softball fields to the woods. Cross the footbridge to the trail. While the trailhead is not marked here, it is marked at the access point south of the dam. The South Shore Trail never leaves the woods that surround Shawnee Mission Lake. It follows the ridge, wrapping around several fingers of the lake, at times descending to cross rocky creekbeds. Erosion has rutted this dirt trail and exposed a network of tree roots that need to be carefully navigated. The trail crosses several creeks which may, after heavy rains, be impassable. Although the trail is not marked by blazes or other markers, it is not hard to follow. Occasionally, however, you may stray off course on the well-worn trails leading down to the lake or up to the Off-Leash Dog Area in an adjacent meadow. The west end of the trail, near picnic shelter 8, is marked by a gazebo and benches.

NORTH SHORE TRAIL: This well-worn, rutted trail and its off-shoots show frequent use by bikers. From the trailhead, the trail climbs a rocky hill north and then forks. We followed the trail to the right (northeast). (The trail straight ahead eventually loops around and reconnects.) This trail intersects with so many side-trails that we could not keep track of the main trail. The southern portion of the trail roughly parallels the park road in a northeasterly direction and at one point comes close to the tennis courts, across the park road from the marina. Past the tennis courts and near a pond, the trail loops back northwest, connecting to another loop. Though we could not follow all of the loops, the Shawnee Mission Park map shows four interconnecting loops. If you continue right at every juncture, you should remain on the outer section of each loop. The trail travels primarily through woodlands, which are especially picturesque in spring and fall.

SERTOMA WOODLAND TRAIL: This is a short, self-guided interpretive trail that circles through woods. Trail brochures are available in the park office.

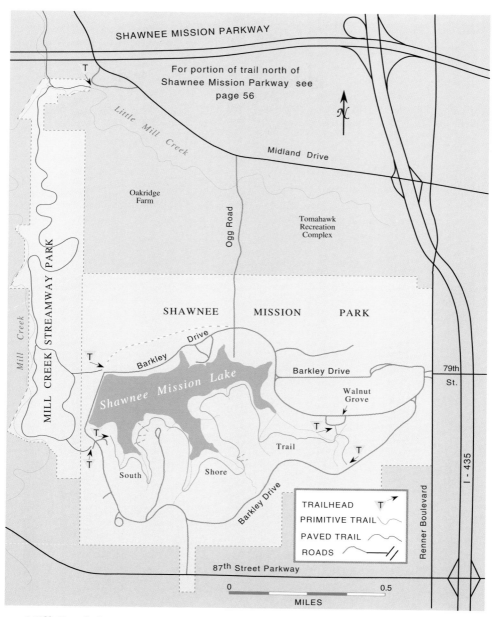

SHAWNEE MISSION PARKWAY

For portion of trail north of
Shawnee Mission Parkway see
page 56

N

Little Mill Creek

Midland Drive

Oakridge
Farm

Ogg Road

Tomahawk
Recreation
Complex

MILL CREEK STREAMWAY PARK

Mill Creek

SHAWNEE   MISSION   PARK

Barkley   Drive

Barkley Drive

79th
St.

Shawnee Mission Lake

Walnut
Grove

Trail

I - 435

South

Shore

Barkley Drive

Renner Boulevard

TRAILHEAD   T
PRIMITIVE TRAIL
PAVED TRAIL
ROADS

87th Street Parkway

0   0.5

MILES

Mill Creek Streamway
and Shawnee Mission Park
South Shore Trails

Horse Trail, Hillsdale Lake

Hillsdale Lake

The trails at Hillsdale Lake cross a highly varied terrain through grassy meadows, cultivated fields, cedar-dotted prairie, rocky, forested hillsides overlooking the lake, and deep wooded valleys, where meandering streams have carved through limestone. Most of the 1.5-mile Hidden Spring Nature Trail winds through scenic woodlands, except for the first section, which cuts a swath through beautiful native tallgrass prairie. The trail on the east side of the lake is used primarily by equestrians but is suitable for hiking. Like most horse trails, however, it is designed to maximize the mileage—it backtracks, loops, and zigzags for 24 miles, all within an area no more than 3.5 miles from north to south and less than a mile from east to west. While the trail is well-worn in most places, the system of trail blazes is hard to decipher and not consistent. Ownership: USACE (913) 783-4366; KDWP (913) 783-4507.

HUNTING REMINDER: The entire horse trail travels through a public hunting area. Check hunting schedules before you hike, and wear bright colors, preferably an orange hat and vest. In February 1997, a hiker's dog was injured by a trap set on the horse trail. Trapping season typically runs from mid-November to mid-February.

HIKE LENGTHS

Hidden Spring Nature Trail .... 1.5-mile loop
Horse Trail .... 24 miles

DIRECTIONS

Hillsdale Lake is about 40 miles southwest of Kansas City and about 37 miles southeast of Lawrence. From I-35, exit south onto U.S. 169 and travel to 255th Street. Turn west and pass through the town of Hillsdale. About 1.75 miles past Hillsdale, watch for the Corps of Engineers Visitors Center on the north side of 255th Street.

⊤ TRAIL ACCESS

Hidden Spring Nature Trail Trailhead

The trail can be reached from the parking area just west of the Visitors Center.

Horse Trail Access

From south to north:

HORSE TRAILER PARKING AREA ACCESS: Turn in at the Visitors Center and continue north for .3 mile to the horse trailer parking area; the trail is west across the road.

253RD STREET ACCESS: Follow the directions to the horse trailer parking area but continue on the gravel road north to the first east-west road, which is 253rd Street; look for the trail near the intersection.

MARYSVILLE BOAT RAMP ACCESS: Follow the directions to the 253rd Street access point; turn right (east) onto 253rd Street, then north on the first road after this intersection. The trail crosses the road near the ramp, as shown on the map.

HARMONY ROAD ACCESS: From 255th Street, turn north on Harmony Road, which is 2.5 miles west of the intersection of U.S. 169 and 255th Street; follow Harmony Road north, past 247th Street, and continue as it curves west. The trail crosses Harmony Road just past Tontzville Road and again a short distance further west.

240TH STREET ACCESS: Follow the directions to the Harmony Road access point, but turn north onto Tontzville Road, which curves east and becomes 240th Street. Shortly after it curves east, watch for the trail to cross the road.

NORTH TRAILHEAD: Follow the directions to the 240th Street access point but continue east on Tontzville Road/240th Street; then north, and back west again, until it intersects Clare Road; go north on Clare Road until it intersects an east-west road leading to the north trailhead, turn left (west) to the trailhead.

ⓘ GENERAL INFORMATION

Hillsdale Lake, built on Big Bull Creek, is the newest and smallest Kansas lake constructed by the Corps of Engineers. It was completed in 1982 and covers 4,580 surface acres. The town of Hillsdale, which is 2.5 miles east of the dam, in north-central Miami County, was platted in 1869 and originally named Columbia. At the beginning of the 18th century, the Kansa and Osage Indians probably hunted along Bull Creek. When the Santa Fe Trail opened in 1812, two branches of it crossed the headwaters of the creek, about two miles north of the present location of Hillsdale Lake. The Shawnee Indian Reservation, a narrow, 2.25-mile strip of land in northern Miami County, is now part of the flood-control pool at the northern end of the lake. Probably the most famous Civil War event in Miami County occurred on Bull Creek. Following his raid on Lawrence, William Clark Quantrill passed through Miami County, whose residents were mostly Free Staters. Residents of Paola prepared an ambush, but Quantrill was warned and when he and his men were about two miles north of Paola, they turned northward and camped on the west side of Bull Creek. A Union force pursuing Quantrill camped at Paola, but the ranking officer refused requests to attack Quantrill, who continued with his men into Missouri.

THE HIKES

Hidden Spring Nature Trail

The trailhead for this self-guided nature trail is at the west end of the Visitors Center parking area. Be sure to pick up a trail brochure at the Visitors Center—it explains the 20 points of interest marked on the first loop. The trail begins by winding through a 5-acre parcel of native tallgrasses, interspersed with prairie wildflowers. After passing a large trail sign and map, the trail enters the woods, where it branches. To follow the interpretive signs in order, take the trail to the left (southwest).

The woods are dominated by oak, hickory, and walnut. Because the trail winds back and forth across a watercourse, the understory is dense. Mosses and lichens grow on fallen wood. When the trail enters the woods, it first descends toward the lake, then travels north and connects via a footbridge (the first of many) to the Eagle Loop, named in recognition of the scouts who cleared it. Watch for the observation deck. When we hiked this trail, the steps up to the deck were loose and had deteriorated. Several footpaths intersect with the main trail on this loop. Eventually, the entire nature trail is to be surfaced with cedar chips. As you return, near the end of the first loop of the trail, watch for the natural spring at marker 17. According to the trail brochure, this spring runs year-round and may have been used as a water source by Indians that once lived along Bull Creek.

Horse Trail

This trail has so many forks, loops, switchbacks, and side-trails that a detailed description would put anyone to sleep. With the map in hand, however, you should have little difficulty. Included below is a general description of each section of the trail, highlighting areas that we found interesting, and pointing out sections we found difficult to follow. We had problems understanding the logic of the colored trail markers. Generally, the brown flex-markers and red (or red-striped) ribbons mark the main trail, and the white and yellow ribbons mark secondary trails. The main trail is mowed, eroded, or marked in most places, but this may be of little comfort when you

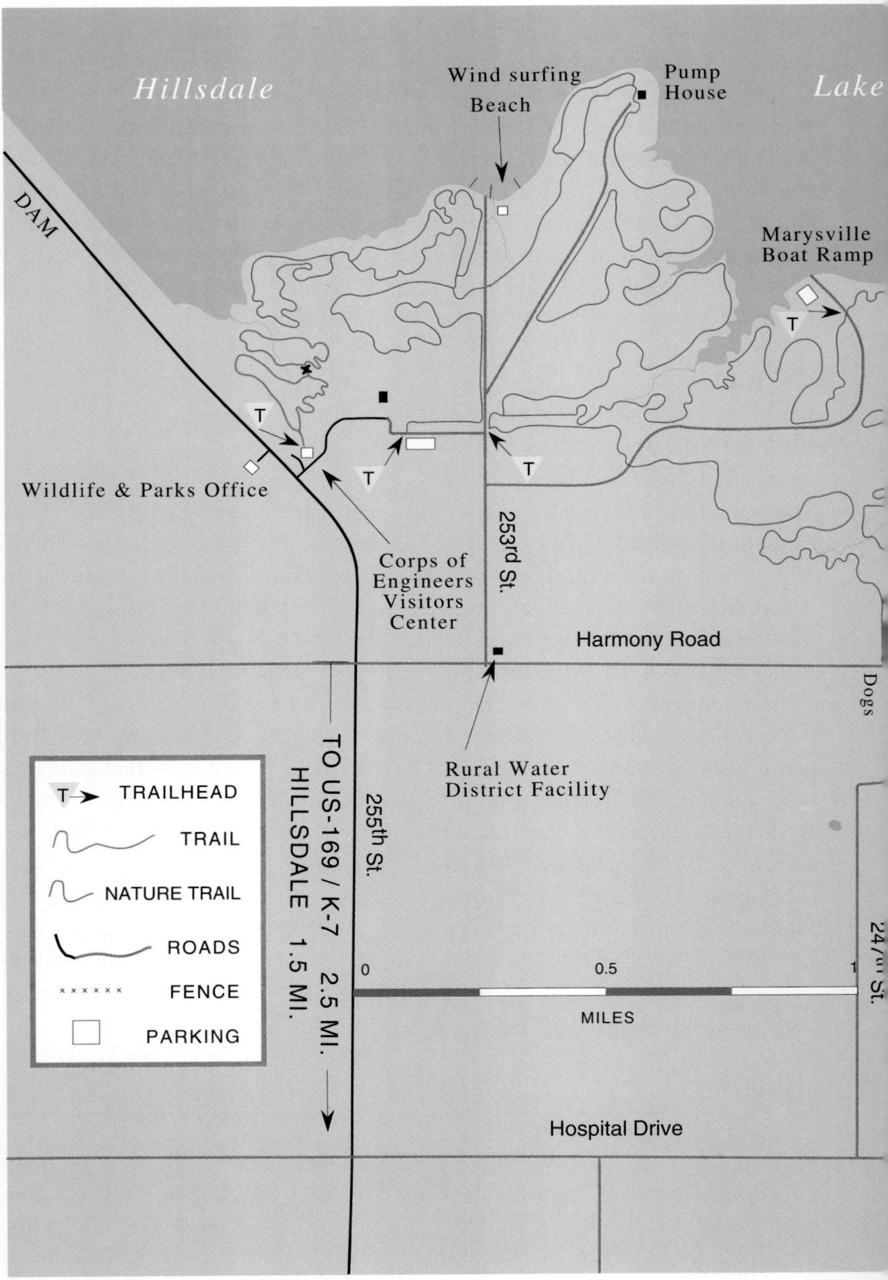
Hillsdale
Lake
Wind surfing Beach
Pump House
DAM
Marysville Boat Ramp
T
T
T
T
Wildlife & Parks Office
Corps of Engineers Visitors Center
253rd St.
Harmony Road
Rural Water District Facility
Dogs
TO US-169 / K-7 2.5 MI.
HILLSDALE 1.5 MI.
255th St.
TRAILHEAD
TRAIL
NATURE TRAIL
ROADS
FENCE
PARKING
0
0.5
MILES
Hospital Drive

Hillsdale Lake Trails

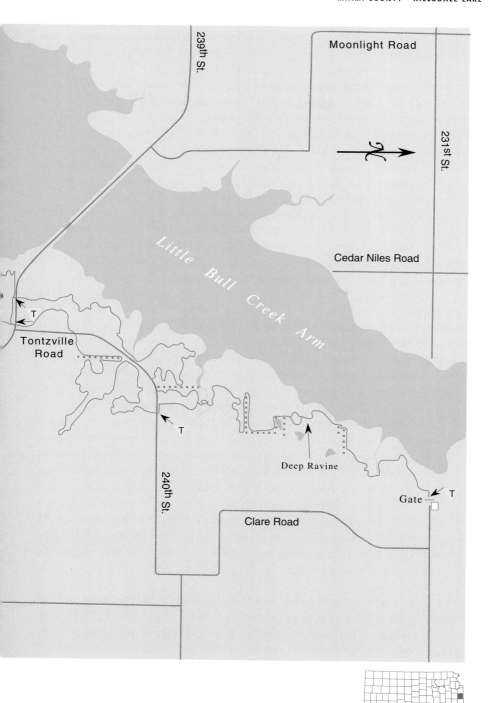

Moonlight Road

239th St.

231st St.

Little Bull Creek Arm

Cedar Niles Road

T

Tontzville
Road

T

Deep Ravine

Gate — T

240th St.

Clare Road

find yourself at a juncture of three equally worn trails. This is when the map will come to your rescue.

TRAIL SOUTH OF 253RD STREET (SEGMENT 1): The first part of this 3.3-mile segment doesn't have much to recommend it. The trail begins across the road from the horse trailer parking area, cutting a narrow passage through thick weeds. After winding for over a mile through a tree-dotted field, with little change in terrain, the trail descends toward the lake. The last 2 miles weave along a rocky, wooded hillside overlooking the lake. This is one of the more scenic areas of the horse trail, although it zigzags so many times up and down the steep ridge that we were dizzy by the time we sighted the windsurfing beach at the north end. The Corps of Engineers plans to close the portion of the horse trail immediately adjacent to the Hidden Spring Nature Trail—hikers on the nature trail have wandered onto the horse trail and become lost. This segment ends just east of the windsurfing beach. Travel east on 253rd Street and then south to return to the parking area, or continue directly north across 253rd Street to hike Segment 2.

LAKE SHORE LOOP—NORTH OF 253RD STREET AND WEST AND SOUTH OF ROAD TO MARYSVILLE BOAT RAMP (SEGMENT 2): This segment connects to the northwestern end of Segment 1. We hiked this 3.75-mile loop clockwise, beginning on the north side of 253rd Street, just east of the windsurfing beach. We ended back at 253rd Street, east of where we started, at the point on the map marked by the letter "T." Three trails meet at this point; this loop follows the west branch. Much of the trail winds through timber, following several fingers of land that reach into the lake. Some of these areas showed signs of flooding. Near the beginning, the trail follows a ridge overlooking the lake, and several paths lead down to it. Before reaching the pumphouse shown on the map, watch for a short loop on the trail—the southwestern side dips down to the lake. After passing the pumphouse, the trail meanders through another finger of land, bordering the lake, then backtracks to the gravel park road leading to the pumphouse. The trail parallels the road for about .3 mile, then heads northwest toward the lake. The brown flex directional markers are particularly helpful because the trail takes so many sharp turns. When the trail emerges from the woods, it travels through open prairie, where tall goldenrod, sunflowers, and other wildflowers bloomed in early September.

MIDDLE TRAIL FROM 253RD STREET NORTH TO HARMONY ROAD/239TH STREET (SEGMENT 3): As noted above, three branches of the trail converge at 253rd Street. This 4.3-mile segment is the middle branch, from 253rd Street north to Harmony Road/239th Street. We hiked this segment from south to north. For a short distance, the trail parallels an abandoned road. This branch too winds in and out of the woods and through open prairie. Parts are hilly. Most of the trail follows the shoreline, providing many views of the lake. As the trail nears Harmony Road/239th Street, it passes through a scenic wooded area near a creek. This segment can be hiked as a 7-mile loop by returning south on Segment 5 (the east branch of the three trails that meet at 253rd Street).

TRAIL NORTH OF HARMONY ROAD/239TH STREET (SEGMENT 4): To hike this 9-mile segment as a loop, be prepared to walk 2.3 miles on a gravel road. Alternatively, if you have two vehicles, park one at the north trailhead on 231st Street and one at the south trailhead on Harmony Road/239th Street, which makes it a 4.2-mile hike. Like the sections described above, this 9-mile loop travels in and out of woodlands, frequently within view of the lake, through prairie, along cultivated fields, into scenic wooded valleys, rocky draws, and gullies and, about a mile south of 231st Street, into a deep ravine. We enjoyed the panoramic views of the surrounding hills, referred to by geologists as the Osage Cuestas.

A sign at 231st Street marks the "Brown Access Hillsdale Wildlife Area." Turn right (east) for about .2 mile to Clare Road, then turn right (south). Clare Road travels south, east, and south again (for a total of about 1.4 miles) before intersecting 240th Street. Turn west and after about .7 mile watch for the trail on the south side of 240th Street. (Note: as shown on the map, just west of here the trail backtracks north from 240th Street, connecting about midway to the lakeside section of this loop.) Although we saw little of the lake as we hiked south from 240th Street, we found this 2.4-mile section a pretty hike through the woods and an especially picturesque valley. Shortly after we began, we crossed into a clearly marked public hunting area. About .3 mile from the end of the loop, the trail crosses Tontzville Road. This loop ends at Harmony Road/239th Street, just east of where you started.

EASTERN BRANCH OF TRAIL FROM 253RD STREET TO HARMONY ROAD/239TH STREET (SEGMENT 5): This 2.7 mile segment is the east branch of the three trails that converge at 253rd Street. We hiked from south to north, parking a car at each end. To hike this as a 7-mile loop, you can return to 253rd Street via the lakeside trail to the west (see Segment 3 above). The first part follows an old farm road, which we had paralleled when we hiked Segment 3. We caught only occasional glimpses of the lake and traveled through large areas of prairie, young timber, and shrubs. A word of advice—two-thirds of the way along, the trail travels up one side of a long cedar shelter belt, then immediately returns down the other side—a senseless jog, and one that we hiked apprehensively as we listened to the fearsome barking of dogs that we hoped were penned. After passing a dry pond, the trail enters the scenic wooded valley and shortly thereafter reaches Harmony Road/239th Street.

Marais des Cygnes River Nature Trail, Melvern Lake

Melvern Lake

Though we had decided not to cover nature trails under one mile, it was impossible to overlook Melvern Lake, with its five well-maintained, scenic trails, including a 1.5-mile hike along an isolated piece of the old Marais des Cygnes River. The trails at Melvern Lake provide access to a variety of ecosystems—from prairie, meadow, and marsh to forest, river, and lake. If you enjoy a primitive hike, take the River Bottom Trail through the dark, hilly woods near the old river channel in the Outlet Park, or the Eisenhower Interpretive Trail through tallgrass prairie in the state park. Alternatively, try the Marais des Cygnes River Nature Trail, which includes a loop through a well-manicured parklike setting, where signs note points of interest. Ownership: USACE (785) 549-3318; KDWP (785) 528-4102.

HIKE LENGTHS

Marais des Cygnes River Nature Trail .... 1.5 miles
River Bottom Nature Trail .... .75 mile
Eisenhower Interpretative Trail .... .5 mile
Overlook Nature Trail .... .6 mile
Breakwater Nature Trail... .6 mile

DIRECTIONS

Melvern Lake is about 33 miles southwest of Ottawa and about 39 miles south of Topeka. From I-35, take Exit 160 and turn north on K-31. At the town of Melvern, turn west to remain on K-31 and watch for the entrance to the lake after crossing under U.S. 75.

⇥ TRAIL ACCESS

MARAIS DES CYGNES RIVER NATURE TRAIL TRAILHEAD: From the lake entrance, follow the signs to the Outlet Park below the dam. Turn right into the camping area (which is past the picnic area) and follow the park road past the fee booth. Continue for .4 mile and watch for the trail sign on the left (northwest) side of the road. Maps to the Outlet Park, including trail locations, are available at the fee booth. Note: the concrete section of this trail is accessible to the handicapped.

RIVER BOTTOM NATURE TRAIL TRAILHEAD: This is also in the camping area of the Outlet Park. Follow the directions above and continue for .5 mile past the trailhead for the Marais des Cygnes River Trail. The trailhead is at the end of the campground loop, across the road from the showers.

EISENHOWER INTERPRETIVE TRAIL TRAILHEAD: From the entrance to Melvern Lake, cross the dam and follow the signs to Eisenhower State Park. Stop at the park office for a map, as well as a trail guide. From the office, go right (southwest) for .4 mile, then left (south) for .7 mile. Watch for the sign pointing toward the trailhead. The trailhead is .2 mile further, on the right (west) side of the road.

OVERLOOK NATURE TRAIL TRAILHEAD: This trail is located in the Coeur d'Alene Park, south of the Administrative Area. Stop at the Corps of Engineers office for a copy of the Melvern Lake Nature Trail Guide, which includes a map of the Overlook Nature Trail, as well as all of the other nature trails at Melvern Lake. You can access the Overlook Trail from the first road into the Coeur d'Alene Park. The trailhead is behind the picnic shelter on the left side of the road. If you reach the swimming beach, you've gone too far.

BREAKWATER NATURE TRAIL TRAILHEAD: This is in the westernmost camping area of the Coeur d'Alene Park, the second road past the picnic-area loop. In the camping area, follow the road north toward the lake. Watch for the trailhead on the right (east) side of the road, before the road loops to the left (west).

ⓘ GENERAL INFORMATION

The Marais des Cygnes (marsh of swans) River was dammed to form Melvern Lake. Before white settlement, this river valley abounded with waterfowl and wildlife, and was valuable hunting and fishing grounds for a number of Indian tribes, including the Kansa, Osage, Shawnee, Chippewa, Munsie, Iowa, Wyandot, Kickapoo, Potawatomie, and Sac and Fox. Later, this land was part of the fifteen-million-dollar Louisiana Purchase, made in 1803 by the United States Government. Federalists grumbled at President Jefferson's decision, even though this purchase from France doubled the size of the nation. Fisher Ames, a representative from

Massachusetts, wrote: "Acquiring of territory with money, is mean and despicable. . . . The Mississippi was a boundary. . . . We were confined within some limits. Now, by adding an unmeasured world beyond the river, we rush like a comet into infinite space."* Almost forty years later, the land where Melvern Lake now sits became part of a reservation for the Sac and Fox Indian tribes.

THE HIKES

MARAIS DES CYGNES RIVER NATURE TRAIL: From the trailhead, the concrete trail leads northwest toward an old section of the Marais des Cygnes River. As one of the trail signs explains, this channel of the river was isolated by the construction of the dam and resembles an oxbow lake. (Natural oxbows are formed when a river cuts a new channel during periods of high water. Without the scouring effect of the river's flow, the water remaining in the old river channel takes on a lake-type ecology.) Just before the trail reaches the river, watch for a sign to the primitive trail, on your left. This .75-mile loop, surfaced with hard-packed limestone screenings, follows the tree-lined old river channel west, to its end. As it loops back on the north side of the river, the trail crosses several bridges. This section of the trail, through mature walnuts, elms, basswoods, silver maples, and oaks, was my favorite. Soon it rejoins the concrete trail, which winds through a scenic park along the river.

RIVER BOTTOM NATURE TRAIL: This is the most primitive nature trail at Melvern Lake, and my favorite. The trail begins at the edge of the woods and never leaves the cool shelter of the trees until the end. The northeastern end of the loop travels within view of the Outlet Park lake. After the trail crosses a bridge over the old river channel, it branches—take the trail to the right (east). Signs identify trees and some of the plants that form the dense understory. After the trail circles back west, it branches again; the trail that continues straight will take you out to the park road, west of the trailhead. The trail to your left will return you to the trailhead.

EISENHOWER INTERPRETIVE TRAIL: While a part of this trail winds through the woods near the lakeshore, this trail showcases the tallgrass prairie that is being restored in this park. This prairie is not as well established or showy as the prairie across from the park office, but the wildflowers that grow among the grasses are plentiful, and the thickets of rough-leaved dogwood, smooth sumac, red cedar, and wild plum are ideal wildlife cover. Be sure to pick up a trail guide at the park office before you hike for information about the 29 markers along the trail.

OVERLOOK NATURE TRAIL: This trail connects the picnic area with the overlook in Coeur d'Alene Park. An added loop through the woods circles a meadow filled with

* From *The Study of American History,* vol. 1, edited by Ernst Kohlmetz (Guilford, Conn.: Dushkin, 1974), p. 255.

dotted gayfeather, which normally blooms from August through September. The trail through the woods is scenic, although a bit swampy. The Corps of Engineers may eventually close this trail because it requires a lot of maintenance.

BREAKWATER NATURE TRAIL: This trail has more climbs than any other at Melvern Lake, climbing up over a ridge and down to the shoreline. Part of the trail is wooded.

Green Memorial Wildlife Area

H istory buffs will especially enjoy this 83-acre wildlife habitat, which was once the site of Uniontown, a trading post for the Potawatomie Indians and the largest settlement in the region. Many of the major westward trails once passed through this area, and the ruts of the Oregon Trail can still be seen on the Oregon Trace Trail, a circular trail in the southern half of the wildlife area. The Post Creek Trail winds through ravines and up hills in the northern half. We enjoyed the scenic view of Post Creek, which runs through the western boundary of the wildlife area. Ownership: KDWP (785) 273-6740.

HIKE LENGTHS
Post Creek Trail .... 1 mile
Oregon Trace Trail .... .75 mile

DIRECTIONS

From I-70, take Exit 346 (8 miles west of Topeka) and travel 2 miles north toward Rossville and Willard. At Willard, turn east onto 2nd Street and travel .4 mile to Gilkerson Street. Turn south and travel .6 miles to the Green Memorial Wildlife Area, on the west side of Gilkerson Street. Parking is available.

GENERAL INFORMATION

Large signs at the entry to the Green Memorial Wildlife Area provide historical information about this site—about .5 mile south of the Kansas River—which was selected by two government agents in 1848 as the official trading post for the Potawatomie Indians.* The agents christened the site "Union Town." In late 1849, a

* The signs excerpt information from *Ghost Towns of Kansas: A Traveler's Guide* by Daniel C. Fitzgerald (Lawrence: University Press of Kansas, 1988).

Green Memorial Wildlife Area

cholera epidemic spread to Uniontown, and the town was burned and abandoned. (A mass burial site for 22 Indian cholera victims is located on private land in the Uniontown cemetery just across the road from the wildlife area.) A year later, Uniontown was rebuilt and became the largest settlement in the region. By 1859, however, trade in Uniontown had declined with the loss of business to Topeka and Tecumseh, and, for reasons unknown, all remaining buildings in Uniontown were again burned. The Green family acquired the land in the 1870s and in 1877 built a house from stone remnants of Uniontown. Near the parking area you can view the dated stone from above the doorway to the Green's home. The California–Oregon Trail, the Fort Leavenworth–Fort Riley Road, the Salt Lake City Trail, and the U.S. Mail Route each branched at one time to Uniontown.

THE HIKES

POST CREEK TRAIL: Both trails start at the parking lot, but the Post Creek Trail heads directly west, while the Oregon Trace Trail veers southwest (left). There is a map of the trails at the trailhead and numbered markers at points of interest along the trails. The Post Creek Trail is circular. We veered right at the outset, traveling the northern, hillier part first. Watch for pink quartzite rock, a metamorphic rock from outcroppings around Sioux Falls, South Dakota, that was deposited here when the glacial ice that once covered this region melted. Parts of this trail were dirt-based and rocky, while other parts, through old farm fields, were mowed. We stopped at the bench overlooking Post Creek and enjoyed the view of the creek and woodlands below. The remainder of the trail is flatter and passes through old farm fields invaded by osage orange and honey locust.

OREGON TRACE TRAIL: From the parking area, this trail heads southwest through tallgrass prairie for about .3 mile before it branches and circles an oak and hickory woodland. We continued straight (south) on the trail rather than taking the branch to the right (west). After entering the woods, watch for marker 13, which marks a noticeable depression—a relic of the Oregon Trail. This depression parallels the trail as it descends to lower, more erodible ground. Here, the path of the Oregon Trail becomes difficult to follow. The trail circles north at the southwestern boundary of the wildlife area and back east to the entry point.

We note that upon our return to the Green Memorial Wildlife Area in June 1996, the trails had not been mown and, in the wooded areas as well as the open fields, were overgrown. We recommend hiking the trails in fall, winter, or early spring.

Shunga Trail

Shunga Trail

The Shunga Trail is a 4.75-mile urban pedestrian/bicycle path through a gallery of Topeka parks. The trail currently ends at the Expocentre in the heart of Topeka, but Topeka Parks and Recreation plans to extend it. Surfaced in concrete and wide enough to accommodate the many walkers, runners, bikers, and skaters that use it, the trail parallels Shunganunga Creek and winds through native tallgrass at Warren Nature Area. Take one of the many mowed paths through the Warren Nature Area, or the Orville Rice Nature Tail, a mowed, and sometimes very muddy, trail that also parallels Shunganunga Creek from Gage Boulevard through the Warren Nature Center and Big Shunga Park, to Washburn Avenue. Ownership: Topeka Parks & Recreation (785) 272-5900.

HIKE LENGTH
Shunga Trail .... 4.75 miles

DIRECTIONS AND TRAIL ACCESS

The Shunga Trail follows the north side of Shunga Creek between Fairlawn Road to the west and Topeka Boulevard to the east. It can be accessed from Crestview Park, Felker Park, Big Shunga Park, and Shunga Glen Park. To reach Crestview Park, exit south on Fairlawn off of I-70 and continue 2.8 miles south to Shunga Drive. Watch for the trail near the creek. Parking is also available at Felker Park, at 25th Street and Gage Boulevard. The Expocentre, at the eastern end of the trail, is off of Topeka Boulevard, between 17th and 21st Streets. The trailhead is just north of 21st Street off of Topeka Boulevard.

ⓘ GENERAL INFORMATION

The Shunganunga Creek was not always bordered by parks. A 1914 picture of the slums along the Shunganunga shows outside privies, wells, dung heaps, and the creek.* The Shunganunga once provided entertainment year-round, from swimming in the summer, to ice-skating and "shinny" in the winter. Shinny was a simple game, often played with cans battered back and forth with homemade hockey sticks. When the waters froze, children gathered to watch employees of the Baughman ice-cream plant drive teams of horses out on the creek to saw off large chunks of ice. During the depression, the widening of the Shunganunga Creek channel was one of the many projects in Topeka undertaken by the Works Projects Administration. The development of the Shunga Trail was proposed in the 1950s by the National Park Recreation Association. The first phase of the trail, in Crestview Park, was not constructed until 1988, and the remainder was completed by 1995.

🥾 THE HIKE

SHUNGA TRAIL: We hiked the trail from west to east, from Fairlawn to Topeka Boulevard. Parking is available off of Shunga Drive, near the Crestview Community Center. Quarter-mile trail markers, a red stripe of brick across the concrete trail, allow you to keep track of your mileage. The trail is fairly flat; the only inclines of significance are at the underpasses, where the trail descends to cross beneath intersecting roads. The many species of trees along the trail between Fairlawn and Gage Boulevard are identified in a guide available through Topeka Parks and Recreation.

The first section of the trail, through Crestview Park, parallels Shunga Drive to the north and Shunganunga Creek to the south. The trail winds and curves with the creek and around trees. Just east of the Crestview swimming pool, the trail jogs to the southwest, where a path splinters off to cross Shunganunga Creek. The trail itself never crosses the creek. At Gage Boulevard, the trail leaves Crestview Park and crosses beneath the Gage bridge. This section can be wet. As you enter the Warren Nature Area, just east of Gage Boulevard, watch for the trailhead to the Orville Rice Nature Trail, a mowed and sometimes muddy trail that also parallels Shunganunga Creek. We remained on the concrete Shunga Trail, which snakes through the towering native grasses. All noise but the wind is muffled by the grasses, which are as tall and dense as those on an open prairie. The wetlands at the Warren Nature Area are a prime bird-watching spot. To the north of the trail, you can see the Veterans Administration Hospital and the Kansas Neurological Institute.

* From *Witness of the Times: A History of Shawnee County* by Douglass Wallace and Roy Bird (Topeka: Shawnee County Historical Society and Shawnee County American Revolution Bicentenniel Commission, 1976). These and many more stories and pictures can be found in *Witness of the Times* and in *Topeka: An Illustrated History of the Kansas Capital* by Roy Bird (Topeka: Baranski Publishing, 1985).

East of the Warren Nature Area, the trail crosses into Big Shunga Park and wraps around McDonald Field. From here, the trail parallels Shunga Drive through a narrow finger of the park that extends to Washburn Avenue. Just before the trail crosses under the road, watch for the bridge over the creek—this leads to College Street on the south side. Past Washburn Avenue, the trail enters Shunga Glen Park, where it travels northeast up to 21st and Fillmore Streets. This part of the trail is noticeably straighter to comply with federal guidelines. At the north end of Shunga Glen Park, the trail takes a jog to the east, along 21st Street, before it dips back southeast to parallel the creek. After crossing 21st Street, the trail travels through the southeast corner of the Expocentre property to Topeka Boulevard, the end of the line for now.

Wyandotte County Lake Trail

Wyandotte County Lake Park

The 8-mile trail that winds around Wyandotte County Lake was designed and is used as a bridle trail. Drainage areas are rough, muddy, and heavily damaged by horse travel. This does not detract, however, from the beauty of the forest. This is a true hardwood forest, part of the eastern deciduous forest that once stretched from the east coast of North America to eastern Kansas. The hickories, oaks, and basswoods that tower over other trees here depend on higher rainfall than occurs further west. As you hike this trail, you cannot help but sense that these woods are old; they are dark and moist and water seems to seep continuously from the limestone underlying the hills. Do not let the fact that this is a bridle trail deter you from enjoying this extraordinary forest. Ownership: Wyandotte County Parks (913) 299-0550.

HIKE LENGTH

Wyandotte County Lake Trail .... 8 miles

DIRECTIONS AND TRAIL ACCESS

Wyandotte County Lake Park is in northwestern Wyandotte County, north of I-70 and east of I-435. From I-70, take I-435 north 2.6 miles to the Leavenworth Road East Exit (Exit 15A). Travel east on Leavenworth Road 1.5 miles to 91st Street (a four-way stop) and turn left (north). The park entrance is .3 mile past this intersection. The trail can be accessed at many points around the lake, as shown on the map. Watch for "Bridle Trail" signs or red flags tied in the trees near the mowed clearings along the park road (frequently the trail leaves the woods and edges these clearings). We entered the trail just west of 93rd Street and parked at the parking area near the road leading to the Visitors Center and boathouse. To reach this entry point, turn left (northwest) at the 91st Street entrance and travel 1.5 miles north. The parking area is just off the road.

The entry point used by horse riders is just off of the park road on 83rd Street, near the 83rd Street park shelter. There is a large sign marking the bridle trail and parking just off of 83rd Street. To reach this entry, turn right (east) at the 91st Street entrance and travel 1.8 miles to 83rd Street. Turn right (southwest) for parking.

[i] GENERAL INFORMATION

Wyandotte County Lake Park, only 13 miles from Kansas City, is a 1500-acre wooded park with a 330-acre lake. This is a Works Projects Administration lake built during the Great Depression. All of the beautiful stone and timber shelters, the boathouse, and other improvements were planned and designed by the National Park Service. The stone and timber were taken from the park. The WPA, created in 1935 by Franklin D. Roosevelt, approved the relief project on October 28, 1935, upon application by the Wyandotte County Commissioners. When construction began on December 17, 1935, approximately 500 men reported for work. This number peaked at 2,000 in 1939.

The construction was not without mishap. On the night of September 19, 1937, when the dam was only days from completion, more than half of it collapsed. Front-page headlines in the *Kansas City Kansan* read: "County Lake Dam Site is Picture of Desolation; Entire Center Section of Huge Earthen Structure Appears to Have Sunk into Abyss; Guard Against Danger to Sightseers." One of the articles described the site as "an earthen 'wreck of the Hesperus.'" The chasm created by the collapse was as deep as 50 feet. The newspaper reported that "the million tons of dirt and stone which appeared to have been 'swallowed up' by the earth, in actuality slipped northward and heaved up the ground and the stone revetment as it went." One engineer commented that the slide may have caused a cornfield a quarter of a mile north of the dam site to rise several inches. The dam had been built on unstable "blue clay," or, as one photojournalist described it, a lot of "mud and muck." When the dam was rebuilt a short distance away (this time under the direction of the Army Corps of Engineers), the mud and muck were excavated and replaced by tons of sand pumped from the Missouri River. Even after the dam was completed, the lake filled slowly due to droughts. When the rains finally came, the waters rose so quickly that heavy equipment was trapped in the construction quarry. It still remains at the bottom of Wilson Cove.

🏃 THE HIKE

The Bridle Trail is circular and weaves in and out of the woods and mowed clearings surrounding the lake. Vistas of the lake are rare—we saw it only briefly, as we neared the lake dam and when the trail emerged at the clearings. The topography resembles the Ozarks of Missouri and Arkansas, and you should not hike this hilly, strenuous trail after rains—the muddy clay becomes slippery, and it's hard to keep your footing. The trail is described in segments for quick reference.

93RD STREET SOUTH TO THE ADMINISTRATION BUILDING: This section of the trail is 1.8 miles. We began the hike in the mowed clearing next to 93rd Street, across

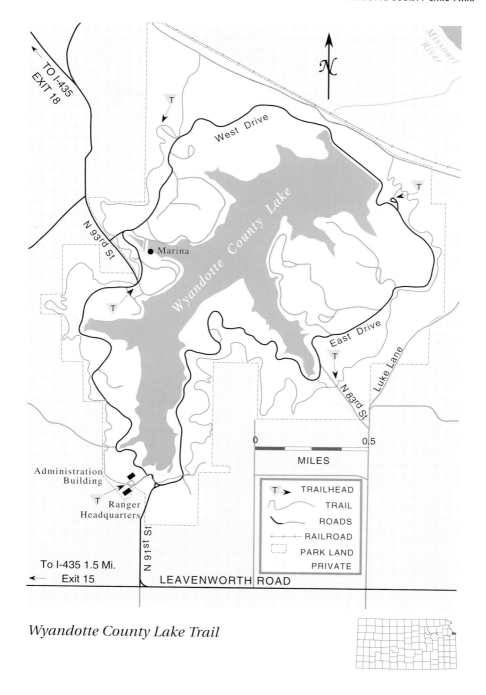

Wyandotte County Lake Trail

the road from the parking area, and followed the flags to the Bridle Trail sign, where the trail enters the woods. The trail first passes through a weedy area—it was not scenic, but we enjoyed the wildflowers—and we had momentary misgivings when we crossed our first muddy "horse-hoof swamp." At .5 mile, the trail briefly emerges at a mowed clearing, then reenters the woods, following a creek. The ravines were beautiful. The spiders had been at work on and off the trail, and an occasional ray of sun illuminated their dartboard-like webs. About .5 mile before the trail reaches the Administration Building, it crosses Hurrelbrink Road, which leads out of the park to 99th Street. After it crosses the street, the trail follows the remains of an old dirt road, with ravines on both sides. The trail emerges at the southwest end of the Ranger Headquarters and playground area.

ADMINISTRATION BUILDING NORTH TO 83RD STREET: From the Administration Building, it is 2.2 miles to 83rd Street, where many horse riders enter the trail. Watch for the red flags dangling from the trees after you leave the woods by the Ranger Headquarters. Cross the park road and turn right (southeast) across the bridge, where a Bridle Trail sign points east across the mowed lawn next to the lake. When you near the park road on the other side, watch for the "Shop Area, Employees Only" sign. Take this road for a short distance and watch for the trail on your left, heading north. We saw a huge buck on this road, moss dangling from its antlers.

The trail on the east side of the lake is wide—8 feet in most places. At 1.2 miles from the Administration Building, it comes to a clearing, within sight of shelter 1. About .6 mile past the shelter, the trail passes through a clearing bordered by woods, where wildflowers bloom profusely. Shortly past this clearing, we heard running water and soon came to a pretty stream. Be sure to look upstream, where the water flows over limestone steps. It is likely, after heavy rains, that the water runs swiftly over this area. From here, the trail soon emerges from the woods and crosses 83rd Street, close to the 83rd Street shelter house.

83RD STREET TO EAST END OF LAKE DAM: This section of the trail is 1.6 miles. After crossing 83rd Street, watch for the red flags in the trees and the Bridle Trail sign at the end of the clearing. A large trail sign and map of the Bridle Trail is located near the parking area. The rocky ascent at the start of this section of the trail is not long. The forest here is old and deep. Watch for red quartzite rocks in the trail, glacial till left by the glaciers that once covered northeastern Kansas. The nearest source of this rock is southeastern South Dakota—over 400 miles away. After about .8 mile, the trail reaches a clearing close to the "3 mile" road sign and shelter 11. Follow the ribbons in the trees edging the clearing. Do not cross the road. After reentering the woods, the trail forks. Only the trail to the left, which travels downhill, is marked with red flags. As you near the east end of the trees, you can catch glimpses of the lake through the foliage. The trail then descends and intersects with a gravel road behind the lake dam.

EAST END OF LAKE DAM TO ARCHERY RANGE: It is 1.2 miles from the east end of the lake dam to the clearing by the archery range. When the trail reaches the gravel road behind the dam, ignore all of the horse trail signs tacked to the utility poles. Turn left (west) on the gravel road and follow it for .8 mile. A railroad track borders the road to the northeast. While this area may not technically be considered wetlands, it is part of the floodplain of the Missouri River—cattails and water grass line parts of the road. At the west end of the road, we passed some impressive bluffs, just before the trail veered left off of the road into the woods. From here the trail climbs .4 mile through dense forest, another of my favorite areas. At the top of the hill, the trail emerges at a clearing by the archery range. Proceed with caution here. While the trail does not come close to the range, there is always a chance of a stray arrow. The open field adjacent to the archery area is a "no leash" area for dogs.

ARCHERY RANGE TO END (WEST OF 93RD STREET): From the archery range back to our point of entry, just west of 93rd Street, it is 1.3 miles. As the trail leaves the clearing by the "no leash" dog area, it enters another section of the forest that makes you wonder whether you are in Kansas. The leaves of some of the young hickories measured 12 inches. The trail emerges from the woods at a clearing behind a home, about .7 mile from the start of this section. Shortly thereafter, the trail passes through a weedy clearing and then reenters the woods. We spotted purple coneflower among the wildflowers. From here, the trail passes in and out of mowed clearings and crosses a road leading to the children's fishing area. When you emerge from behind shelter 10, next to 93rd Street, you have finished, although the trail ribbons direct you across 93rd Street and back to the point of entry.

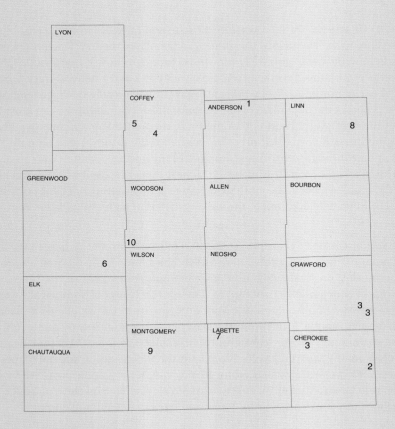

SOUTHEAST REGION

1. Prairie Spirit Trail (see Northeast Region)
2. Spring River Wildlife Area
3. Mined Land Wildlife Area
4. John Redmond Reservoir
5. Flint Hills National Wildlife Refuge
6. Fall River Lake
7. Big Hill Lake
8. Marais des Cygnes Wildlife Area
9. Elk City Lake
10. Toronto Lake

SOUTH

Southeast
R E G I O N

EAST

Spring River Wildlife Area

The 424-acre Spring River Wildlife Area is the only state-owned wildlife area in the Ozark Plateau, a unique 50-square-mile region in the far southeastern corner of Kansas (Kansas covers 82,282 square miles). As its name suggests, the Ozark Plateau is part of the Ozarks, which cover southern Missouri and northern Arkansas. Dense hardwood forests blanket the rocky hillsides, where brooks and springs seep and flow over some of the oldest exposed rock strata in Kansas. Spring River, which has its source in Missouri and its mouth in Oklahoma, forms the eastern border of the wildlife area. Rising above the river is a forested sandstone ridge, where in spring and summer woodland wildflowers bloom profusely in the dense understory of ferns, may-apples, buckbrush, greenbrier, golden currant, and wild gooseberry. Kansas Wildlife and Parks mows about 2 miles of trails (most are abandoned farm roads) along the western edge of the 200-acre forest. The wildlife area also includes about 70 acres of native prairie and 90 acres of restored grasslands, as well as 55 acres of cropland. Over 100 species of plants, including many showy wildflowers, have been identified in a prairie meadow in the northwest corner of the wildlife area. Ownership: KDWP (316) 231-3173.

HUNTING REMINDER: Spring River Wildlife Area is open to public hunting. It is always advisable to wear bright colors when you hike—preferably an orange hunting vest and hat.

HIKE LENGTH
Mowed paths cover about 2 miles, but the entire wildlife area is suitable for hiking.

DIRECTIONS

From Pittsburg, take U.S. 400/69 Alternate south to K-96 and turn east. Travel 3 miles on K-96 to 100th Street and turn north. If you cross Spring River, you have

Spring River Wildlife Area

gone too far east. Travel .25 mile north on 100th Street to the south parking area, marked by a large sign for the Spring River Wildlife Area. (Note: in April 1997, there was no sign for the wildlife area on K-96.) The south parking area is closest to the mowed trail into the woodlands. The north parking area, which borders the native prairie and grasslands area, can be reached by turning west off of 100th Street onto Salisbury Road, then north onto 97th Terrace, west on Stone Road, then north again on 95th Street, a total of 1.25 miles from the south parking area. The north parking area is just north of Bethlehem Road on the east side of 95th Street.

ℹ GENERAL INFORMATION

Here in the extreme southeast corner of Kansas, thousands of feet of rock have slowly weathered away, exposing the oldest sedimentary rock that appears at the surface in Kansas. As you walk through the lush woodlands at the Spring River Wildlife Area, the landscape bears little resemblance to the rest of Kansas. This area receives more than 40 inches of precipitation in an average year (compared to a statewide average of 26.95 inches); temperatures have averaged 2.4 degrees above statewide averages; and the growing season is nearly 200 days long, 40 days longer than in the northwestern corner of Kansas. It is not surprising that the flora and fauna here are unique. Among the more common oaks, hickories, elm, and hackberry trees, you

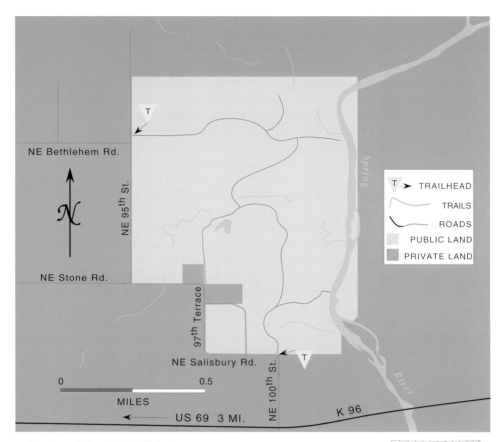

Spring River Wildlife Area

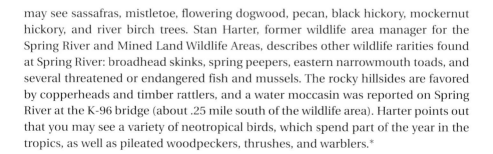

may see sassafras, mistletoe, flowering dogwood, pecan, black hickory, mockernut hickory, and river birch trees. Stan Harter, former wildlife area manager for the Spring River and Mined Land Wildlife Areas, describes other wildlife rarities found at Spring River: broadhead skinks, spring peepers, eastern narrowmouth toads, and several threatened or endangered fish and mussels. The rocky hillsides are favored by copperheads and timber rattlers, and a water moccasin was reported on Spring River at the K-96 bridge (about .25 mile south of the wildlife area). Harter points out that you may see a variety of neotropical birds, which spend part of the year in the tropics, as well as pileated woodpeckers, thrushes, and warblers.*

* In "Kansas Ozarks? Spring River Wildlife Area" by Stan Harter in *Kansas Wildlife and Parks,* July/August 1995.

THE HIKE

At the south parking area, look for the mowed trail behind the large park sign. For a short distance, the trail passes through savanna, a transition area where groves of hickories and oaks are intermixed with prairie grasses and other plants. We followed the trail across a creek and then veered east into the forest. As we neared Spring River, the trail ended, and we rambled on through the woods, following deer paths where we could find them. This may not be advisable in the summer, when poison ivy takes hold, and the tangled undergrowth makes navigation difficult. In mid-April 1997, prairie and marsh phlox, violets, golden groundsel, and many other woodland flowers brightened the woods. Take time to walk down to the river bank—in spring, we saw rapids. From south to north, you can follow the woodlands along the Spring River for about a mile.

We did not travel far before hiking back up the ridge, where we intersected the mowed path that winds along the western edge of the woods. From the trail, we could see the tallgrass prairie through the trees. The prairie meadows are filled with wildflowers from spring through fall. There is little topographical relief on the mowed trail through the woods. Watch for the trail to branch into the tallgrass prairie. We followed this branch for a short distance to its end, then returned to the woods. Soon after this, the trail reaches a scenic clearing and crosses a sandstone shelf, where shallow, clear waters trickle over the rocks. From here the trail gradually shifts from north to west, then as it leaves the woods, the trail crosses a shallow draw and turns south. Watch for the pond to the east. Shortly after this, we traveled through a corridor of trees, between two windbreaks, before we realized that it would be difficult to reach the bordering county road (Stone Road) without trespassing on private property to the west and south. To remain on the public land, we gingerly forded a bramble patch—a route we do not recommend. In hindsight, we should have returned on the original path. After we had completed our fieldwork, the wildlife area manager informed us that additional trails have been mowed, as shown on the map.

Mined Land Wildlife Area

The Mined Land Wildlife Area covers 14,500 acres spread out across Crawford, Cherokee, and Labette Counties in southeastern Kansas. This unique area is riddled with more than 200 clear lakes, once strip mines, set within the wooded hills of the Cherokee Lowlands. Mining began here in the late 1800s and continued into the 1970s, and coal shovels have left long, fingerlike trenches, sometimes 50 feet deep and 100 feet wide, as well as open pits. Prior to the passage of stringent federal and state legislation, strip mines were abandoned once the coal was removed and allowed to fill with water. Mining companies considered the land useless and donated thousands of acres to the state of Kansas. Trees, brush, and grasses have grown around the glassy lakes. While there are just a few short, established trails here, old mining roads and animal trails offer additional hiking opportunities. Ownership: KDWP (316) 231-3173.

HUNTING REMINDER: The Mined Land Wildlife Area is open to hunting and trapping. Hikers should check with the wildlife area manager about regulations, maps, and hunting seasons, and wear bright colors when hiking, especially hunter orange. In spring turkey season, avoid wearing bright blue, red, or white, especially in combination, due to the similarity to the colors of a male turkey.

DIRECTIONS AND TRAIL ACCESS

The Kansas Department of Wildlife and Parks has divided the Mined Land Wildlife Area ("MLWA") into 46 numbered areas in three general locations: the West Mineral Areas, near the town of West Mineral; the Pittsburg Areas; and the Scammon Areas, near the town of Scammon. The map shows areas 1 and 21, where we recommend hiking, although there are many other areas to hike, including MLWA 3, MLWA 4, and MLWA 6 (each located in the "Pittsburg Areas").

Mined Land Wildlife Area (MLWA 1)

MLWA 1: This is located just north of Frontenac at the junction of U.S. 69 and U.S. 160, in the "Pittsburg Areas." The entrance is just east of the junction. The wildlife area contains about 2.5 miles of gravel road in addition to about 1 mile of fishing access/hiking trails.

MLWA 3: Although not shown in detail on the map, this site is easy to find. It lies along the Missouri state line, directly east of Pittsburg. From U.S. 69, turn east at U.S. 160, as if going to MLWA 1. Continue east on U.S. 160 about 5 miles to the state line, then turn south and proceed 1.5 miles on the gravel road to the parking area for MLWA 3, on the west side of the road. The parking area is small, and signs may be difficult to see, as vandals routinely destroy or remove them. Hiking is also possible at the south end of MLWA 3.

MLWA 4: This area is located immediately south of MLWA 3, and is accessed from two different parking areas. The east parking area is approximately 1 mile south of the parking area for MLWA 3. The west parking area is approximately 2.5 miles south of U.S. 160 on South 260th Street. There is a sign on the east side of the road.

MLWA 6: This area is located about 2.5 miles west of the junction of U.S. 69 Bypass and 20th Street, on the south side of the road. When entering the area, take the first left turn on the wildlife-area road and follow it until you reach the trailhead on the east side of the road. A second trail is located farther south along the road and has two parking sites. Additional information about these trails is available at the Mined Land Wildlife Area Main Office, also located near MLWA 6.

MLWA 21: This area is southwest of Pittsburg in the "West Mineral Areas." From Pittsburg, take U.S. 69 south to U.S. 160/400; turn right (west) for 7 miles to K-7; turn left (south), go 4 miles to K-102; turn right (west), go 5 miles to NW 50th Street; turn left (south), go 1.7 miles to Star Valley Road; turn right (west), go 3 miles to NW 80th Street; turn left (south), go .6 mile to the "Deer Trace Canoe Trail" sign on the east side of the road. Follow the wildlife-area road east to the end of the turn-around to hike the "Fishermen's Trail" marked on the adjacent map, or take your canoe and enjoy the canoe trail.

To explore other areas within the Mined Land Wildlife Area, stop at the Mined Land Wildlife Area main office near MLWA 6 (507 E. 560th Avenue) or at the field office (7545 NW Belleview Road, Columbus) for detailed maps.

GENERAL INFORMATION

The mining of coal is interwoven with the history and development of southeastern Kansas. A series of bituminous coal-bearing rock formations, called the Cherokee Group, lie close to the surface throughout the region (in northeastern Kansas, the coal is around 700 feet deep) and has been commercially mined since the 1860s. At the peak of mining in Crawford County, 14,000 miners were digging 7,000,000 tons of coal annually in 65 mines.* Pittsburg, founded in 1876, is an old mining town, named after Pittsburgh, Pennsylvania because of the large quantities of coal, lead, and zinc found in the area. Between 1890 and 1910, more than 100 coal camps and company towns, such as Coalvale, Scotts Camp, Camp 50, and Red Onion, were built near mine-shafts or road junctions throughout southeastern Kansas. Much of U.S. 69 from Arma to Pittsburg is undermined. Eventually, strip-mining production exceeded underground mining. New regulations now require mining companies to refill the strip pits and return the land to pasture or farming.†

🏃🏃 THE HIKES

MLWA 1: The quiet woods and tranquil, almost idyllic, lakes make this an especially scenic area, and the shaded roads are good for hiking. There are also plenty of opportunities to follow fishermen's trails or animal paths to or around the lakes, although the dense undergrowth makes hiking through the woods difficult in the summer. Oaks and hickories dominate the woods, where redbuds and dogwood bloom in the spring. Woodland wildflowers are also plentiful. You're sure to see a variety of wildlife, including waterfowl, bobwhite, wild turkey, and white-tailed deer, particularly if you hike in early morning or evening.

MLWA 3 AND 4: This remote area of the Mined Lands sits on the Missouri border, east of Pittsburg. We did not hike in MLWA 3, but the map provided by the wildlife manager shows a mowed trail from the road that branches after about .25 mile and leads to several small lakes. We did hike in MLWA 4, where an old mining road (just under a mile) runs through the middle and is bordered by lakes and streams. The only reminder of civilization is a large power line that crosses this area. As we continued down the road, we nearly jumped at the loud honk of a large Canada goose in the lake ahead of us. A number of geese were enjoying the still water in a tree-shrouded cove. The eastern half of the road is more scenic than the western—it follows a wooded creek. The road at the eastern end of this area is the Missouri border.

MLWA 6: While we did not hike in this area, the wildlife manager suggested hiking two mowed loops that lead to several strip lakes in this area, as described in the Directions section on page 101.

---

* From *Kansas: Historical Tour Guide* by D. Ray Wilson (Carpentersville, IL: Crossroads Communications, 1994).

† Rex C. Buchanan and James R. McCauley's *Roadside Kansas: A Travelers Guide to Its Geology and Landmarks,* the source of many of the above facts, includes a number of fascinating stories about the coal mines, towns, and history of southeastern Kansas, as well as a geologic history of the area (Lawrence: University Press of Kansas, 1987).

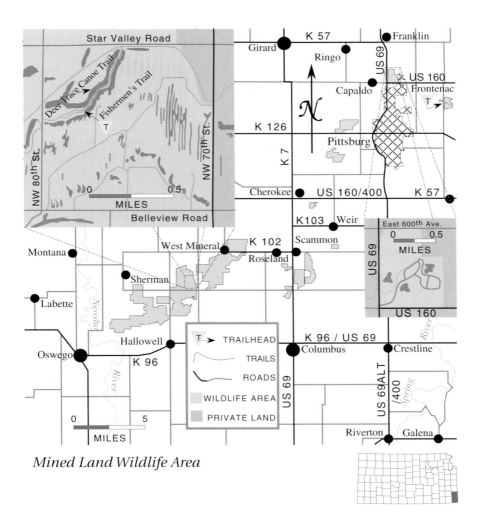

Mined Land Wildlife Area

MLWA 21: The landscape of this Mined Land Wildlife Area, within the West Mineral Area, is completely different from that of MLWA 1 and 4. Rolling, open prairies border the clear finger-lakes to the east and north. A short fishermen's trail, marked on the map, runs adjacent to the Deer Trace Canoe Trail, a 2-mile trail through the strip lakes. The worn fishermen's trail follows a narrow ribbon of land between two strip lakes.

Hickory Creek Trail, John Redmond Reservoir

John Redmond Reservoir

C learing the 14-mile Hickory Creek Trail at John Redmond Reservoir was not an easy task. Twice in 1993 and once in 1995 the trail was damaged by high water levels in the reservoir, resulting from heavy rains. With perseverance and many hours of work by volunteer crews, including the North America Trail Ride Conference and the Kansas Trails Council, the lower, lakeside loops of the trail were moved to higher ground. The trail was worth waiting for; the landscape and terrain are diverse. Whether you prefer a hike through the open prairie, hilly woodlands, or lush river valley, if you stay on this trail long enough, you will not be disappointed. The trail wraps around a number of interesting features, such as Massasauga Mound (a haunt of rattlesnakes), Reemers Point, Fire Tower Pond, Screech Owl Pond, the Log, and Anglers Rest. Ownership: USACE (316) 364-8614.

HIKE LENGTH
Hickory Creek Trail ....14.1 miles (one-way)

The main trail, which is blazed in blue, is 7.9 miles one-way; the lake-side loops, blazed in white, and the land-side loops, blazed in orange, total 6.2 miles.

DIRECTIONS

John Redmond Reservoir is about 55 miles south of Topeka and 37 miles southeast of Emporia. From I-35, take Exit 155 and travel south on U.S. 75. The entrance to the reservoir is on the west side of the road at New Strawn. At the project office, pick up a copy of the 11" × 17" Corps of Engineers trail map, showing the location of each of the numbered trail markers (1–26), the mileage between each marker, and water crossings subject to flooding, as well as trail rules and camping and hiking tips. The project director indicated that the Corps is working on a larger-scale map-update that is easier to read and less confusing.

⚑ TRAIL ACCESS

OVERLOOK TRAILHEAD: This trailhead, at the southeastern end of the trail, is located in the Damsite Area, past the project office, on the west side of the road, where parking is available.

REDMOND COVE TRAILHEAD: Do not turn off into the Damsite Area, but continue west from New Strawn about 1.4 miles; just before the road turns north, watch for the park road on the left (south) side of the road, leading to Redmond Cove (the trail crosses the park road as shown on the map).

HICKORY CREEK TRAILHEAD: Follow the directions to the Redmond Cove Trailhead but continue on the paved road as it turns north. After 1 mile, watch for the gravel road on the left and turn west. This road leads to the Hickory Creek East Recreation Area shown on the map. After 1 mile, the gravel road turns north. Follow this road for another .25 mile and watch for the trail, which is located slightly off of the road. As the map shows, the trail (actually, a lakeside loop blazed in white) follows this gravel road north for about another .25 mile, where it intersects with the main (blue-blazed) trail.

ℹ GENERAL INFORMATION

John Redmond Reservoir impounds the Neosho River, which is also dammed in Oklahoma to form the Grand Lake of the Cherokees. The 18,500-acre Flint Hills National Wildlife Refuge borders the reservoir on the northwest. The normal water pool at John Redmond Reservoir is about 2,400 surface acres larger than its nearest neighbor, Melvern Lake. Flooding in the Neosho River Valley was common prior to the completion of the John Redmond Dam in 1964. The town of Strawn, founded sometime in the early 1870s, was frequently inundated and now lies beneath the reservoir waters. Strawn was booming in 1910 and was the second largest shipping point on the Neosho division of the M.K.T. Railroad. As fields were cleared and drained for cultivation, however, the floods grew worse as the Neosho River over-flowed its banks. After a dam site on the Neosho River was selected, and the residents of "old" Strawn realized that their town was located within the pool area of the John Redmond Reservoir, they moved Strawn 6 miles eastward to higher ground and named it New Strawn.* The reservoir is named after John Redmond (1920–1953), who was trained under William Allen White and eventually became the publisher of the *Burlington Daily Republican.* John Redmond was one of the first to campaign for flood control and water conservation on the upper Neosho.

* This and more information can found in *Faded Dreams: More Ghost Towns of Kansas* by Daniel C. Fitzgerald (Lawrence: University Press of Kansas, 1994).

THE HIKE

HICKORY CREEK TRAIL: The key is understanding the blazing code. The main trail is blazed in blue. Branching off of the main trail are five white-blazed "lakeside" loops, none of which exceeds 1 mile, and four orange-blazed "landside" loops, two of which are shortcuts to shave mileage off the main trail. The southernmost orange loop is 1.6 miles, but the rest are no more than .6 mile. The trail is relatively flat, although at the northern end, it climbs a wooded ridge overlooking Hickory Creek. Lake views are infrequent. The trail is located in the Neosho River Valley, of which part is wooded, part is cultivated, and part is in native prairie grasses. In fall the big bluestem, Indian grass, switch grass, and sideoats grama turn varying hues of brown and orange—a spectacular sight when the sun shines through the tall plumes. When we hiked in October 1996, wet weather had prevented the Corps from using its equipment to keep the trails clear, and parts of the trail were overgrown. The trail is used by horses, and several areas, especially through the prairie, are rough and pitted by hooves. According to the Corps, the trail has smoothed out with use.

We started at the Overlook Trailhead and traveled the mowed trail through a tree-dotted field before we intersected with the first orange loop at marker 1. The longer orange loop travels through open prairie, around Massasauga Mound and an old, now dry, rearing pond. The field in late October was speckled with scarlet-colored sumac, and a few hardy wildflowers were still in bloom. We enjoyed the distant view of the lake, which we rarely saw on the remainder of the trail. The blue trail between markers 1 and 5 will take you through some prairie as well as woodlands. At marker 2 watch for the trail to branch left. This side trail will take you to the Damsite North Trailhead (shown on the Corps map but not reserved for hikers only, like the Overlook Trailhead) and the Pin Oak Group Camping Area, less than .2 mile west. If you are hiking with children, be aware that both the orange loop and the blue trail cross the road before reaching marker 5 and that the blue trail crosses the road again before the Redmond Cove Trailhead.

At the northernmost point on the blue trail north of the road, it crosses a stream. The Corps map shows this as subject to flooding. Between markers 5 and 6, the trail travels through woodlands. At marker 6, a white loop branches to the left, passing near a pond. The blue trail passes through what the Corps map calls the "South Slope Prairie Area." At marker 8, watch for the .3-mile white loop (the Corps map marks this as the "narrows loop") through cedars. Less than .3 mile further, the orange trail branches off at marker 10 for a .3 mile shortcut. For the next 2 miles the blue trail winds in and out of scenic woodlands, dipping down and across old streambeds and across prairie. This area and the hickory woodlands on the ridge at the north end of the trail were our favorite sections. We found the section around markers 13 and 14 confusing. If you are on the white trail, you can rejoin the blue trail at marker 13 by heading north, or continue on the white trail to marker 16 by continuing south. The entire white loop from marker 12 to 16 is 1.1 miles, while the blue section is about 2 miles.

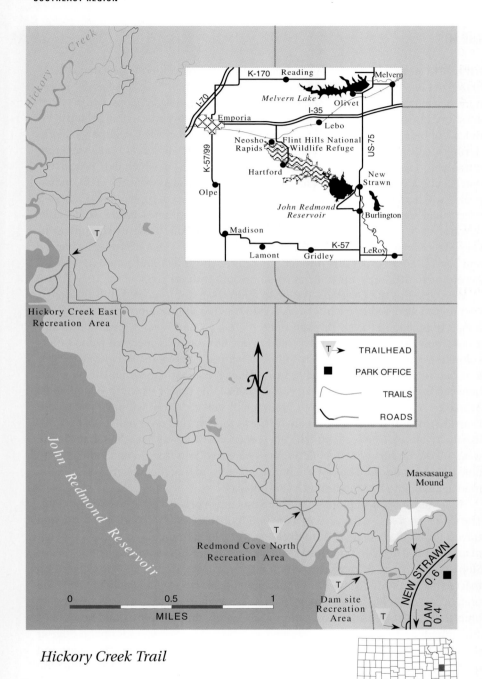

Hickory Creek Trail

Back on the blue trail, just past marker 17, the trail passes Screech Owl Pond and crosses a gravel road, continuing north. From here, the white trail runs east-west, just north off of the road, and then turns and runs north through cottonwood trees to a road gate and trailhead. If you opt for the blue trail, it passes through prairie and some trees. At marker 18 on the blue trail, watch for the orange .6-mile loop to the east—this loop was fairly rough and weedy. At marker 19, the blue trail travels on the road for a short distance before it turns west to loop down toward Hickory Creek. At marker 22, the blue trail follows the road again for a short distance before turning east to head toward a ridge overlooking Hickory Creek. Just before marker 23, the trail crosses a gravel road, and then the white trail branches to the north. We followed the blue trail first and returned on the white trail. We never saw marker 26, which marks the end of the trail. According to the Corps of Engineers, marker 26 keeps disappearing. The first part of the return trip on the white loop was overgrown, and we navigated with the help of the blazes on the trees. This area of the trail, along the wooded ridge overlooking Hickory Creek, was one of the more scenic.

NOTE: The Corps permits primitive overnight camping for trail users at the Hickory Creek East Recreation Area, but no facilities are available.

Flint Hills National Wildlife Refuge

Flint Hills National Wildlife Refuge

T he Flint Hills National Wildlife Refuge is an 18,500-acre area in the Neosho River Valley, about 12 miles southeast of Emporia. This wide, flat river valley is a mixture of wildlife habitats, including bluestem prairie, hardwood timber, marshes, sloughes, and croplands, managed primarily for migratory waterfowl. The refuge is located just upstream from John Redmond Reservoir and is within the Central Flyway, a migratory route from warm wintering grounds in South and Central America to cooler summer homes in Canada and the Arctic. Although the refuge is named after the Flint Hills, which lie about 25 miles to the west, it is located in the physiographic region known as the Osage Cuestas (Spanish for hills or slopes). Several hiking options are available: you can hike the short loop trails scattered across the refuge or the isolated roads. We recommend hiking the Dove Roost Trail, a scenic 1-mile trail through tallgrass and woodlands, where you are likely to see a variety of wildlife. Note: for map see John Redmond Reservoir. Ownership: USACE (administered by U.S. Fish and Wildlife Service) (316) 392-5553.

HUNTING REMINDER: Parts of the Flint Hills National Wildlife Refuge are open to hunting and trapping. Be sure to pick up the map available at the refuge office (see Directions below), which shows the public hunting areas. It is always advisable to wear bright colors when you hike—preferably an orange hunting vest and hat.

HIKE LENGTHS
The Hartford Trail, Burgess Trail, and Dove Roost Trail are all short nature trails—none exceeds a mile.

DIRECTIONS

Stop first at the refuge office for a public-use map showing the location of marshes, ponds, and areas that might be closed during waterfowl season. From I-35, take

Exit 141 (K-130), which is about 8 miles east of Emporia. Travel south 8 miles on K-130 to Hartford High School and turn right (west). After three blocks, turn right (north) to reach the refuge office.

⚑ TRAIL ACCESS

THE HARTFORD TRAIL: Continue north on the road from the office for .25 mile, then go right (east) for about .4 mile to the trail.

THE BURGESS TRAIL: This was under construction when we visited in late fall 1996. To reach this trail from K-130, go north from Hartford 1 mile; before you leave the refuge, turn left; follow the road .2 mile south to the trailhead parking lot.

DOVE ROOST TRAIL: From Hartford, travel east on the road leading to the Hartford Recreational Area and boat ramp. Do not turn off, however, into this recreational area. Cross the Neosho River and travel 4 miles east; turn right (south), go .5 mile; turn left (east), go 2.1 miles, then turn right (south) and go 1 mile to the trailhead. Watch for the signs along these roads to the Dove Roost Nature Trail.

[i] GENERAL INFORMATION

At the refuge office, pick up the brochure "Birds of Flint Hills National Wildlife Refuge." This lists 291 species of birds found in the refuge, including 88 species that nest there. The peak of waterfowl migration occurs in November, an ideal time to hike with your binoculars. The Neosho River snakes through the middle of the Flint Hills National Wildlife Refuge, from the northwest corner to the southeast end, where the river is impounded to form John Redmond Reservoir. Many record-setting and unusual fish have been found in the river, such as the state record flathead catfish, 86 pounds 4 ounces and 55 inches long, caught in August 1966. Paddlefish, or spoonbill, which have long, spoon-shaped snouts, no bones, no scales, and feed exclusively on plankton, also are found in the river. The largest paddlefish caught in Kansas was taken from the Neosho River; it weighed 73 pounds and measured 69 inches long. The Neohso River is also one of the few places where the endangered Neosho madtom can still be found. This unusual catfish, only a few inches in length, has been hurt by pollution and the impoundment of the river.*

🥾 THE HIKES

The terrain at the Flint Hills National Wildlife Refuge is flat and open, although trees line the creeks, ponds, and river. As the refuge public-use map shows, marshes cover

---

* This and more information about the Neosho River and its fish can be found in *Fishes in Kansas* by Frank B. Cross and Joseph T. Collins (Lawrence: University Press of Kansas, 1995).

a significant portion of the refuge, which sits in the broad floodplain of the Neosho River. The refuge brochure warns that water levels fluctuate seasonally and that deep channels may not be visible. Several sections of road travel through the marshes, where you are likely to see a variety of waterfowl. On foot, you can readily scan the cattails, sedges, and rushes for waterfowl, which enjoy the cover. Several great blue herons took flight within several yards of the road where we were walking. While the landscape at the refuge is somewhat stark, and in late fall and winter somewhat brown and foreboding, this only enhances the beauty of the Kansas skies and provides a good backdrop for spotting the abundant wildlife.

HARTFORD TRAIL: Close to the refuge headquarters, this is a short walk through some river-bottom timber, where a glimpse of a deer or wood duck is likely.

BURGESS TRAIL: Handicapped accessible, this trail was not completed when we hiked at the refuge in October 1996. It opened in September 1997 and runs on top of a dike. The trail was designed to provide excellent views of wetlands.

DOVE ROOST TRAIL: Circling a pond near a bend in the Neosho River, this is a pleasant hike through tallgrass prairie as well as woodlands. At dusk or early morning, you may see deer. We heard a variety of songbirds in the woods and especially enjoyed the view of the Neosho River.

Post Oak Trail, Fall River Lake

Fall River Lake

F all River Lake lies between the Chatauqua Hills on the east and the Flint Hills on the west, in the Osage Cuestas. The Post Oak Trail, in the Quarry Bay area of Fall River State Park, is a short, scenic loop through woods of post oak and blackjack oak and several open meadows. Points of interest include occasional limestone outcroppings. Kansas Wildlife and Parks is developing plans for two additional trails—the Catclaw Trail, a loop that will connect to the Post Oak Trail across the park road, and the Bluestem Prairie Trail, a loop that will connect to the Catclaw Trail. The new trails will provide an additional 2.5 miles of trails at Fall River. Ownership: KDWP (316) 637-2213; USACE (316) 658-4445.

HIKE LENGTH
Post Oak Trail.. .75 mile (new trails will add 2.5 miles)

DIRECTIONS AND TRAIL ACCESS

Fall River Lake is in southeastern Greenwood County, about 4 miles northeast of the town of Fall River and about 17 miles southeast of Eureka. From the intersection of K-99 and K-96 (which is about 6.5 miles south of Climax), travel 7.5 miles east on K-96 to the entrance to Fall River Lake. Turn north. The Post Oak Trail is northeast of the Fall River Dam. Follow the park road across the dam and continue northeast up the hill on the road leading to the state park office/maintenance facility. (Note: the intersection just past the dam is confusing. The road to the far left [northwest] leads to the Quarry Bay camping/picnic area.) Watch for the trail sign on the east side of the road, just before the park office. The trailhead is well marked.

[i] GENERAL INFORMATION

Fall River is a tributary of the Verdigris River. Fall River Lake is one of the older and smaller Corps of Engineers lake projects in Kansas. It was completed in 1949, only one year after Kanopolis Dam, the first Corps of Engineers dam in Kansas. Fall River Lake covers a surface area of only 2,450 acres (Milford Lake, the largest in Kansas, has 15,700 surface acres of water). Five other lakes, including Toronto, Elk City, and Neodesha Lakes in Kansas, occupy the Verdigris River Basin.

Fall River derives its name from its waterfalls. Early settlers of Greenwood County were attracted to its clear waters and abundant wildlife. The elderberries, wild grape, strawberries, gooseberries, pawpaws (small trees with banana-like fruit), plums, persimmons, mulberries, and walnuts that grew along the river added variety to an otherwise dull and often meager diet. In 1872, a 15-year-old boy hunting squirrels on Otter Creek (which flows into Fall River east of Climax, where the Fall River State Wildlife Area is now located) shot a panther stretched out on a tree limb. Gray wolves roamed the area until the disappearance of the bison. Between 1850 and 1900, certain game, including bison, elk, black bear, antelope, white-tailed deer, and wild turkey were hunted so extensively that they were either eliminated or drastically reduced in the county. In 1858, salt springs were discovered a mile northwest of the town of Fall River. Three barrels of water from the springs yielded one barrel of salt. The salt won a $50 prize at the Territorial Fair in 1862 for the best salt exhibited. The town of Salt Springs, established after the organization of a town company in 1869, was short-lived—one of the organizers refused to deed over half of the acreage on which the town was situated.*

🚶🚶 THE HIKES

POST OAK TRAIL: This grass-covered trail circles a wooded hillside in Fall River State Park. While there are no overlooks or views of the lake, the woods are quiet and lush. Watch for the post oak, a small, scraggly oak that grows well in the sandstone areas of eastern Kansas. As the name suggests, post oaks are used for fence posts and rail fences. I hiked the northern side of the loop first, veering left at the trailhead. The trail gradually descends through the woods, eventually coming within view of Craig Creek, an intermittent stream. Here the trail turns and climbs back up the hill, winding through limestone outcroppings. Not surprisingly, petroglyphs have been discovered in southeastern Greenwood County, on a large stone outcropping. An 1880 article in the *Eureka Herald* described petroglyphs found on upper Fall River, which included tracks of a turkey, a pony or a mule, a deer, moccasins, and an impression of a hand or paw. The land where Fall River Lake is now located once belonged to the Osage Indians, who were removed from Missouri around 1810 and moved to southeastern Kansas.

* This and more information can be found in the two-volume *History of Greenwood County*, compiled by the Greenwood County Historical Society (Wichita: Josten's Publications, 1986).

CATCLAW TRAIL: Eventually, the Post Oak Trail will tie into a new trail, the Catclaw Trail, directly across the road. The Catclaw Trail will travel through tallgrass prairie, along sandstone ridges, and across wooded and open floodplains. At the the north end of the Catclaw loop, near the rock pit, the Catclaw Trail will connect to the Bluestem Prairie Trail.

Ruth Nixon Memorial Trail, Big Hill Lake

Big Hill Lake

The Ruth Nixon Memorial Trail travels along a beautiful forested ridge overlooking Big Hill Lake. We hiked this trail in the fall, when the oaks, hickories, and walnut trees were varying shades of yellow and red. Big Hill Lake sits in a valley cut by Big Hill Creek, surrounded by the hills sometimes referred to as the Labette County Ozarks. The entire trail is within view of the lake, offering plenty of opportunities to view migratory waterfowl. A 17-mile horse trail winds around three-fourths of the lake, but we did not hike it because the section we could see appeared overgrown. It may be worth checking on in the winter, but be warned that all of the horse trail is in a public hunting area. The Corps of Engineers map of the lake shows the route of the horse trail. Ownership: USACE (316) 336-2741.

HIKE LENGTH
Ruth Nixon Memorial Trail... 1 mile (one-way)

DIRECTIONS AND TRAIL ACCESS

Big Hill Lake is located 4.5 miles east of Cherryvale, in northwestern Labette County. From U.S. 169, turn east onto Main Street in Cherryvale and travel 1 mile to a T intersection. Turn north and travel .8 mile to County Road 5200, then turn east to the lake. At Cherryvale Parkway, a paved park road, turn south and travel past the Corps of Engineers project office, to the Overlook Area. The south trailhead is just east of the parking area and is well marked by a large sign and map. The north trailhead can be accessed by turning north on Cherryvale Parkway. It is north of Cherryvale Park, at the fishing berm.

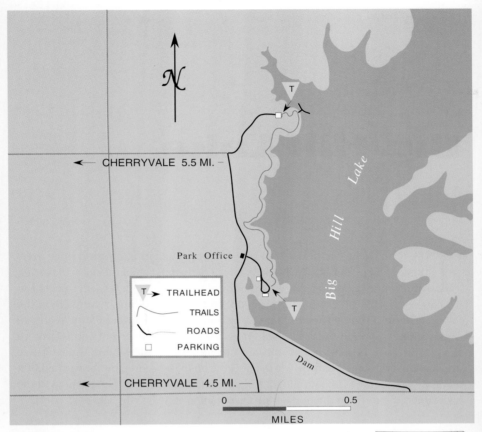

Ruth Nixon Memorial Trail

i GENERAL INFORMATION

The area surrounding Big Hill Creek was inhabited by various tribes and bands of Indians long before white settlers arrived in Kansas. Nomadic bands of hunters and gatherers frequented this area during the Paleo-Indian period (10,000–6,000 B.C.), as evidenced by artifacts and human remains. Before impoundment of lake waters began, archaeologists excavated three Cuesta Indian sites, which included four lodges and numerous artifacts now displayed at the project office. In more recent history, the Osage Indians lived on the banks of Big Hill Creek, named after one of the leaders of the Osage, Paˊlˊˊn-No-Pa-She (Not Afraid of Long Hairs) or Big Hill Joe, as he was dubbed by white settlers. In the summer of 1868, the Osage, who once dominated the territory between the Arkansas and Red Rivers, ceded most of their remaining lands in Kansas and moved to reservations in Oklahoma. At the turn of the twentieth century, the town of Cherryvale, about 4.5 miles west of Big Hill Lake, had become a leading brick manufacturer. Kilns at the six brick plants in town turned out an estimated 500,000 bricks per day, made from shale quarried from the extensive mounds throughout the area. The famous "Don't Spit on Sidewalk" bricks were manufactured at the Cherryvale brickyards. A Topeka doctor introduced this slogan as part of a campaign begun in 1908 against tuberculosis.*

THE HIKE

RUTH NIXON MEMORIAL TRAIL: From the south trailhead, the trail winds along a scenic, oak-dominated ridge parallel to the shoreline. It emerges twice, only briefly, from the woods. Less than .2 mile from the start, watch for a side-trail to your left (west) leading up to the overlook shelter. As the trail edges closer to the lake, the panoramic views through the trees are spectacular. Twin footbridges are located at the halfway point, where the trail branches for a short loop to a resting spot closer to the shoreline. A short distance past this loop, several side-paths travel west up the ridge to a shelter and picnic facilities. The trail ends at the fishing berm, where it turns west up the ridge to the north trailhead.

The trail is dedicated in memory of Ruth Nixon, a promotor and benefactor of Big Hill Lake. The trail brochure, available at the trailhead, rates the trail as moderately rugged. We found the main trunk of the trail to be easy, but the climb up the ridge can leave you winded.

* See Cherryvale Centennial 1871–1971, "A New Century Beckons."

Marais des Cygnes Wildlife Area

Marais des Cygnes Wildlife Area

The 7,235-acre Marais des Cygnes (pronounced *mare-de-zeen*) Wildlife Area, in the broad floodplain of the Marais des Cygnes River in Linn County, features natural and manmade wetlands, scenic hills blanketed by mature hardwood forests, native prairie, and croplands. French explorers gave the river its name, which means "marsh of the swans." While there are no established hiking trails, Kansas Wildlife and Parks periodically mows a path around several of the marshes. In addition, the 3.7-mile gravel road that encircles the isolated 485-acre marsh designated "Unit G," in the far northwestern corner of the wildlife area, offers a prime vantage point for observing a wide variety of waterfowl. Over 300 species of birds have been identified here. Call ahead for information about spring and fall migrations, when as many as 150,000 birds have been observed in the wildlife area. Ownership: KDWP (913) 352-8941.

HUNTING REMINDER: Much of the wildlife area is open to hunting, although hunting from the dikes, levees, and roads is prohibited. If you plan to hike off the roads, be sure to pick up the map available at park headquarters, which shows the public hunting areas. It is always advisable to wear bright colors—preferably an orange hunting vest and hat.

DIRECTIONS

Marais des Cygnes Wildlife Area is just off of U.S. 69, about 60 miles south of Kansas City and about 30 miles north of Fort Scott. We recommend stopping at the park headquarters (clearly marked by a sign on the west side of U.S. 69) to inquire about current conditions of the marshes and any "hotspots" for migratory birds. Each year, Kansas Wildlife and Parks drains selected marshes, while others may be burned, disked, or mowed. At the park headquarters, ask for a map of the wildlife area before you hike off-road. The wildlife area is spread out over several sections, not all of which are contiguous. Below are directions to some of the marshes.

UNIT A (602 ACRES): From the entrance to the park headquarters, continue south on U.S. 69 for 1.4 miles and turn west shortly after crossing the Marais des Cygnes River. Watch for the sign for Unit A (on the south side of the road) just after you turn, and watch for the gravel road that borders the marsh, leading southwest from the sign.

UNITS F1 (115 ACRES) AND F2 (476 ACRES): The best access point is about 3 miles south of the entrance to the park headquarters, off of U.S. 69, on the west side of the highway. This is not a public road but is the second designated parking area past the Marais des Cygnes River on the west side of the highway.

UNIT G: Follow the directions to Unit A. After turning off of U.S. 69, continue 2.9 miles on the gravel road that borders Unit A to the west, and the Marais des Cygnes River to the east. Turn right (north) before crossing the railroad tracks near the town of Biocourt. After .7 mile, the road passes under the railroad tracks, and in another .7 mile it reaches Unit G.

NOTE: Units B and C1 are refuges and are closed to all activities, including hiking.

ⓘ GENERAL INFORMATION

The Marais des Cygnes Wildlife Area is one of several wildlife areas established in Kansas to protect, maintain, and enhance naturally occurring wetlands and other wildlife habitats that have long been a stopover for migratory birds. Recently, the U.S. Fish and Wildlife Service acquired 7,300 acres to the east of this site to establish the Marais des Cygnes National Wildlife Refuge. As of June 1997, Congress had not appropriated funds for improvements to, or the operation of, this refuge, and it was not open to the public. About 65 miles due west from here is the 18,500-acre Flint Hills National Wildlife Refuge, and another 145 miles further west are the 19,857-acre Cheyenne Bottoms Wildlife Area and the 21,820-acre Quivira National Wildlife Refuge. These wildlife areas and refuges, located in the Central Flyway (a major north-south migratory route), are critical refueling points for migratory birds. Hike in the Marais des Cygnes Wildlife Area in fall or spring to observe migratory waterfowl such as pelicans, double-crested cormorants, snow geese, Canada geese, white-fronted geese, and varieties of herons, egrets, and ducks.

🚶🚶 THE HIKES

All of the accessible hiking areas in the wildlife area are through open prairie and wetlands, at least in the growing seasons. While the hilly woodlands are picturesque, especially in the spring when woodland wildflowers and redbuds are in bloom, the dense understory of woody vegetation and ground cover makes hiking difficult. If you don't mind hiking gravel roads, we recommend hiking the 3.7-mile road that wraps around Unit G. The pool and surrounding wetlands are secluded, and you are likely to encounter a variety of wildlife.

UNIT G: From the entrance I turned left (west). The road is bordered on the south by forest, and by lake (or pool) on the north. After the road turns north and intersects with a road to the west, continue straight. (The property on the west side of the road is privately owned.) This is about the only section that does not have a good view of the pool. Turn right (east) at the next intersecting road to complete the loop around the marsh. This section, on the east side of the marsh, borders the Marais des Cygnes River to the east. The park map indicates that this section of the road may be closed seasonally.

UNIT A: Another accessible marsh pool, this is bordered by a gravel road, the northern section of which may also be closed seasonally. This is the largest unit in the wildlife area. The hike from the southeastern end (starting at the large park sign, traveling south, west, and then north) to the northern end of the marsh pool is about 3.25 miles. In June 1997, this marsh consisted of shallow sheet water and mud flats, a favored habitat of shorebirds.

Directions to Units F1 and F2 appear above because the park periodically mows a path around them. When I visited these pools in June 1997, the paths were too overgrown to hike.

Elk River Hiking Trail, Elk City Lake

Elk City Lake

The trails at Elk City Lake without a doubt rank among the top five in Kansas. *Outside* magazine lists the 15-mile Elk River Hiking Trail as the best hike in the state.* This trail, which winds along a rocky ridge on the north side of the lake, travels along sheer rock walls, under rock canopies, through rock tunnels and chambers, up rock steps to bluffs overlooking the lake, and around giant boulders, sometimes balanced precariously on end, in seeming defiance of gravity. We were fascinated by the mushroomlike rocks, table rocks, ledges, and a rock hollow carved by a small waterfall. Hikers have a wide selection to choose from at Elk City Lake: five trails around the lake range in length from .66 mile to 15 miles and in difficulty from easy to strenuous. Ownership: USACE (316) 331-0315; KDWP (316) 336-2741.

HUNTING REMINDER: The Elk River Hiking Trail and the Timber Ridge Trail are both in public hunting areas. Check hunting schedules before you hike and wear bright colors, preferably the orange hat and vest worn by hunters.

HIKE LENGTHS
Elk River Hiking Trail (blazed in blue) .... 15 miles (one-way)
Table Mound Hiking Trail (blazed in blue) .... 2.75 miles (one-way)
Green Thumb Nature Trail (blazed in white)......................... 1 mile (round-trip)
Post Oak Nature Trail (blazed in orange) .... .66 mile (round-trip)
Timber Ridge Hiking Trail (blazed in blue) .... 2.33 miles (round-trip)
Squaw Creek Multi-Use Trail .... 1 mile (one-way)

DIRECTIONS

The main entrance to Elk City Lake is approximately 1 mile west of Independence, north off of U.S. 160. Watch for the small lake sign on the north side of the highway.

* "America's Top Hikes: The Finest in Every State," *Outside* magazine, April 1996.

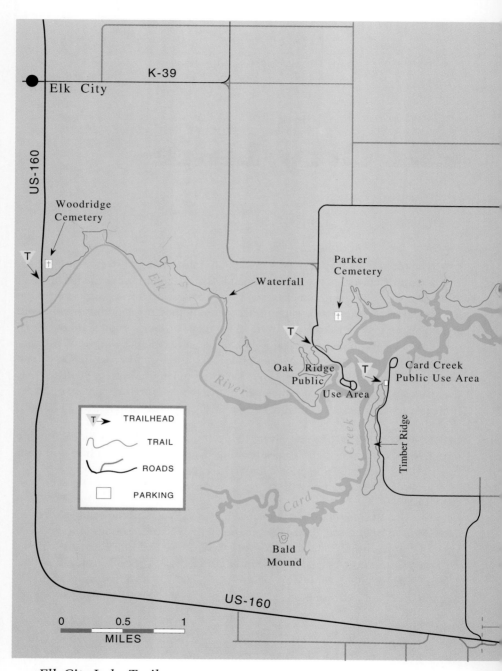

Elk City Lake Trails

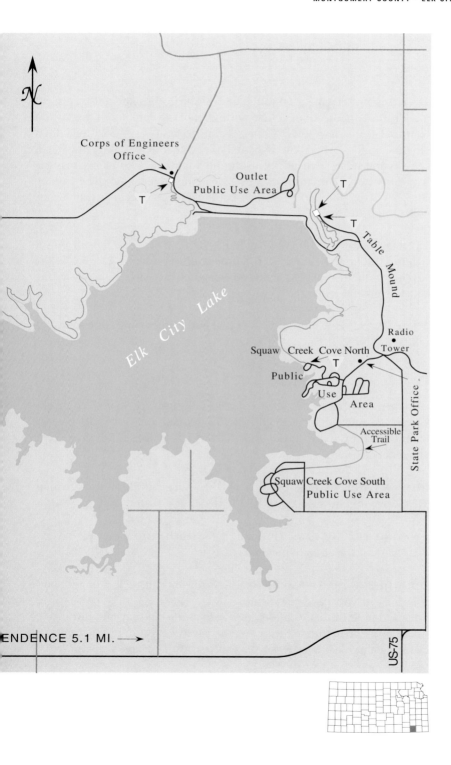

N

Corps of Engineers
Office

Outlet
Public Use Area

T

T

T

Table Mound

Elk City Lake

Radio
Tower

Squaw Creek Cove North

T

Public

Use

Area

State Park Office

Accessible
Trail

Squaw Creek Cove South
Public Use Area

ENDENCE 5.1 MI. →

US-75

TRAIL ACCESS

Elk River Hiking Trail

EAST TRAILHEAD: This is located 100 yards south of the Corps of Engineers project office (across the park road), about .5 mile northwest of the dam. From the turnoff on U.S. 160, travel 1 mile north to a T intersection; go left (west) for .3 mile, then right (north) for 1.5 miles, where the road intersects with a road to the right (east). Curve left (west) and travel west/northwest for an additional 3.3 miles across the dam and watch for the road on the northwest side of the project office. The parking by the trailhead is across the park road, south of the project office. The trail begins by the large trail sign and map.

OAK RIDGE TRAILHEAD: This is in the Oak Ridge Public Use Area. After turning at the park road on the northwest side of the project office, travel 4.75 miles to the trailhead, as shown on the map. The trailhead is marked by a large sign, just off the road. Parking is available.

WEST TRAILHEAD: This is just off of U.S. 160, about 2 miles south of Elk City, as shown on the map.

Other Trails

TABLE MOUND HIKING TRAIL ACCESS: This trail is in Elk City State Park, on the east side of the lake, and can be reached either from Memorial Overlook, just east of the dam, or from the Squaw Creek Public Use Area, northwest of the state park office, as shown on the map.

GREEN THUMB NATURE TRAIL ACCESS: While this trail is not shown on the map, it is a 1-mile loop at the southern end of the Table Mound Hiking Trail.

POST OAK NATURE TRAIL ACCESS: This trail can be reached from the parking area by Memorial Overlook, just east of the dam.

TIMBER RIDGE HIKING TRAIL TRAILHEAD: This is the only hiking trail on the south side of the lake. From Independence, remain on U.S. 160 for 4 miles past U.S. 75. Watch for the sign to Card Creek on the north side of the highway and turn north. Travel 1.3 miles north, then turn left (west) on the paved road and travel 1.7 miles to the trailhead (note: this road travels west, then curves north). A large sign is posted at the trailhead.

SQUAW CREEK MULTI-USE TRAIL TRAILHEAD: This asphalt-paved trail connects the north and south portions of Elk City State Park. From the turnoff on U.S. 160, travel 1 mile north to a T intersection; turn west and follow this road to the Squaw Creek Cove South Public Use Area. The trailhead is shown on the map.

GENERAL INFORMATION

Elk City Lake lies in the physiographic region known as the Osage Cuestas, where alternating beds of shale and limestone were deposited by shallow seas during the Pennsylvanian period, about 250 to 300 million years ago. As you look west from Elk City Lake, particularly from the Memorial Overlook area on the Table Mound Trail, you will be able to see the beautiful tree-covered Chautauqua Hills on the horizon.

The most striking features of the landscape along the Elk River Hiking Trail and the Table Mound Hiking Trail are the outcroppings of gray limestone and shale along the ridge overlooking the lake and Elk River. Limestone, in its purest state as crystals of calcite (calcium carbonate) is white or buff-colored. Such stone is commonly found in eastern Kansas and is used for building. Impurities, such as organic remains, clay, or other minerals, create colored limestone, such as that found at Elk City Lake. The Elk River Hiking Trail and the Table Mound Hiking Trail travel along a narrow band of exposed shale and limestone formations of varying shades and colors. My research yielded little explanation for the actual formations, as opposed to the composition, of the rocks along the trail, other than the freeze-thaw effects of entrapped water and wind erosion. The distinctive stratified or banded rock formations along the trails may be "algal" limestone: when thick deposits of algae form limestone, the resulting rock can take on the form of the algae, creating irregularly shaped, stratified, and banded formations. Algae has formed, in part, at least half of the limestone of the Pennsylvanian and Permian rock found in eastern Kansas.*

THE HIKES

ELK RIVER HIKING TRAIL: This trail is rated as rugged because of the rocky and some-times steep climbs and descents on the ridge overlooking the lake. Just past the east trailhead, the trail, which is blazed in blue, crosses a creek on a board. As you climb the first of many switchbacks, you will see outcroppings of the incredible rock that sets this trail apart from all others in Kansas. As the trail nears the top of the ridge, it skirts caverns eroded from the bluffs, passing through rock chasms and into chambers. The woods along the rocky hillside are dominated by many varieties of oaks, including bur, blackjack, Shumard's, chestnut (also known as chinquapin), post, red, and black. The ragged-looking blackjack oak, with its paw-shaped leathery leaf, is hard to miss. Other native trees to watch for on the hillsides and along the many small creeks include western buckeye (a small flowering tree, distinguished by its 7-leaflets and famous for its red-brown, slightly poisonous, eye-like seeds—buckeyes) and hawthorn (which

---

* For more information about the lake and trails, see "Elk City's Pathways in Paradise" by Marc Murrell in *Kansas Wildlife and Parks,* July/August 1995.

has egg-shaped, dark green, glossy leaves, clusters of white flowers in early spring, and grows only 7 to 13 feet high).

About 1.3 miles from the start, the trail climbs to a large table rock overlooking the lake. Occasionally, the trail leaves the woods and travels through prairie dotted with red cedar, woody shrubs, wildflowers, and even cactus. Here you are likely to see one of the many varieties of *Buteo* or open-country hawks common to this area, such as the red-tailed hawk and the ferruginous hawk. When the trail is not traveling along the bluffs over the lake, it often drops into scenic wooded valleys where clear creeks can cool hot, tired feet. The rocks are an ideal habitat for copperheads and scorpions. Look before you grab any rocks or sit down.

The 5.6-mile hike from the Oak Ridge Trailhead to the end is not as scenic overall as the first 9.4 miles, but it has some singularly beautiful sections. A half mile past the trailhead, a large sycamore, which appears to grow out of rock, stretches over a mossy stream, beckoning hikers to sit at its base and dangle their feet over the water. From Oak Ridge to the end, the trail parallels and frequently climbs the bluffs for panoramic views of Elk River. The rock in this area reminded us of the remarkable formations at the very start. A notable stopping point is a small waterfall, where water from the overhanging rock trickled into the rock hollow below. Not far from here, the trail travels past an area where cars and other debris have been dumped, but then it quickly moves into a picturesque hollow. In the last 2 miles the trail climbs across rocks and drops into the old river channel. Watch for a small cave in the bluffs. About 1 mile from the end, the trail drops down to the river, one of the most scenic areas of the hike. When you reach the road, turn right to cross the bridge, then look for the trail to your left to complete the remaining .6 mile of the hike.

TABLE MOUND HIKING TRAIL: This trail is a condensed version of the Elk River Hiking Trail and like it travels along a rocky, wooded ridge overlooking the lake. It provides many opportunities to climb through, across, and under incredible rock formations. The trail is marked by blue blazes and is rated moderately difficult, although the climb up the rocks toward Memorial Overlook was rugged and strenuous. Double, or stacked, blazes on a tree indicate that the trail takes a sharp turn. At times, as the rocky trail winds through groves of old, tall cedar, and you hear the wind whistling in the boughs, you could mistake this trail for one in Colorado.

Along the trail, southern black haw trees, with their nearly black bark and dark green, shiny, oval leaves, are a striking contrast against the rocky surroundings. At about 2 miles, the trail crosses the busy park road leading to the dam. If you are hiking with children, warn them to wait at the road—cars speed through this area. After crossing the road, the trail begins its ascent to the Memorial Overlook. Before the trail reaches the top, it winds in and out of rock crevices, beneath a rock canopy, and through a rock tunnel, as it wraps around the hill overlooking the lake. The views of the lake from here are spectacular. The climb through a narrow rock chimney to the top of Memorial Overlook was an appropriate finish.

GREEN THUMB NATURE TRAIL: This 1-mile circular trail is reached from the Squaw Creek Cove Campground, by the trailhead of the Table Mound Hiking Trail. It is the only trail at Elk City Lake that is blazed in white. Don't let the length of this trail deceive you—the climb for a sweeping view of the lake is moderately strenuous. At one point, when the trail crossed a rocky area, I had difficulty following it until I saw the white blazes painted on the rocks below. Most of the trail winds through a scenic oak/hickory forest.

POST OAK NATURE TRAIL: After hiking the Table Mound Trail, take time to walk over to the Post Oak Trail, at the opposite end of the Memorial Overlook parking lot. The Post Oak Trail is a short, easy, self-guided nature trail that loops through the scenic woods and other habitats atop the limestone bluff known as Table Mound. The trail is blazed in orange.

TIMBER RIDGE HIKING TRAIL: The sign at the trailhead rates this 2.3-mile trail as "easy to rugged." The rugged section is the western side of the loop, above Card Creek, where the trail climbs into the rocks and travels along a ridge. From the trailhead, we took the side of the loop closest to, and parallel with, the park road. This section, sometimes within view of the road, is not as scenic as the west side of the loop, where the trail overlooks Card Creek and the pastoral river valley.

The trail first winds through young timber, woody vegetation, grasses, and wildflowers. About .3 mile from the start, watch for a white-blazed crossover trail, as shown on the map. By .6 mile, the trail reaches the top of a ridge, where you will find several table rocks on which to sit to view the beautiful valley below. Just past a mile, the trail begins a rocky and steep descent. While the rock formations on this trail are not as remarkable as those along the Table Mound and Elk River Trails, they are still formidable, particularly the huge boulders lying just off the trail. At 1.9 miles, watch for the white crossover trail heading east to connect to the east side of the loop, as shown on the map. The remainder of the trail travels through the woods back to the trailhead.

SQUAW CREEK MULTI-USE TRAIL: While we did not hike this 1-mile, asphalt-paved trail, the brochure indicates that it connects the north and south portions of Elk City State Park and that a variety of shorebirds and wildflowers can be seen from the trail.

Chautauqua Hills Trail, Toronto Lake

Toronto Lake

Toronto Lake, in the beautiful Verdigris River Valley, is surrounded by the Chautauqua Hills—a narrow finger of sandstone-capped hills that extends north from the southern border of Kansas. More than 8 miles of well-designed hiking trails show off the canyons, bluffs, streams, and trees unique to this area. The sandstone outcroppings throughout the canyon in Woodson Cove and along sections of the Chautauqua Hills Trail are unlike any others we have seen. These are sandstones deposited during the Pennsylvanian period (about 300 million years ago) in a broad river channel that drained to the south. Wildlife is diverse—many come to Toronto Lake to birdwatch. Ownership: KDWP (316) 637-2213.

HUNTING REMINDER: Public hunting is permitted in sections around Toronto Lake. Parts of the Chautauqua Hills Trail pass through a restricted hunting area. While the Woodson Cove Overlook Trail does not pass through a hunting area, hunting is permitted across the road from the cove. We recommend that whenever you hike, you wear bright colors—invest in an orange hunting vest and hat.

HIKE LENGTHS
Chautauqua Hills Trail
    Blue Trail .... 1.5 miles
    Yellow Trail .... 4.0 miles
Woodson Cove Overlook Trail .... 1.25 miles
Blackjack Ridge Trail .... 1 mile
Oak Ridge Trail... .5 mile

DIRECTIONS

Toronto Lake is south of U.S. 54, between K-99 to the west and U.S. 75 to the east. From U.S. 54, take K-105 south, through Toronto.

TRAIL ACCESS

CHAUTAUQUA HILLS TRAIL TRAILHEAD: This trail is in the Toronto Point Public Use Area. At the eastern boundary of Toronto proper, watch for the signs on K-105 to the Toronto Point Area in Toronto State Park. Turn south on Point Road and travel 1.4 miles. Turn left at the park road and travel .1 mile. Veer left again at the next park road (leading to the trailer park electric hook-ups) and follow this road to the trailhead, marked by a large sign.

WOODSON COVE OVERLOOK TRAIL TRAILHEADS: From the town of Toronto, continue south on K-105 to the lake dam. (K-105 turns west to cross the dam.) There are two trailheads. One is located in the Woodson Cove Area west of the parking lot. We started at the trailhead in the Overlook Area, on the southeast end of Toronto Lake, just east of the dam. If you cross the dam, you have gone too far. The trail starts to the right (northeast) of the shelter overlooking the lake.

BLACKJACK RIDGE TRAIL TRAILHEAD: Follow the directions to Woodson Cove, but continue west on K-105 across the dam. Just past the dam, you will pass the Toronto State Park office and self-pay station on your right. Continue on K-105 until it reaches a fork. Follow the sign to the Holiday Hill Area. In about .2 mile, you will reach another intersection—the road to the right (east) leads to boat ramp 3, and the gravel roads to your left lead west and northwest away from the state park. Veer north on the paved park road to the north end of the Holiday Hill Area, where the trailer hook-ups are located. The trailhead is on the left (south) side of the road, across from the trailer hook-up/campground area and toilets. There is a sign at the trailhead.

OAK RIDGE TRAIL TRAILHEAD: Although this trail is not shown on the map, the trailhead is just west of the shower and toilet facilities on the park road leading to boat ramp 3. Follow the directions to the Blackjack Ridge Trail, but at the juncture past K-105, turn right (east) toward the lake and watch for the entrance to the shower facilities.

GENERAL INFORMATION

Toronto Lake lies close to the northern boundary of what was once an Osage Indian reservation. Pursuant to an 1825 treaty with the Kaw and the Osage, the Osage were moved out of their traditional homeland, along the Osage River in what is now western Missouri, to lands along the Neosho River. Their reservation comprised much of the southern quarter of what is now Kansas and stretched as far west as Clark County in southwestern Kansas. The area along the Verdigris River, where Toronto Lake is now located, was once choice hunting and camping grounds for the Osage. When the Kaw and the Osage entered into the 1825 treaty, they demanded that the treaty allow them to hold the lands as long as "the grass should grow and the water should run." The Osage, a Siouan-speaking people, named the river after the green and gray bark of the sycamore trees that grew along it. The name was later translated into French.

The Verdigris River, whose waters are dammed at Toronto Lake, slices through the northern tip of the Chautauqua Hills, best known for their dense cover of oak, hickory, and other timber and for their thick cap of sandstone. The sandstone is the residue of sediments deposited at the mouths of rivers and streams that flowed into ancient seas in this region during the Pennsylvanian period. Erosion eventually exposed the sandstone seen along the trails. The Chautauqua Hills region reaches only 60 miles north into Kansas from the Oklahoma border and at its widest spot is only 20 miles from east to west. The pioneers referred to the region as the "Cross Timbers Area" because of the stands of post and blackjack oak that they crossed here on their journey across the prairie.

THE HIKES

CHAUTAUQUA HILLS TRAIL: For those who prefer a shorter and less strenuous hike, the Chautauqua Hills Trail has been designed with a shorter loop, blazed in blue. Those who hike the longer trail, blazed in yellow, can follow one side of the blue loop on the way out, and the other side of the loop on the way back. This trail was designed by Dolores Baker of La Fountaine and Virginia Lefford of Fredonia, who also assisted in its construction. The trail is well maintained by the Kansas Department of Wildlife and Parks. The sign at the trailhead rates the trail as moderately difficult.

A short distance from the trailhead is a substantial pedestrian bridge over an inlet of the lake. From here to the northwest end of the Blue Trail loop, the trail passes through scenic woodlands. We traveled the east side of the loop of the Blue Trail (the right branch) first, where large sandstone outcroppings follow the ridge above the inlet. We especially enjoyed crossing the stony gullies and climbing up water-carved sandstone steps. When we reached the north end of the Blue Trail loop at .8 mile from the trailhead, we continued northeast on the Yellow Trail, which soon enters a tallgrass prairie. In places, the big bluestem and Indian grasses towered several feet over our heads. Even in October, wildflowers were blooming here, including purple aromatic aster and yellow partridge pea. After .5 mile, the trail leaves the prairie momentarily to cross a wooded creekbed, then reenters the grass on the other side. Much of the trail on the eastern side of the inlet travels through prairie, sometimes skirting the edge of the woods. The parts in the woods often parallel a ridge littered with enormous sandstone boulders and unusual sandstone outcroppings. As the trail nears the loop at the southern end, watch for the cairn of rocks in the middle of the field. I thought it might be a turnaround marker, but the trail continues, though we had some difficulty following its short loop into the woods. We returned the way we came, except that when we reached the loop of the Blue Trail, we traveled the west side, which passed through prairie and cedar-dotted fields and was not as scenic as the eastern side.

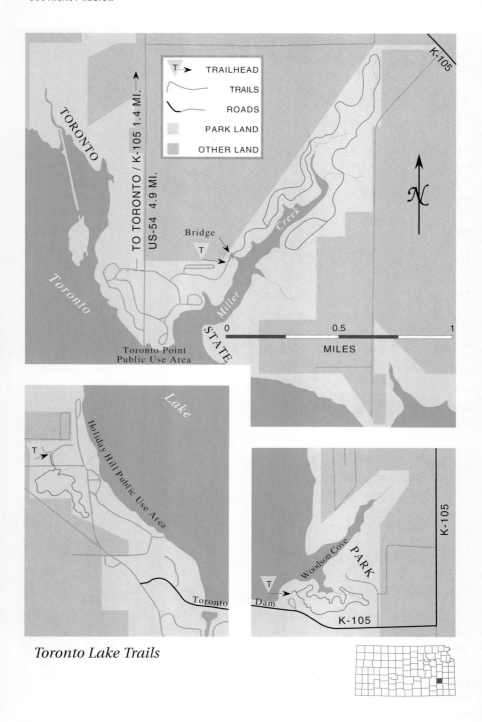

TORONTO

TO TORONTO / K-105 1.4 MI.

US-54 4.9 MI.

TRAILHEAD
TRAILS
ROADS
PARK LAND
OTHER LAND

K-105

Toronto

Creek

Bridge

Miller

N

Toronto Point
Public Use Area

STATE

0   0.5   1

MILES

Lake

Holiday Hill Public Use Area

Toronto

Woodson Cove

PARK

K-105

Dam

K-105

Toronto Lake Trails

WOODSON COVE OVERLOOK TRAIL: We lost all of our short-trail prejudices when we hiked this 1.25 mile trail. The scenery along this trail was spectacular, as it passes through hickory and oak woodlands where the trees appear almost artfully groomed and spaced. The climbs make it more strenuous than any other trail at Toronto Lake.

About 100 yards from the trailhead, the trail begins its loop. We veered right and recommend this direction because of the beautiful vista of the lake it will provide. The trail edges a wooded, rock-strewn gulch where we saw deer. We stopped many times to look at the fascinating sandstone outcroppings. When we reached the northern end of the loop, I was surprised to see that we were traveling along a cliff overlooking the lake.

BLACKJACK RIDGE TRAIL: The scenery on this trail is not as diverse or as dramatic as along the Woodson Cove Overlook Trail or the Chautauqua Hills Trail, but we enjoyed the hike through the woods and another opportunity to view the sandstone ridges and canyons unique to this region. While there are some moderate climbs, for the most part it's an easy hike. From the trailhead, the trail heads into the woods and immediately branches to start the loop. We took the right branch (which travels southwesterly), although the trail is marked from both directions. The woods are dominated by oak, especially blackjack oak. At one point, toward the southeastern end of the loop, where the trail emerges from the woods into a tree-dotted field, we momentarily lost track of it. I tried to follow the trail along a rock shelf by a stand of cedar trees and missed the turn into the woods. Beyond this turn, the trail travels through woods back to the trailhead.

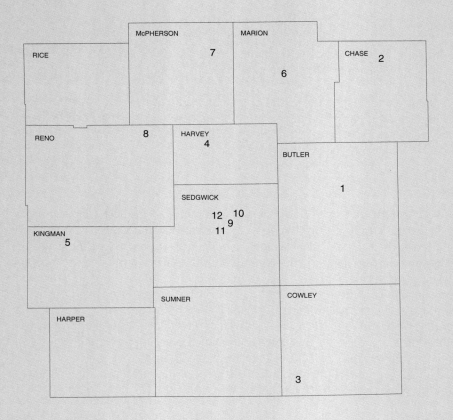

SOUTH CENTRAL REGION

1. El Dorado State Park and Wildlife Area
2. Z-Bar/Spring Hill Ranch
3. Chaplin Nature Center
4. Harvey County West Park
5. Kingman State Fishing Lake and Byron Walker Wildlife Area
6. Marion Reservoir
7. Maxwell Wildlife Refuge
8. Sand Hills State Park
9. Arkansas River Path
10. Chisolm Creek Park
11. Pawnee Prairie Park
12. Sedgwick County Park

SOUTH CE

South Central

REGION

El Dorado State Park and Wildlife Area

T he 12-mile Boulder Bluff Horse/Hiking Trail along the west shore of El Dorado Reservoir travels predominantly through tallgrass prairie in view of the lake. While there has been some invasion of trees and woody vegetation, much of this bluestem prairie is treeless. From spring through early fall, wildflowers bloom on the prairie. The Boulder Bluff Trail is a mowed loop, with many crossovers between the east and west sides. The east side of the loop parallels the lakeshore, traveling through camping/picnic areas in the Boulder Bluff Public Use Area, and the west side travels west of the park road, parallel to the railroad tracks. Take time to hike the scenic .75-mile Teter Nature Trail, which winds down a rocky, wooded ridge southeast of the dam. Ownership: KDWP (316) 321-7180.

HIKE LENGTHS
Boulder Bluff Horse/Hiking Trail.. 12 miles (round-trip)
Teter Nature Trail .... .75 mile (round-trip)

DIRECTIONS

El Dorado State Park and Wildlife Area is located northeast of El Dorado, off the Kansas Turnpike (I-35). Take Exit 76 and travel south on U.S. 77 to Meyers Road, which leads to the lake. Turn left (east) for 1.6 miles to the park road circling the reservoir.

TRAIL ACCESS

BOULDER BLUFF HORSE/HIKING TRAIL TRAILHEAD: Turn north off of Meyers Road and travel about 2 miles to the north trailhead, located in camping area 1. The trailhead is marked by a large sign, and there is parking available. As shown on the map,

Boulder Bluff Trail, El Dorado State Park and Wildlife Area

the trail can also be accessed from each of the camping areas north of Meyers Road and south of camping area 1, as well as from the Walnut River camping area near the dam.

TETER NATURE TRAIL TRAILHEAD: From Meyers Road, turn right (south) on the park road. Continue past the dam and past 12th Street (which leads to the Honor Camp). Watch for the trail parking on the south side of the road. The trailhead is marked by a large sign.

ⓘ GENERAL INFORMATION

El Dorado Reservoir, one of the newer reservoirs in Kansas, was completed in 1981 by the U.S. Army Corps of Engineers, which then turned over the management of the fisheries and wildlife resources to the Kansas Department of Wildlife and Parks. The lake covers 8,000 surface acres and is built on the Walnut River in the Flint Hills Uplands physiographic region, although it lies south of what most consider the heart of the Flint Hills—Chase and Morris Counties. The El Dorado oil field, which has produced more than 300 million barrels since 1915, the most produced by any field in Kansas, is just a few miles southwest of the lake. Daniel Fitzgerald, in *Ghost*

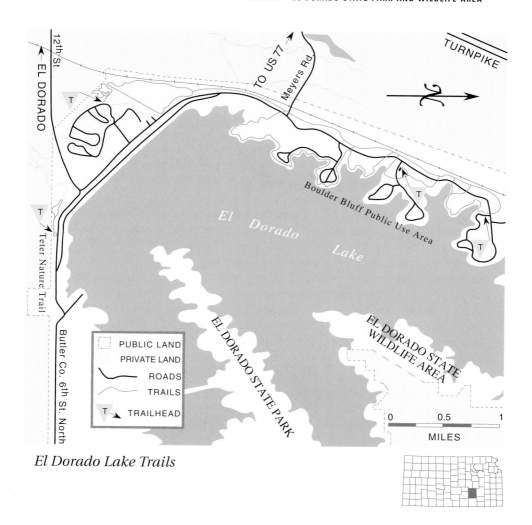

El Dorado Lake Trails

Towns of Kansas, traces the history of two boom-and-bust towns—Oil City, to the west of the lake, and Midian, further west and south. Midian, where an estimated 6,000 people came and went from 1917 to 1920, prospered until 1925 (only 9 years after it was built), when the oil production began to subside. It is now a ghost town located on private property. Oil Hill, a Cities Service town, and in 1934, the head-quarters of Empire Gas and Fuel Company, boomed until 1950, but in 1969 the last business closed.* Four miles southwest of the El Dorado Lake exit, the turnpike passes over Oil Hill Road.

* This and more information can be found in *Ghost Towns of Kansas: A Traveler's Guide* by Daniel C. Fitzgerald (Lawrence: University Press of Kansas, 1988).

👫 **THE HIKES**

BOULDER BLUFF HORSE/HIKING TRAIL: We began at the north trailhead in camping area 1. As you enter the state park off of Meyers Road, you will have a bird's-eye view of much of the prairie through which the north end of the trail passes. Only a short segment of the trail is shaded; the remainder crosses open, relatively flat, prairie. There are no overlooks and few changes in the terrain. The most striking features include the views of the reservoir, seen from most parts of the trail, as well as the spectacular Kansas skies, which provide a constantly changing backdrop. We watched red-tailed hawks soar overhead. In winter, watch for bald eagles, which perch in the dead timber in the lake.

As the map shows, the east side of the trail travels out to each peninsula in the Boulder Bluff area, following the shoreline. The trail, which winds predominantly through big bluestem and other native tallgrasses, is mowed and well-marked. Several cut-across trails (shown on the map) link the trail along the shoreline to the trail west of the park road, parallel to the railroad tracks. We preferred the lakeside. When we hiked this trail in March 1997, we could see a few high-water areas, where the trail was difficult to follow, primarily in camping area 4, the southernmost peninsula in Boulder Bluff. After following the lakeshore, the trail turns northwest and crosses the park road, just south of Meyers Road. This section leading toward the dam is about a 1-mile piece that you will travel both out and back. At the northwest end of the dam, the trail loops—the trail to the left (heading southeast) parallels the road, then turns southwest; the trail to the right (heading south), parallels the railroad. Eventually, the two branches meet near a scenic wooded area across from the Walnut River camping area. From here, the trail meanders through woodlands bordering the river. This section was still under construction when we hiked.

TETER NATURE TRAIL: You wouldn't know that this short but scenic nature trail is located in the same park! It begins in the tallgrass prairie but quickly leads into woodlands blanketing a steep, rocky ridge, down which the trail winds. These 8 acres are known as the Butler County Historical Society Wilderness Area, containing one of the most diverse collections of plant life in Butler County, according to the brochure at the trailhead, which includes a map, trail history, and a description of six points of interest along the trail. To follow the signs in sequence, take the trail to the right at sign 2, where the woodlands loop begins. Just west of sign 4, which marks the pawpaw patch (small trees, with bananalike fruit), be sure to take the "spring loop," which reconnects to the main trail near sign 5, marking a riverbank grapevine over 60 feet in length. The trail soon returns to the prairie ridge, an ideal vantage point to view the outlying Flint Hills and the stream channel far below.

Z-Bar/Spring Hill Ranch

The Southwind Nature Trail is a 1.75-mile self-guided trail on the historic 10,894-acre Z-Bar/Spring Hill Ranch. In October 1996, Congress established 180 acres of this ranch as the Tallgrass Prairie National Preserve, the first national park in Kansas. Located in the middle of the Flint Hills, the ranch is surrounded by miles of open prairie. A path leading to the trailhead starts in front of the hand-cut native white limestone ranchhouse built in 1881 and now listed on the National Register of Historic Places. The mowed trail travels north along the base of a ridge, across tallgrass prairie to the Lower Fox Creek School, a one-room limestone schoolhouse built in 1882. After crossing a tree-lined creek, the trail begins a gradual ascent to a ridge overlooking the ranch, Fox Creek, and the beauty of the Flint Hills. Ownership: Tallgrass Prairie National Preserve (316) 273-8494 and National Park Trust.

HIKE LENGTH

Southwind Nature Trail.. 1.75 miles

DIRECTIONS AND TRAIL ACCESS

The Tallgrass Prairie National Preserve is 2 miles north of Strong City and 17 miles south of Council Grove on K-177. (Strong City is 20 miles west of Emporia on U. S. 50.) Turn north off of U.S. 50 onto K-177. The ranch and Southwind Nature Trail are on the west side of the highway.

GENERAL INFORMATION

The Southwind Nature Trail was named after the Kansa Indians, whose tribal name has been translated as "People of the South Wind" or "Wind People." William Least Heat-Moon writes in *PrairyErth* that even before the great migration of the Kansa from the upper Ohio River Valley to the junction of the Kansas River and the

Southwind Nature Trail, Z-Bar/Spring Hill Ranch

Missouri River, "the word Kansa referred to a gens whose totem was the wind; that the Kansa would one day give their name to a state famous for its winds is only a wonderful coincidence."* In 1876, Stephen F. Jones emigrated from Colorado to Chase County, Kansas, and bought 7,000 acres of prairie along Fox Creek. He built his three-story, eleven-room, twin-gabled, red-mansard-roofed ranchhouse near the spring that issued from a hilltop. Three garden terraces, walled by cut limestone, were built around the house; a short, wrought-iron fence topped the lowest terrace; and a circular stone fountain (at one time filled by the spring but now filled with soil) was built on the highest terrace. Jones also built a three-story, cut-limestone barn large enough for a four-horse team to enter and turn full circle. After completing the barn, Jones learned that it lacked 2 feet to make it the largest in Kansas. Other improvements to the ranch included a chickenhouse, a cut-limestone three-seated privy (one half-sized for his children), and a combined smokehouse-springhouse connected to the kitchen by a 30-foot tunnel. According to William Least Heat-Moon, while there were rumors that the tunnel was part of the underground railroad (even though the Civil War had ended 16 years earlier), "the truth is that Louisa Jones, after witnessing a tornado strike the house during construction, wanted a storm cellar, one she could reach without getting wet."† Twenty-six miles of stone fence surrounded the Spring Hill Ranch. Only twelve years after arriving in Kansas, Jones sold Spring Hill Ranch and moved to Kansas City, Missouri.

The purchaser, a wealthy Strong City man, moved his cowhands into the ranch-house. Nineteen years later, the ranch was sold again. After that, the ranch was sold four more times, and the house was occupied mainly by tenants. The last owner used the brand Z—. In 1989, the Audubon Society purchased an option on the ranch, as well as on the 10,894 acres of surrounding prairie, and in 1994, the National Park Trust, an affiliate of the National Parks and Conservation Association, purchased the ranch. The 104th Congress, in 1996, established the Tallgrass Prairie National Preserve, comprising 180 acres of the ranch, including the house, the barn, and the school. Rangers and park guides, as well as a visitors center, are provided by the National Park Service. Additional trails may be added in the future.

THE HIKE

SOUTHWIND NATURE TRAIL: A trail guide, which includes a map of the trail, is available at the trailhead, as well as at the large sign at the entrance to the ranch. The trail is a mowed loop through the prairie and can be hiked in either direction. To reach the trailhead from the parking near the barn, follow the path parallel to K-177, in front of the rock wall surrounding the ranchhouse. The only side-trail leads to the school-house. The trail is not difficult and climbs only once, to the top of a ridge for a panoramic view of Fox Creek, the Lower Fox Creek School, and the Flint Hills.

---

* *PrairyErth* by William Least Heat-Moon (Boston: Houghton-Mifflin, 1991), p. 121.
† *PrairyErth*, pp. 165–66.

River Trail, Chaplin Nature Center

Chaplin Nature Center

More than 4 miles of trail weave through prairie and woodlands and along a spring-fed creek at the 200-acre Chaplin Nature Center, about 5 miles northwest of Arkansas City. One of the trails showcases the Arkansas River, traveling for a short distance on the sands at the river's edge. Driftwood is scattered across the sandbars, and grand cottonwoods shade the beaches. Another trail at the nature center climbs to a bluff for a scenic view of Spring Creek and the wooded valley that borders it. In spring, the woods are lit by blossoming redbuds and daffodils, while in fall, the foliage of sumac, elms, walnuts, cottonwoods, and sycamores colors the river valley. The Chaplin Nature Center is owned by the Wichita Audubon Society. Ownership: Wichita Audubon Society (316) 442-4133.

HIKE LENGTHS

River Trail (Trail D) .... 1.9 miles (round-trip)
Prairie Trail (Trail E) .... .8 mile (round-trip)
Bluff Trail (Trail F) .... .6 mile (round-trip)
Wildlife Homes Trail (Trail G)... .3 mile (round-trip)
Spring Creek Trail (Trail H)... .5 mile (round-trip)

DIRECTIONS

Chaplin Nature Center is about 50 miles southeast of Wichita and 5 miles northwest of Arkansas City. From Wichita, take the Kansas Turnpike, or U.S. 81, about 38 miles south to U.S. 166. Go east on U.S. 166 for 13.5 miles (from the turnpike) and watch for the sign on the side of the road. Go north for 2 miles to the nature center.

The trails at Chaplin Nature Center are designated by the letters D–H and are marked by letter on the map. (Note that the red-and-white-dashed trail shown on the map was open when we hiked but is being closed.)

ⓘ GENERAL INFORMATION

The land that is now the Chaplin Nature Center was homesteaded in 1874 by relatives of the late Mrs. C. Stedman (Hazel) Chaplin, whose grandfather purchased the land in 1901. The Chaplins worked to preserve and enhance the wildlife habitats on their farm and hoped to convert it someday into a nature center. In 1973, they sold the property to the Wichita Audubon Society, which then established the nature center. Not surprisingly, the Chaplin Nature Center, located next to the Arkansas River, is in the physiographic region known as the Arkansas River Lowlands. The lowlands appear on a physiographic map as a wide swath that generally follows the course of the Arkansas River, from Hamilton County, on the Colorado border, east to Hutchinson, then south through Wichita to the Oklahoma border. Most of the lowlands have been flattened by the river, which carried and deposited sand and other sediment from the Rocky Mountains, where the Arkansas River originates. Sand dunes, some of which are active and continue to be reshaped by wind and erosion, are found in parts of the lowlands.

🏃 THE HIKES

From the Visitors Center parking, we headed west on the Prairie Trail (E). This is the only trail that leaves directly from the parking area. The trail passes the horse barn. The short loop near the start is "Chappie's Bunting Trail," only about .25 mile in length. As its name suggests, the Prairie Trail winds through prairie, where you will see some invasion of smooth sumac, red cedar, and woody vegetation, as well as a variety of wildflowers. At the north end of the loop, the trail travels through a wooded area, then reaches the northern end of an old farm pond, where it intersects with a trail that continues straight (north) marked "H." This is the Spring Creek Trail. If you turn right (southeast) and follow along the pond, you will intersect the gravel road shown on the map and return to the parking.

We continued straight on the Spring Creek Trail (H). This area, through the mature woodlands along Spring Creek, can be muddy in wet weather. We saw evidence of flooding at marker 22. The Chaplin Nature Center has attracted 225 species of birds, as well as a variety of other wildlife.* At the north end of the Spring Creek loop, the trail crosses the creek and heads back southeast, intersecting with the River Trail (D). At this intersection, you can turn right (southwest) and cross Spring Creek, to intersect the Wildlife Homes Trail (G), which then intersects with the Bluff Trail (F). Alternatively, you can continue on the gravel road, which leads back to the parking area. We opted to take the trail left (northeast), which is the River Trail.

The River Trail (D) edges a prairie, then heads into the wooded river valley. The trail splits, but is circular; we went straight (east) and followed the trail clockwise.

---

* See *Watching Kansas Wildlife: A Guide to 101 Sites* by Bob Gress and George Potts (Lawrence: University Press of Kansas, 1993).

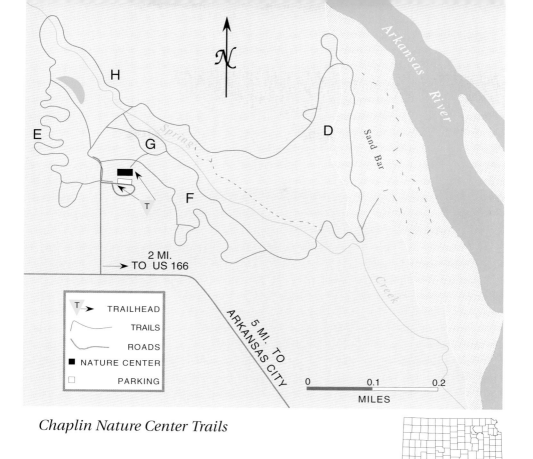

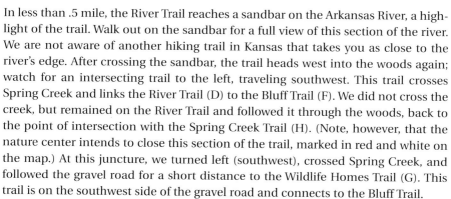

Chaplin Nature Center Trails

In less than .5 mile, the River Trail reaches a sandbar on the Arkansas River, a highlight of the trail. Walk out on the sandbar for a full view of this section of the river. We are not aware of another hiking trail in Kansas that takes you as close to the river's edge. After crossing the sandbar, the trail heads west into the woods again; watch for an intersecting trail to the left, traveling southwest. This trail crosses Spring Creek and links the River Trail (D) to the Bluff Trail (F). We did not cross the creek, but remained on the River Trail and followed it through the woods, back to the point of intersection with the Spring Creek Trail (H). (Note, however, that the nature center intends to close this section of the trail, marked in red and white on the map.) At this juncture, we turned left (southwest), crossed Spring Creek, and followed the gravel road for a short distance to the Wildlife Homes Trail (G). This trail is on the southwest side of the gravel road and connects to the Bluff Trail.

The Bluff Trail (F) is the only trail at the nature center that offers a steep climb. This trail parallels Spring Creek, passing through a pretty section of the woods, then climbs to a bluff overlooking the creek and scenic valley below. The trail follows along the top of the bluff, then takes you back to the Visitors Center.

Harvey County West Park

Harvey County West Park

Harvey County West Park, the oldest park in Harvey County, is a 310-acre, multi-use park, replete with a swimming pond, fishing lake, ball diamond, camping areas, and a 135-acre natural history preserve, through which several miles of hiking trails wind. The whimsical, wire-mesh suspension footbridge leading over the fishing lake to the hiking trails seems almost to skim the surface of the water as you walk across. The 1-mile Lakeside Nature Trail follows the wooded southern perimeter of the lake. Thirty-seven numbered guideposts correspond to an information-packed booklet available at the ranger station. The mowed trails on the western half of the park, called the Sand Hills Natural History Preserve, circle the grass-covered sandhills that give this preserve its name. Ownership: Harvey County (316) 835-3189.

HIKE LENGTHS

Lakeside Nature Trail .... 1 mile
Mowed interpretive trails .... 2 miles

DIRECTIONS AND TRAIL ACCESS

Harvey County West Park is located about halfway between Newton and Hutchinson. From Newton, take U.S. 50 west for about 13 miles to Halstead Road (formerly Harvey County Road 801), or from Hutchinson, take U.S. 50 east to North River Park Road (formerly Harvey County Road 793), which is 4 miles east of Burrton. A blue park sign marks each of these roads. Turn north on either Halstead or North River Park Road and travel 3 miles to 24th Street (formerly Harvey County Road 566) to reach the south entrance of the park. The park is .75 mile east of North River Park Road and .25 mile west of Halstead Road on the north side of 24th Street. To reach the trailhead from the south entrance, continue north on the main park road past the ranger station to the parking area near the swimming pond and fishing lake. You can't miss the suspension bridge, marking the start of the trail. The north, or main, entrance to the park is a mile further north on either North River Park Road or Halstead Road, on the south side of 36th Street (formerly Harvey County Road 564). Take the park road south, past the ball diamond and the ranger station as described above.

ℹ GENERAL INFORMATION

Harvey County was named after James M. Harvey, governor of Kansas (1869–73) at the time the county was created. According to Walter Enns, who was supervisor of Harvey County Park from 1937 to the late 1970s, the land acquired for the park in 1938 was originally farmland and grassland, and two farmhouses once stood in the western part of the park. The park was constructed by the Works Projects Administration, with supervision and a crane provided by Harvey County. The bombing of Pearl Harbor halted construction, and work did not resume until after the war. Enns noted that construction of the Little Arkansas River dam (at the southern end of the park), built with rock quarried near Florence and El Dorado, was completed just before the shut-down. Park workers even built a storm shelter into a hill north of the ranger's house. That shelter holds up to 100 people and has been used in emergencies. The suspension bridge over the 16-acre fishing lake was built in 1967. Previously, visitors crossed the lake by a floating bridge, built over drums. According to Enns, the suspension bridge was built to last—oil-field cable supports it, and the pilings, sunk 30 feet deep, are anchored in concrete.

🥾 THE HIKES

LAKESIDE NATURE TRAIL: The trail begins at the suspension bridge and forks just after crossing it. Follow the trail straight. (The trail to the right, or northeast, leads to the mowed interpretive trails through the western side of the park.) This is an easy, well-marked trail, with no hills or rough terrain. The trail forks again at marker 2. Take the trail to the left (southwest). (Again, the trail to the right, which continues west, leads to the mowed interpretive trails.) From marker 2 to marker 24, the trail closely parallels the lake, and much of it is shaded. Watch for American elm (also called white elm), rough-leaved dogwood, cottonwood, bur oak, green ash, catalpa, willow, and honey locust trees. At several points along the Lakeside Nature Trail—at markers 15, just past 16, 19, 23, 25, and 31—side-trails radiate out to the longer mowed interpretive trails on the western side of the preserve. If this sounds confusing, remember that the Lakeside Nature Trail hugs the lake. Near the start of the trail is a large park map of the trails, also shown in the booklet available at the ranger station.

　　The lake trail passes through a variety of habitats, including mixed-grass prairie, marsh, and riparian. I saw several blue herons and a variety of other birds around the lake. At marker 24, the trail crosses a boardwalk over a marsh, then travels through prairie. At marker 31, the trail branches—the trail to your right, leading south, will take you to a loop of the mowed interpretive trails at the southern end of the preserve. To remain on the Lakeside Trail, take the trail to the left, which will shortly reach the parking area near the suspension bridge.

OTHER INTERPRETIVE NATURE TRAILS: The mowed trails through the Sand Hills Natural History Preserve on the western half of the park consist of three loops. As I hiked, I sometimes felt I was in a maze, not sure whether I was walking in circles, because so much of the trail winds through grasses and weedy vegetation. I suggest starting at the suspension bridge and following the trail northwest along the lake. (Note: the nature trail travels straight from the bridge.) This scenic stretch travels along the northern end of the fishing lake, where you are likely to see a variety of birds. Eventually, the trail curves west, away from the lake, and passes through a wooded area, then curves south through prairie. When I hiked in mid-August 1996, the trails were well maintained and had been recently mowed. This section of the preserve is wilder and less traveled than the Lakeside Trail, but not as scenic. The terrain is relatively flat, and most of the trails pass through open prairie. In August, there were not many wildflowers in bloom, but I could see their dried heads among the prairie grasses, suggesting a colorful display when blooming.

Kingman State Fishing Lake

Kingman State Fishing Lake and Byron Walker Wildlife Area

The 3-mile nature trail that circles Kingman State Fishing Lake travels across prairie and marsh and through woodlands that border the lake. While the surrounding landscape is unexceptional, wildlife abounds. *Watching Kansas Wildlife: A Guide to 101 Sites,* describes the Byron Walker Wildlife Area (of which Kingman State Fishing Lake is a part) as one of the premier wildlife spots in Kansas.* The 144-acre lake was rehabilitated in 1993, and when we hiked in March 1996, water levels were still low and parts of the lake were marshy. Ownership: KDWP (316) 532-3242.

HUNTING REMINDER: Certain areas around Kingman State Fishing Lake, and nearly all of the Byron Walker Wildlife Area, are open to public hunting. It is always advisable to wear bright colors when you hike—preferably an orange hunting vest and hat.

HIKE LENGTH
Kingman State Fishing Lake Nature Trail.. 3 miles

DIRECTIONS AND TRAIL ACCESS

Travel 7 miles west from Kingman on K-54. (Kingman is about midway between Pratt to the west and Wichita to the east.) The turnoff to the lake is on the north side of K-54. Follow the park road north to the second intersecting park road and turn left. This road leads to the picnic areas down by the lake. Before the road circles back to the entrance, watch for the trailhead on the edge of the woods (beyond the toilets).

 * *Watching Kansas Wildlife: A Guide to 101 Sites* by Bob Gress and George Potts (Lawrence: University Press of Kansas, 1993).

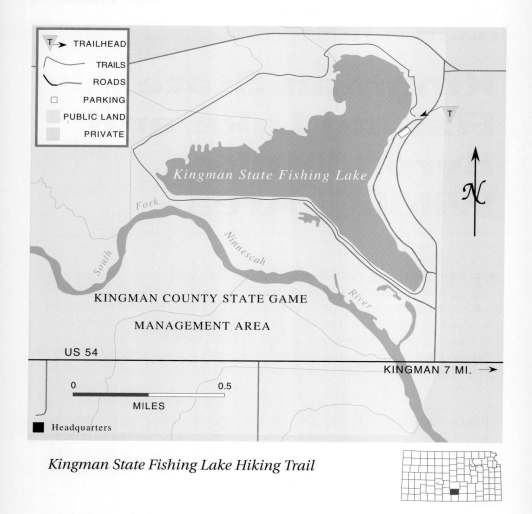

LEGEND

- T→ TRAILHEAD
- TRAILS
- ROADS
- □ PARKING
- PUBLIC LAND
- PRIVATE

Kingman State Fishing Lake

Fork

Ninnescah

South

River

KINGMAN COUNTY STATE GAME

MANAGEMENT AREA

US 54

KINGMAN 7 MI. →

0   0.5

MILES

■ Headquarters

Kingman State Fishing Lake Hiking Trail

ⓘ GENERAL INFORMATION

The Kingman State Fishing Lake and the Byron Walker Wildlife Area lie within the easternmost reaches of the High Plains physiographic region. The geologic history of the High Plains is interwoven with the formation of the Rocky Mountains. As these mountains were uplifted by movement of the earth's crust, streams flowing from the mountains into Kansas carried away massive amounts of rock debris, which spilled out from the stream valleys and were deposited across the uplands. By the end of the Tertiary period (which lasted for about 60 million years, ending about 2 million years ago), the sand, gravel, and other sediments carried by wind and water had formed a vast plain, which sloped eastward from the base of the Rockies to the west slope of the Flint Hills. This slope is so gradual that a traveler driving from the lowest point in Kansas (700 feet in Montgomery County in southeastern Kansas) to the highest point (4,039 in Wallace County on the Colorado border) might not notice it. The High Plains represent the uneroded remains of the large plain that once covered all of western Kansas, which has since been dissected by past and present watercourses. Beneath its surface are layers of sand, gravel, and porous rock, known as the Ogallala Formation, where huge supplies of ground water are stored. The land on which Kingman State Fishing Lake is located was purchased in 1930, and the lake was built in 1933. Originally, the lake was to have been a reservoir, with its dam on the Ninnescah River. These plans fell through, and the state built an 88-acre fishing lake. In 1955, the dam was raised to create the present 144-acre lake. In 1962, the state purchased an additional 2,900 acres of land, and with later, smaller acquisitions the Kingman State Fishing Lake and Byron Walker Wildlife Area grew to 4,529 acres. From 1947 to 1987, the site was managed by Byron Walker, after whom the wildlife area was later named.

THE HIKE

KINGMAN STATE FISHING LAKE NATURE TRAIL: When we hiked in March 1996, the first part of the trail was marshy, even after a dry winter. The lake was dotted with ducks and other water birds. At points, the shrubs and plants along the trail serve as a natural blind for watching the wide variety of wildlife that lives in the diverse habitats that surround the lake. As the trail wraps around the northwest corner of the lake, it is bordered by timber on the lake side and prairie on the other. The woodlands are an ideal habitat for many nesting birds.

On the south side of the lake, the trail dips close to the South Fork of the Ninnescah River, a sandy-bottomed river known for its clear waters. The river reportedly received its name from the Indian word for "good water" or "clear water."* The Ninnescah was once considered an ideal location for mills—the natural fall of the river, at 7 feet per mile, provided ample power to turn the mill machinery. Soon the trail intersects with an unimproved road and runs parallel to the south shore of the lake. Midway across the lake, the unimproved road leads into a gravel road. Follow this back to the park road leading to the trailhead.

---

* See *Roadside Kansas: A Traveler's Guide to Its Geology and Landmarks* by Rex C. Buchanan and James R. McCauley (Lawrence: University Press of Kansas, 1987).

Willow Walk Trail, Marion Reservoir

Marion Reservoir

arion Reservoir sits in the Cottonwood River Valley, at the western edge of the Flint Hills. The terrain on the 1-mile Willow Walk Trail at Cottonwood Point, on the west side of the lake, is relatively flat. We enjoyed the views of the lake along the western section of this looped trail along the marshy lakeshore. The eastern side of the loop travels through an area that is gradually returning to tallgrass prairie. Spring, fall, and winter are the preferred hiking seasons. In spring and fall, hikers can view the many water birds, including pelicans and great blue herons, that frequent Marion Reservoir. In winter, the combination of wind, waves, and water spray often creates bizarre ice sculptures along the shoreline. The Willow Walk Trail is ideal for a family with younger children or older persons with limited mobility. Much of this nature trail is covered by gravel, but it can be muddy after rains. Ownership: USACE (316) 382-2101.

HIKE LENGTH
Willow Walk Trail .... 1 mile

DIRECTIONS AND TRAIL ACCESS

Marion Reservoir is located north off of U.S. 56, about 4 miles west of Marion and about 6 miles east of Hillsboro. Watch for signs to the entrance to the reservoir and turn north on the paved road leading to the dam. Continue for 1 mile past the dam and turn west at the road leading to Cottonwood Point. Take this road .5 mile to the gate shack/pay station and turn right (northwest). Go .5 mile to the stop sign. Turn left (south) for .3 mile, then go west .1 mile to the trailhead, which is well marked by a large sign and map of the trail. An informative brochure with a map of the trail is available at the trailhead.

ℹ GENERAL INFORMATION

Marion Reservoir is named after the county in which it is located and the nearby town of Marion, once called Marion Center. In the 1880s Marion Center was known as "The Stone City" because nearly 50 public buildings, businesses, and homes had been constructed from the native limestone. The town and county derive their name from a Revolutionary War hero, General Francis Marion, commonly known as the "Swamp Fox." General Marion was a guerrilla commander who, after the British captured Charleston in 1780, raided enemy outposts in the coastal marshes of South Carolina, keeping the rebel cause alive there. The county of Marion, created by an act of the Territorial Legislature on February 17, 1860, was at the heart of cross-country travel. The historic Santa Fe Trail, the Chisholm Trail, the Kaw Indian Trail, and, later, a branch of the Santa Fe Railroad crossed through Marion County. Mennonites from Germany were among the early settlers of Marion County and of the town of Hillsboro, about 6 miles west of the reservoir.

Marion Reservoir, which dams the Cottonwood River, was completed in 1968 and, along with John Redmond Reservoir and Council Grove Lake, provides flood protection for the Grand (Neosho) River Valley. The lake covers about 6,200 surface acres of land. The Kansas Department of Wildlife and Parks holds a license to 4,166 acres, maintained as a public hunting area, and an additional 462 acres, maintained as a waterfowl refuge with no public access. The total project acreage of Marion Reservoir is 12,667 acres.

🚶 THE HIKE

WILLOW WALK TRAIL: This is a well-maintained, well-marked, flat trail within the flood pool of Marion Reservoir. Occasionally, it will be completely inundated. Much of the trail is graveled, but following rains it is muddy, and in summer the insects can swarm in the marshy areas. From the trailhead, I followed the west branch to the lakeshore, by far the more scenic part. When I hiked in the summer of 1996, it appeared that high waters had damaged some of the vegetation and trees near the shore. At .25 mile, watch for a crossover trail leading to the east side of the looped trail. Cottonwoods frame your view of the water as the trail travels out to several isolated points on the lake, perfect for watching birds. Marion Reservoir attracts a variety of waterfowl and shorebirds, including egrets, ducks, pelicans, great blue herons, Canada geese, and belted kingfishers (which, if you are lucky, you may see plunging headfirst into the water for fish). The return trip on the eastern side of the loop is not shaded. The trail travels through tallgrasses, including switchgrass, Indian grass, and big bluestem. Interspersed in the grasses are weeds, wildflowers, and woody vegetation.

Maxwell Wildlife Refuge

The 1.5-mile Gypsum Creek Nature Trail is located in an area of the 2,560-acre Maxwell Wildlife Refuge that is not grazed by the bison and elk that roam the remainder of the refuge. Because the road across the refuge to the trail crosses several miles of hilly, nearly treeless, tallgrass prairie, we were surprised to find that the nature trail winds through dense woodlands, near Gypsum Creek. At one point, the trail leaves the woods to climb a sandy hill, providing a panoramic view of the outlying prairie, before reaching its destination—the clear, tree-shrouded waters of Gypsum Creek. Ownership: KDWP (316) 628-4592.

HIKE LENGTH

Gypsum Creek Nature Trail.. 1.5 miles (round-trip)

DIRECTIONS AND TRAIL ACCESS

From I-135, take McPherson County Road 429 (Exit 72) 10.5 miles east to Roxbury. At the stop sign in Roxbury, turn right (south) on County Road 304 (also called 27th Avenue) 5 miles to the entrance to the Maxwell Wildlife Refuge/McPherson State Fishing Lake, marked by a sign on the west side of the road. (The entrance is 6 miles north of Canton.) Turn right (west) into the refuge on Pueblo Road and follow this road 3 miles around the north end of the lake, then south. The lake road intersects with Pueblo Road, which leads west off the refuge. Continuing straight south, the lake road immediately forks again, looping around the camping/picnic area. Take either branch to the south end of the loop and watch for the parking area and a large sign marking the trailhead.

Gypsum Creek Nature Trail, Maxwell Wildlife Refuge

ℹ️ GENERAL INFORMATION

Maxwell Wildlife Refuge is located just west of the Flint Hills, in the Smoky Hills region, as evidenced by the sandstone boulders that litter the pastures and the occasional sandstone outcroppings from the Dakota Formation (a rock formation usually identified with sandstone, but which also includes clay and shale), seen along the ridge tops and on knolls. The Dakota Formation at the refuge is heavily cross-bedded—angled lines indicate it was deposited by flowing water. In places, the sandstone is naturally cemented together and stained dark, almost black, in deposits known colloquially as "ironstone." The refuge is best known for the bison and elk herds that roam within a fenced 3.5-square-mile area. Ten bison, brought from the Wichita Mountains National Wildlife Refuge in Oklahoma, formed the nucleus of the herd in 1951. The herd now averages around 200, and about 55–65 bison are auctioned each year by the Kansas Department of Wildlife and Parks. An elk herd, introduced to the refuge at about the same time, numbers about 65. In the fall, particularly in the evenings and mornings, you may hear the distinctive bugle of the bull elk.

The Maxwell Wildlife Refuge derives its name from Henry Irving Maxwell, a McPherson businessman who envisioned the preservation of the surrounding native prairie and the creation of a wildlife refuge. By 1944, his estate had acquired 2,560 acres of land, which it deeded to the Kansas Forestry, Fish, and Game Commission, now the Kansas Department of Wildlife and Parks. The refuge was eatablished 10 years later.*

THE HIKE

THE GYPSUM CREEK NATURE TRAIL: The trail begins at the edge of the woods that line Gypsum Creek. I was immediately struck by the redness (caused by deposits of iron oxide in some of the rocks) of the silty, highly erodible soil along the trail. Be sure to pick up the booklet at the trailhead, which includes information on the trees, native grasses, and wildlife habitats found on the trail. At .2 mile, the trail branches (this is a short loop, and the branches soon rejoin and travel concurrently to Gypsum Creek). We followed the lower (left) branch, which soon leaves the woods and travels by a thicket of chickasaw plum, also known as sand plum or sandhill plum. (The upper branch crosses prairie, which edges the woods.) Eventually the trail climbs a sandy hill, a good vantage point for viewing the creek below and spotting bison and elk on the refuge. Dozens of species of wildflowers, such as yucca, sunflowers, and gayfeather bloom on this open prairie.

When we hiked this trail in June 1996, it was lined with a healthy crop of poison ivy, which often sent shoots across the trail and, like the sandhill plum, seemed to flourish in the sandy soil. The poison ivy was especially thick by Gypsum Creek, where the trail ends. We made our way around it only because our kids saw the sandy creek, strewn with large boulders, and would not turn back. (The creek's name refers to the deposits of gypsum found in the Wellington Formation, a rock formation created later in the Permian period by the evaporation of the shallow inland sea that had covered central Kansas. In the late 1800s, gypsum was mined near the towns of Solomon and Hope and was used in plaster.) We waded in the creek and enjoyed the quiet of the surrounding woods as the sun set.

* For more information, see "Maxwell Wildlife Refuge: A Glimpse of Kansas Past" by Cliff Peterson in *Kansas Wildlife and Parks,* January/February 1992, and "At Home on the Range" by Shawna Bethel Paramore in *Kansas!* (2) 1996.

Sand Hills State Park

Sand Hills State Park

The sand-dune landscape at Sand Hills State Park more closely resembles the Outer Banks of North Carolina than Kansas. From the top of the 40-foot sand dune on the Prairie/Dune Trail, the trails appear as narrow ribbons of sand through the grass-covered dunes. The panoramic view of the surrounding dunes is striking. When we hiked these trails in February 1996, the tall and short prairie grasses were varying hues of gold and copper. Wildflowers bloom in the grasses in spring and summer. The 1,123-acre park contains approximately 40 sand dunes, ranging from 10 to 40 feet tall. While one section of trail passes through woodlands, most of the trails meander through the sand prairie. Ownership: KDWP (316) 542-3664.

SPECIAL NOTES: Kansas Wildlife and Parks imposes a $2.50 per person per day charge for hiking these trails. An annual permit may be purchased for $10.00 per person. Bow hunting (deer, turkey, and upland game) is allowed near (but not within 100 feet of) the Pond Trail on the east side of the park. The Dune, Prairie, and Cottonwood Trails are in a no-hunting area. It is always advisable to wear bright colors when you hike—preferably an orange hunting vest and hat.

HIKE LENGTHS
Dune Trail .... .9 mile
Prairie Trail .... 1.8 miles
Cottonwood Interpretive Trail .... .6 mile
Pond Trail .... 1.5 miles

DIRECTIONS AND TRAIL ACCESS

Sand Hills State Park is northeast of Hutchinson. From Hutchinson, take K-61 northeast. The trails can be accessed from either the south parking area (trailhead for the Prairie and Dune Trails) or the north parking area (trailhead for the Cottonwood Interpretive Trail). The Prairie and Dune Trails can also be accessed from the Cottonwood Trail. To reach the south parking area, turn right (east) off of K-61 onto 56th Street. Exercise caution: the road immediately crosses the Southern Pacific Railroad tracks. To reach the north parking area, continue on K-61 to 69th Street (1 mile past 56th Street) and turn right (east). Access to the Pond Trail is off of 69th Street, east of the north parking area. Watch for the second horse gate past the north parking area. In the summer of 1997, the Kansas Department of Wildlife and Parks indicated that it had expanded the parking lot on 69th Street and the Pond Trail access, as well as the parking area on 56th street, just east of its maintenance building, to allow for additional horse-trailer parking and equestrian access to the fireguard trails and to the Pond Trail.

i GENERAL INFORMATION

Sand Hills State Park lies in the Arkansas River Lowlands. While glaciers were moving in and out of northeastern Kansas during the Pleistocene epoch—often referred to as the Great Ice Age—the Arkansas River carried and deposited millions of tons of sand and gravel from the eroding Rocky Mountains across Kansas. This river, the third-longest in the United States, originates in Lake County, Colorado, above Leadville, along the Continental Divide. Strong, southwesterly Pleistocene winds blew the sands out of the Arkansas River Valley, forming a band of sand dunes across southern Kansas from Hamilton County, on the western border of Kansas, east to Harvey County in south-central Kansas, and southeast to Cowley County on the southern border of Kansas, where the Arkansas River enters Oklahoma. Initially, these dunes were active. Winds eroded, moved, and sculpted the loose sand until grasses and shrubs rooted and stabilized the dunes.*

🥾 THE HIKES

DUNE, PRAIRIE, AND COTTONWOOD TRAILS: The brown carsonite flex markers posted along the trails color-code them: orange circle, Dune Tail; green diamond, Prairie Trail; blue square, Prairie/Dune Trail; and red triangle, Cottonwood Interpretive Trail. The Dune and Prairie Trails, laid out in a figure-eight pattern, connect to the Cottonwood Interpretive Trail at the north end. The Cottonwood Trail can also be accessed directly from the north parking area. These trails are well marked and easy to follow, and the only steep climb is up the 40-foot dune on the Dune Trail.

From the trailhead at the south parking area, the Dune Trail travels north toward a 40-foot sand dune, one of the tallest in the park. At the base of the sand dune, the trail

---

* For an extensive description of the park and its flora and fauna, as well as several beautiful photographs, we recommend "Oasis in the Sand: Sandhills State Park" by Jerry Schmidt in *Kansas Wildlife and Parks,* September/October 1990.

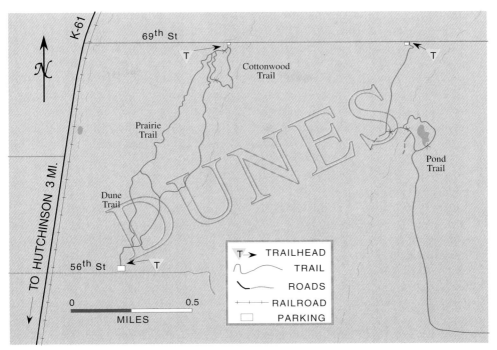

Sand Hills State Park

splits—the trail to the right, heading east, circles behind the dune. We followed the trail up the railroad-tie stairs to the top of the dune. The view from here is spectacular in any season. After descending, watch for the trail to branch. We continued north, to hike the west side of the Prairie Trail loop. To remain on the Dune Trail, however, take the branch heading right (east) until it branches again. Veer right (south) to return to the trailhead in the south parking area. (The north branch, to your left, is the east side of the Prairie Trail loop.) As we continued on the west side of the Prairie Trail loop, we noticed the changes in vegetation in the lower areas (called playas) between the dunes. After rains, these areas may fill with water because of denser soils beneath the sands. Here you will often find woody vegetation such as buttonbush and roughleaf dogwood, as well as water grasses. When we reached the north end of the Prairie Trail loop and veered right (east) to connect to the Cottonwood Interpretive Trail, the vegetation began to change. Soon we were in a woodland area close to a stream, where cottonwoods towered overhead. Black locust, Siberian elm, green ash, osage orange, and hackberry trees also can be found in this belt of trees.

After we completed the Cottonwood Trail loop, we returned to the Prairie Trail and followed the east side of the loop back to the trailhead. This section also passes through sand prairie. (Grasses thrive in this desert-like environment, yet the key to their success is not apparent on the surface. Unlike the wildflowers and shrubs on this prairie, which grow from the ground up or from the tips of branches out, grasses' growth tissue lies beneath the ground, enabling them to survive prairie fires, droughts, and blizzards. Their extensive root systems allow them to store water and nutrients until they are needed, so when conditions are poor, they can lie dormant for years.) When you reach the south end of the Prairie Trail loop, continue straight to return to the trailhead via the east side of the Dune Trail loop. The branch to the right (west) will take you back to the west side of the Dune Trail loop.

POND TRAIL: From the horse gate, the trail travels south. In February 1996, the beginning was mowed, but it was virtually impossible to follow after we crossed the cattleguard over the creek (heading east) to loop around the ponds. There were also several open pits at the south end of the larger pond that were not marked. There were no trail markers. The terrain on the Dune and Prairie trails to the west is much more interesting and scenic.

The Kansas Department of Wildlife and Parks, in July 1997, explained that several years ago the pond dams were damaged, and therefore the trails around them were severed. Until recently, funds and personnel were not available to properly repair the problems. According to the park manager, federal trail money is being used to repair the dams and to expand and build the parking lots referenced in the Directions section above. When these repairs are completed, there will be a trail around the ponds, and the ponds will have water in them. The open pits that we encountered in 1996 were former wildlife viewing stations. These are to be renovated and made into wildlife viewing stations again through Eagle Scout projects in the fall or winter of 1997/1998. The trails will also be re-marked for easier access, which will most likely be an Eagle Scout project.

Arkansas River Path

This unique 9-mile urban trail follows the Arkansas River through the middle of Wichita. Yet because the trail edges several parks and travels so near the water, you are often not aware of the city commotion just beyond the banks of the river. This asphalt path is well used by walkers, runners, bicyclists, and roller-bladers but is rarely congested. Near downtown, the trail passes the confluence of the Little Arkansas and Arkansas Rivers, where the city of Wichita originated. Here the Wichita and other related Indian tribes settled in 1864, drawing frontier traders such as James Richard Mead, Jesse Chisholm, and William "Dutch Bill" Greiffenstein to the Arkansas River. Today "The Keeper of the Plains," a 44-foot, 5-ton sculpture by the late Blackbear Bosin, overlooks the river near the Mid-America All Indian Center and can be seen from the path west of the Douglas Street Bridge. The path also skirts Old Cowtown Museum—a reminder that Wichita was once "cow capital" of Kansas. Ownership: Wichita Department of Parks and Recreation (316) 268-4361.

HIKE LENGTH

Arkansas River Path ....9 miles (one-way)

DIRECTIONS AND TRAIL ACCESS

The Arkansas River Path is in Wichita and follows the Arkansas River from 21st Street North to a point about .3 mile south of 31st Street South (1.3 miles south of Pawnee Avenue). The path can be accessed from many points along the river, although there are no designated parking areas, except at the 21st Street trailhead. As the map shows, the river path crosses several bridges; some sections of the path travel on the east side of the river and others on the west.

Note: at the north end, the Arkansas River Path connects to a bicycle lane on Westdale Drive, which runs parallel to I-235. The bicycle lane then connects to Zoo

Arkansas River Path

Boulevard and ends at 21st Street North and Ridge Road. This is a 3-mile extension, providing access to the Sedgwick County Zoo and the bicycle/walking paths in Sedgwick County Park. In addition, a 1-mile path connects the Arkansas River Path to the central business district along Central Street.

ℹ️ GENERAL INFORMATION

The Arkansas River, the third-longest river in the continental United States, is one of two Kansas rivers that originate in the Rocky Mountains. Its source is along the Continental Divide, above Leadville, Colorado. The history of Wichita unfolds as you walk the path along the river. Before the Wichita Indian Confederation of tribes settled along the Arkansas River in 1864, James Richard Mead hunted game at the juncture of the Little Arkansas and Arkansas Rivers, an area rich in wildlife. Mead's first 1863 trip lasted three weeks and yielded "3,500 lbs. of tallow, 330 buffalo hides, and large numbers of wolf and elk skins, together worth about $400."* With the onset of the Civil War, the Wichita Indians and other related tribes were driven north from the Indian Territory (what is now Oklahoma) by tribes sympathetic to

* From *Wichita: The Magic City,* by Craig Miner (Wichita: Wichita–Sedgwick County Historical Museum Association, 1988).

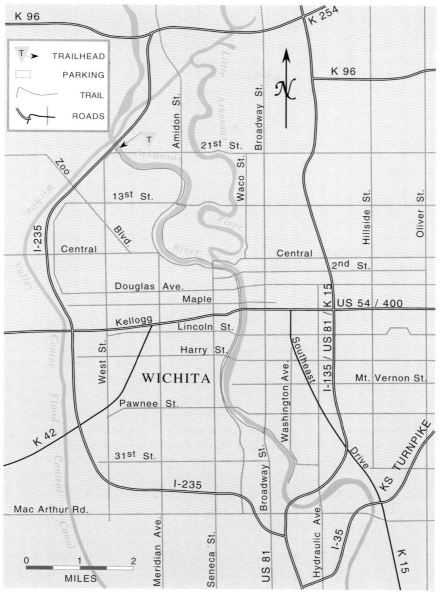

Arkansas River Path

the Confederate cause. They settled in 1864 at the mouth of the Little Arkansas River. As you near the juncture of the rivers, west of the Seneca Street Bridge, watch for Old Cowtown Museum, a recreated frontier village depicting the early years of Wichita, from 1865–80. About .75 mile further south is the Douglas Avenue Bridge, the site of the first bridge across the Arkansas River, built in 1872 by the Wichita Bridge Company. The original, essential to the establishment of Wichita as a cattle thoroughfare, was a toll bridge—passage cost five cents a head for cattle and fifty cents a team for a farmer with wagons. Ten years after it was built, the timber-truss span had rotted through and had to be replaced by a steel bridge.

🏃🏃 THE HIKE

ARKANSAS RIVER PATH: We began at the north trailhead off of 21st Street North. Although this section of the path travels within view of commercial buildings and apartments, the river itself remains untouched. The sandbars are near enough to see the cattails, reeds, sedges, and other riverside plants that provide cover for wildlife. As the trail nears 13th Street, it leaves the river's edge briefly, then crosses the 13th Street Bridge to travel on the east side of the river. From here, the trail borders the Arthur D. Sim Memorial Park, a 183-acre park that includes a municipal golf course. We enjoyed the shade and quiet of the park, which still remains primitive in some areas. A short walk from here is Botanica, a botanical garden where paths weave through spectacularly groomed gardens, as well as an area of native wildflowers.

The next feature seen from the trail is the Old Cowtown Museum. Just east of here, the trail crosses the Seneca Street Bridge and travels on the west side of the river. The confluence of the Little Arkansas and Arkansas Rivers is just east of the bridge. Over 130 years ago, this wedge of land was dotted with tents and grass huts of the tribes of the Wichita Indian Confederation. The trail then heads into the heart of downtown, where you will see, across the river, the scenic A. Price Woodard Park that borders Century II (identified by its sky-blue roof). For the next 3 miles, the trail remains on the west side of the river, which is bordered by a mixture of commercial and residential developments. We enjoyed this quiet section of the river, where an occasional cottonwood towers over the water. Just past the Pawnee Avenue Bridge, the river is bordered on the northeast by Herman Hill Park and on the southwest by Watson Park. The path then crosses the Broadway Bridge and continues for about 1.25 miles on the east side of the river, which is bordered by a residential area. As the map shows, the trail ends before the river bends east, about half a mile from I-135.

Chisholm Creek Park

This 280-acre park in northeast Wichita includes a unique, 2-mile paved nature trail that winds across and around Chisholm Creek, passing through a wide range of habitats, including wetlands, tallgrass prairie, and riparian woodlands. The elevated boardwalk and observation decks allow you to walk "through" the wetlands, a feat that typically requires waist-high wading boots. The trail is linked to the newly constructed Great Plains Nature Center, an impressive educational facility. As you hike, take time to follow some of the many dirt paths that lead from the trail to the creek or through the woods. Ownership: Wichita Department of Parks and Recreation (316) 268-4361 or (316) 683-5499 (Great Plains Nature Center).

HIKE LENGTH
Chisolm Creek Park Nature Trail .... 2 miles (dirt paths add additional mileage)

DIRECTIONS AND TRAIL ACCESS

Chisholm Creek Park is located at 3238 N. Oliver Street and is bordered by K-96 on the north, Oliver Street on the west, 29th Street North on the south, and Woodlawn on the east. From K-96, exit south at Oliver to the entrance to the park on the east side of Oliver Street. Travel east on the park road for less than .2 mile to the first parking area to the south. The trailhead is by the picnic shelter. The trail can also be accessed from the Great Plains Nature Center, at 6232 East 29th Street North. The Great Plains Nature Center is contiguous with Chisholm Creek Park and is linked to the 2 miles of wheelchair-accessible nature trails in the park.

Chisholm Creek Park

ℹ️ GENERAL INFORMATION

Chisholm Creek is named after Jesse Chisholm, a frontier trader who in 1863 established a trading post, cabins, and a corral in Wichita, several miles downstream from the present location of Chisholm Creek Park. This may have been the first business in Wichita. Chisholm was born in 1805 in Tennessee to a Scottish father and Cherokee mother. He is probably most famous for establishing the Chisholm Trail, from Wichita to the Red River area in Texas. This 600-mile trail, which Chisholm cut after the Civil War, passed through sections of Indian territory and was used by traders, cattle drovers, and the military. In 1868, Chisholm died gruesomely of food poisoning after eating rancid bear grease that had sat overnight in a brass kettle. Chisholm Creek Park, which is owned by the City of Wichita, is contiguous with the Great Plains Nature Center. It was built as a result of a unique partnership among the United States Fish and Wildlife Service, the Kansas Department of Wildlife and Parks, and the City of Wichita Department of Parks and Recreation. The center is linked to the nature trail at its eastern end, near the wetlands. Take time to detour from the trail to see the 2,400-gallon aquarium, the wildlife observatory, the prairie dioramas, and other interpretive and interactive exhibits of wildlife and habitats in the Great Plains.

THE HIKE

The trail is paved, handicapped accessible, and well marked with directional signs and mileage markers. Just past the picnic shelter next to the parking lot, a "Hiking Trails" sign directs you to the right, along a row of red cedars. Soon the trail crosses Chisholm Creek, via the first of many artfully designed wooden pedestrian bridges. The stream, lined by a narrow band of trees called a gallery forest, is the east fork of Chisholm Creek. The trail forks after crossing the bridge. Follow the arrow and continue straight (east). (The trail to the left travels north, or clockwise, around the loop.) The trail soon reaches an open area where wildflowers are interspersed in the prairie grasses. Watch for another bridge across Chisholm Creek—this is a shortcut back to the trailhead. At the half-mile marker, the trail meets a concrete walk to the south. This is the western end of the trail leading through the wetlands area in the eastern section of the park. After traveling southeast, the trail through the wetlands curves east and then northwest to intersect with the easternmost pedestrian bridge on the nature trail. To avoid missing a section of the nature trail, remain on the asphalted trail to the second walkway to the south, leading to the wetlands. Long stretches of boardwalk take you through the heart of the wetlands, one of my favorite sections of the trail. Eventually, the trail loops back to the half-mile marker.

The eastern end of the wetlands loop intersects with the nature trail as it crosses north over Chisholm Creek and loops back to the west. Much of the trail on the north side of Chisholm Creek travels through open prairie, including a "prairie restoration" area. At the 1.25-mile marker, watch for the pedestrian bridge heading southwest over Chisholm Creek; continue straight to complete the nature trail loop. Shortly after the bridge, the trail passes a pond, then travels beneath a canopy of osage orange trees. Log benches make this a great rest stop. When you reach a fork in the trail, an arrow points straight ahead. (The other fork, to the right, will take you over a bridge to a picnic shelter and parking area northeast of the trailhead.) Continuing straight, the trail crosses Chisholm Creek again, then curves north, then south, before intersecting with the trail just east of the pedestrian bridge you crossed at the start. Cross the pedestrian bridge to return to the trailhead.

Pawnee Prairie Park

Pawnee Prairie Park

Fifteen years ago, Pawnee Prairie Park was a labyrinth of foot trails. Much has changed since then. The first nature trail at the park was only 1.25 miles; by 1982, it had been expanded to 3 miles. But as traffic across the highly erodible soil increased, the park became riddled with trails on both sides of the creek. Today, the main trail through this 625-acre park is more than 5 miles long and color-coded. So long as you remain on the blazed trail and follow the arrows, you should have no difficulty finding your way back. One mile of the trail, from the shelter house on the west side of the park to the nature center on the east side, is surfaced in concrete. This section winds through the woods that line Cowskin Creek and edges a tallgrass prairie. Ownership: Wichita Department of Parks and Recreation (316) 721-9418.

HIKE LENGTH

About 5 miles round-trip, following the posted trail. The park brochure states that there are 8–10 miles of trail in the park.

DIRECTIONS AND TRAIL ACCESS

Pawnee Prairie Park is in west Wichita, on the south side of U.S. 54 (Kellogg) between Tyler Road to the east and Maize Road to the west. You can access the trails from either the east or west:

PAWNEE ENTRANCE: From U.S. 54, take Maize Road south to Pawnee Street; turn east and watch for the park entrance on the north side of the road. The trail starts just east of the picnic shelter.

TYLER ENTRANCE: Take U.S. 54 to Tyler Road; turn south and go about 1.5 miles to the entrance on the west side of the road. Both the concrete trail leading around the nature center and the mowed trail through the prairie start from the parking area.

GENERAL INFORMATION

Cowskin Creek, a tributary of the Arkansas River, was originally called Crooked Creek, an appropriate name. The creek has since been straightened and channelized through and around Wichita to prevent flooding. The channel through Pawnee Prairie, however, is unaltered. The renaming of Cowskin Creek can be traced to the Chisholm Trail, a trail cut by Jesse Chisholm from his trading post on the Little Arkansas River through Indian Territory to the Red River in Texas. Hundreds of thousands of cattle were driven up this trail between 1867 and 1871 to railheads in Wichita, Newton, Caldwell, Abilene, and Ellsworth. The Texas longhorns carried a type of pneumonia, spread by ticks, which did little harm to the longhorns, but caused "Texas" or "splenic" fever in epidemic proportions in the cattle imported by Kansas ranchers. As cattle died on the Chisholm Trail near Cowskin Creek, their hides were left to dry on its banks.

Pawnee Prairie derives its name from the Pawnee Indians, one of eight tribes that inhabited Kansas during the 1700s and 1800s. Several trading posts were established on Cowskin Creek in the 1860s to cater to the bands of Wichita Indians and related tribes that settled around 1863 at the confluence of the Little Arkansas and Arkansas Rivers. These tribes were displaced from Indian Territory, in what is now Oklahoma, by other tribes sympathetic to the Confederate cause. James Richmond Mead started a trading post on Cowskin Creek in 1865, west of the Wichita village located on the Little Arkansas River. William "Dutch Bill" Greiffenstein, who achieved fame as a trader and later was instrumental in building the first bridge across the Arkansas River, also built a trading post on the Cowskin. These traders established a lucrative business, trading flour, coffee, sugar, tobacco, broadcloth, calico, knives, beads, shells and other goods for buffalo robes and furs.*

THE HIKE

PAWNEE PRAIRIE PARK NATURE TRAIL: As posted, the trail is a sequence of three loops: yellow (south), blue (middle), and red (north). We found the trail surprisingly easy to follow, even with the many side-paths. For the most part, the trail to the north of the picnic area, off of the Pawnee Avenue entrance, is more primitive, a dirt trail through the woods that skirts both sides of Cowskin Creek and in wet weather can be muddy. The trail to the south is paved in concrete, although one offshoot, on the west side of the creek, is a mowed path. From the park shelter, we followed the concrete trail east, then south, along Cowskin Creek. The woods along the creek were lush in spring, not what some might expect in an area known for its treeless prairies and vast wheat fields. The southern end of the concrete trail edges a prairie,

* For more historical information about this area, we recommend *Wichita: The Early Years, 1865–1880* (Lincoln University of Nebraska Press, 1982) and *Wichita: The Magic City* (Wichita: Wichita–Sedgwick County Historical Museum Association, 1988), both by Craig Miner.

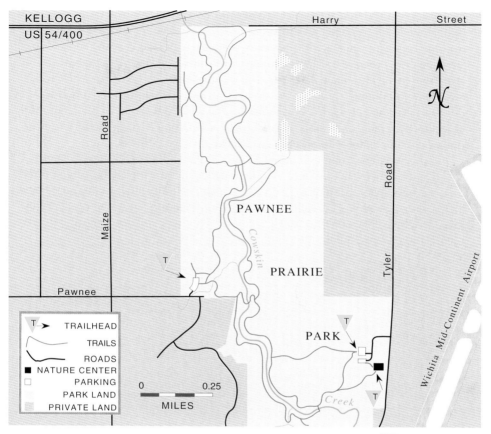

KELLOGG
US 54/400
Harry Street

Road

Maize

Pawnee

PAWNEE

PRAIRIE

PARK

Cowskin

Tyler Road

Wichita Mid-Continent Airport

Creek

T→   TRAILHEAD
      TRAILS
      ROADS
■ NATURE CENTER
□   PARKING
      PARK LAND
   PRIVATE LAND

0   0.25
MILES

Pawnee Prairie Park Trail

where you will see a variety of native grasses, including little and big bluestem, switchgrass, and Indian grass, as well as many prairie wildflowers. The concrete trail ends at the nature center, off of Tyler Road, where a mowed path tunnels through the prairie from the parking area. This trail intersects with the concrete trail near the creek; turn right (north) and backtrack to connect to the northern, primitive part of the trail. As the map shows, if you cross Cowskin Creek, you have gone too far on the concrete section and missed the dirt trail.

The dirt trail, marked by steel posts, continues north from the concrete trail just before the concrete trail dips down to cross the creek. One confusing spot is near a cobblestonelike drainage area, where bags of concrete have been laid near the creek to prevent erosion. After this, watch carefully for a blue arrow. From here, the trail travels primarily through the woods that line Cowskin Creek or skirts the edge of the woods next to the prairie. To travel just half of the northern section of the trail, take the bridge at the halfway point to the west side of Cowskin Creek and turn left (south) onto the blue-blazed trail. Otherwise, continue north to the bridge near the end of Harry Street on the red-blazed trail. On the way, you will pass a wetlands, a favorite haven for great blue heron and other waterfowl. The trail on the west side of Cowskin Creek is less wooded and winds through fields dotted with red cedar, sumac, and rough-leaved dogwood. At points, you will be able to see the steep dirt banks of the creek, and abandoned sections of the trail, which have caved in as the bank eroded. This area is riddled with footpaths—follow the signs back to the picnic shelter.

Another section of the trail parallels the west side of Cowskin Creek, south of Pawnee Avenue. Just before the concrete trail dips to cross the creek, watch for the yellow arrow. This section reconnects to the concrete trail at the southern end by a bridge over the creek. This side of the creek is not as wooded or scenic. When we hiked this trail in March 1997, the bridge was still under construction, and part of the trail was hard to follow.

Sedgwick County Park

Four miles of asphalt trail wrap around several sandpit lakes and run through open prairie and along a narrow slough in the 480-acre Sedgwick County Park. Some of you might have plunged from the 30-foot diving platform that once towered over Horseshoe Lake, at the north end of the trail, or jumped into the lake from its giant swing. Moss Lake, between Horseshoe Lake and Tom Scott Lake, is another old swimming hole that some might remember as Lagoona Beach. Over time the lake has filled with silt, and cottonwoods, bald cypress, and willows now shroud its shallow waters. Most of the trail is unshaded, although occasionally it passes through tunnels of trees, at the south end of the trail and near Moss Lake. This is a popular urban trail, used by walkers, runners, bikers, and roller-bladers. Ownership: Sedgwick County (316) 943-0192.

HIKE LENGTH
Sedgwick County Park Trail .... 4-mile loop

DIRECTIONS

Sedgwick County Park is located in northwestern Wichita, adjacent to and west of the Sedgwick County Zoo. The park is bordered on the south by 13th Street and on the north by 21st Street, and is located between Ridge Road to the west and Zoo Boulevard to the northeast. You can enter the park and find parking just off of either 13th Street or 21st Street. The asphalt trail connects to each parking area. Be sure to stop at the park office to pick up a map that shows the trail (labeled "Biking Trail"), the lakes, and various recreational facilities. The park office is about midway between the parking areas, north of Tom Scott Lake and just south of Moss Lake.

Sedgwick County Park

ℹ️ GENERAL INFORMATION

Sedgwick County derives its name from John M. Sedgwick, a major general in the United States Army during the Civil War, killed at the battle of Spotsylvania on May 9, 1864. The 480-acre county park lies in the Arkansas River floodplain, a little more than a mile west of the Arkansas River, and just west of the Wichita Valley Center Flood Control Canal (commonly referred to as the "Big Ditch"). In light of the history of flooding of the Arkansas River, it is not surprising that the Sedgwick County Park was once the site of several sand excavation operations. Vic's Lake, in the northwest corner of the trail loop, was excavated to about 30 feet for sand. The sand had been carried in over several million years by the Arkansas River, which lies just to the northeast of the park. This river originates near Leadville, Colorado, in the Rocky Mountains, where the river's swift current carved the Royal Gorge. Through western Kansas, however, the river is torpid and at times dries up. O. J. Reichman points out that the outline of the Arkansas River Lowlands, the physiographic region in which the Sedgwick County Park is located, demarcates the past and present courses of the Arkansas River.* In the past, the Arkansas River, like most slow-moving rivers in flat terrain, frequently flood-

---

* In *Living Landscapes of Kansas* by O. J. Reichman; photographs by Steve Mulligan (Lawrence: University Press of Kansas, 1995).

ed and meandered, forming a broad floodplain. Today, the river is almost as far north as it has ever meandered; consequently, there is a wide swath of floodplain to the south of the river covered by hundreds of feet of sand and silt.

THE HIKE

We began from the south entrance, off of 13th Street, and headed north, toward the windmill. (Don't mistake the fitness trail, which travels east from the parking area, for the asphalt bike trail.) After the trail passes the windmill, it tunnels through what appears to be an old shelter belt of trees. The lengthy stretch of trail along the east side of the park crosses open prairie adjacent to the Sedgwick County Zoo. In spring, summer, and early fall, the wildflowers are plentiful, and by winter the native tall-grasses have turned varying hues of copper, gold, and brown. You are likely to hear a number of foreign cries and calls from animals and birds in the zoo. At the north end of Tom Scott Lake, the trail enters an area of young timber, and then it branches. The trail to the left (west) travels between Tom Scott Lake and Moss Lake and inter-sects with the road leading to the park office. We continued north, walking in view of Moss Lake (formerly Lagoona Beach), a shallow lake favored by waterfowl. At the north end of Moss Lake, the trail again branches. The trail to the left (west) travels by the tennis courts, playground, and horseshoe pit. We continued north around Horseshoe Lake. At the north end of the lake, the trail branching to the right (east) leads to the zoo and is part of a bike trail that eventually links up with the Arkansas River Trail. We continued on the trail to the left (west), which turns south at the Kid's Pond (actually the northwest end of the horseshoe, designated as a fishing area for children) and crosses the park road. If you are hiking with children, caution them about the traffic.

   The trail next reaches Vic's Lake, the deepest lake at the park. From here, to the south end of the loop, the trail parallels the Big Slough, a waterway where you may spot blue herons, ducks, or other waterfowl hiding behind cattails. As the trail nears 13th Street, past the tennis courts, it branches. The branch to the left, which travels southeast, is a shortcut back to the start. Whether you take this or the longer branch to the right, watch for traffic where the trail crosses the park road.

GREELEY | WICHITA | **7** SCOTT | LANE | NESS | RUSH | BARTON

3

HAMILTON | KEARNY | FINNEY | HODGEMAN | PAWNEE | STAFFORD **8**

GRAY

FORD

STANTON | GRANT | HASKELL | EDWARDS | KIOWA | PRATT

MEADE | CLARK **5** | BARBER

MORTON | STEVENS | SEWARD | COMANCHE | **2** **1**

4

6

SOUTHWEST REGION

1. Barber State Fishing Lake and Wildlife Area
2. Gypsum Hills Scenic Drive
3. Cheyenne Bottoms Wildlife Area
4. Big Basin Prairie Preserve
5. Clark State Fishing Lake and Wildlife Area
6. Cimarron National Grassland
7. Lake Scott State Park
8. Quivira National Wildlife Refuge

SOUTH

Southwest
REGION

WEST

Barber State Fishing Lake and Wildlife Area

The 1.75-mile Red Cedar Nature Trail loops through woods and prairie surrounding a 77-acre watershed lake in a 190-acre wildlife area. While this is within the Red Hills physiographic region, the characteristic red mesas, bluffs, and buttes are several miles southwest of the lake. The cedar-chip trail is well maintained, and the artfully designed trail signs provide information about the wildlife, soil, and other points of interest. Our favorite area was the footbridge and dike on the north end of the lake, a good spot for wildlife. The southern third of the trail follows the gravel lake road. Ownership: KDWP (316) 227-8609.

HIKE LENGTH
Red Cedar Nature Trail ....1.75 miles

DIRECTIONS AND TRAIL ACCESS

The Barber State Fishing Lake and Wildlife Area is just north of Medicine Lodge. From the junction of U.S. 160 and U.S. 281 take 281 north and watch for the lake sign on the east side of the road. Turn east on the lake road and travel .2 mile. The west trailhead is on the north side of the road, marked by a large sign with a map of the trail. The east trailhead can be reached by following the lake road south, then west across the dam. Just north of the dam, near a grove of trees, watch for the trail sign and map.

GENERAL INFORMATION

Barber State Fishing Lake and Wildlife Area is in northeastern Barber County, between the Medicine Lodge River to the southwest and Elm Creek to the east. About 2 miles south of here, in October 1867, the famous Medicine Lodge Indian Peace Treaty was signed by five Plains Indian tribes—the Apache, Arapaho,

Red Cedar Nature Trail, Barber State Fishing Lake and Wildlife Area

Cheyenne, Comanche, and Kiowa. The leaders of these tribes met with a treaty commission formed by Congress to bring peace to the plains, while 15,000 Indians waited in nearby camps in the natural basin formed by the confluence of the Medicine Lodge River and Elm Creek. The commissioners spoke of reservations and limited hunting rights, while the Indians expressed concerns about the encroachment of white settlers. Journalists reported the eloquent speeches of the Indian chiefs, including that of Ten Bears, the Comanche chief, who stated: "You said you wanted to put us upon a reservation, to build us houses and make us medicine lodges. I do not want them. I was born on the prairie where the wind blew free and there was nothing to break the light of the sun. I was born where there were no inclosures and where everything drew a free breath. I want to die there and not within walls."* As a result of the treaty, the Comanches and Kiowas signed away 60,000 square miles of their homeland in return for 5,000 square miles of reservation land in southwestern Oklahoma and hunting privileges south of the Arkansas River in southern Kansas.

THE HIKE

RED CEDAR NATURE TRAIL: We entered the trail at the east trailhead and hiked north through a corridor of tall red cedars. Elms, cottonwoods, and black willow trees also provide shade in many places. The trail crosses the park road on the east side of the lake four times. After the first crossing, the trail passes through an area of native prairie grasses infiltrated by red cedar. Stands of pampas grass also grow along the trail. A trail sign identifies the soil as Woodward loam, the "soft red silty soils found in the Gyp Hill area." Watch for the field of Illinois bundle flower, which averages 3 feet tall, but may grow to 5 feet in fertile soil. This plant, which has a fern-like appearance and tiny white flowers, is used in prairie restoration and provides nourishment for livestock and wildlife.

After half a mile, the trail reaches the dike at the north end of the lake. We had some difficulty following the trail at this point and mistakenly crossed the road over to the vault toilets. The map at the trailheads shows a loop here—a turnaround point for a shorter hike. We could not find the loop. The trail turns south before it crosses the road and follows the footbridge to the dike. At the end of the dike, turn left (east). Do not cross the road. The trail on the west side of the lake passes through areas of young timber as well as open prairie, where various native grasses are labeled.

* From *Medicine Lodge: The Story of a Kansas Town* by Nellie Snyder Yost (Chicago: Swallow Press, 1970).

Gypsum Hills Scenic Drive

Gypsum Hills Scenic Drive

The striking beauty of the Gypsum Hills, also aptly named the Red Hills, compeled us to find a hike here. We were disappointed to learn that there is no park or other public access. The hike described below follows part of the Gyp Hills Scenic Drive, a gravel road that showcases the red buttes and mesas, peaks, bluffs, pyramids, and other unusual geological formations characteristic of the Gypsum Hills. Hiking along a road is somewhat akin to window shopping, but with scenery this beautiful, you won't mind.

HIKE LENGTH: About a 30-mile loop. We suggest hiking only on the gravel road, which is a 14.4-mile segment, and in particular the sections noted below.

DIRECTIONS

The Gypsum Hills Scenic Drive begins 10.8 miles east of the western boundary of Barber County, south off of U.S. 160 (directly across from the turnoff to Lake City). A sign on U.S. 160 points to the scenic drive. From Medicine Lodge, take U.S. 160 about 14 miles west to the scenic drive. Note that you will first intersect Gyp Hill Road, a paved road about 3.5 miles west of Medicine Lodge, and the eastern end of the Gypsum Hills Scenic Drive.

GENERAL INFORMATION

The Gypsum Hills are steeped in legend and folklore. Before you turn south off of U.S. 160, scan the horizon to the east for Flowerpot Mound, a distinctive, gypsum-capped, flat-topped butte on the north side of the highway. According to legend, a buffalo hunter camped at the top of the butte and in the night was awakened by unearthly cries and the radiant light of a blazing fire. Indians surrounded the fire, in which two humans were bound to a stake. The vision passed, but later a voice

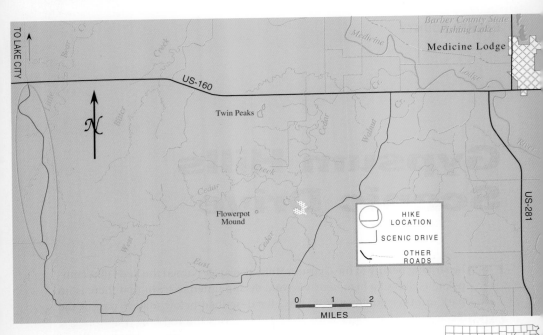

Gypsum Hills Scenic Drive

directed him to a box, buried beneath a stone, where the hunter found the diary of Lenora Day. The diary told of the journey of Lenora Day and 31 other members of her party, who were on their way in 1849 from St. Louis to California. Sixteen of the travelers died in a flood on the "White Medicine River," and the remainder were later captured by a band of Kiowa Indians and burned at the stake on top of Flowerpot Mound.*

Believing that healing spirits dwelled in these hills, Indians called them the "Medicine Hills." There is some basis for their belief. The springs and streams here contain natural salts, including calcium and magnesium sulfate (Epsom salt), dissolved from gypsum and dolomite beds. The healing qualities of some of these natural compounds were especially appreciated before the discovery of antibiotics. Epsom salts were often diluted and drunk as a tonic, applied to wounds to draw out an infection, or poured in a soaking bath to heal bruised muscles.†

---

* The legend of Flower Pot Mountain is recounted in *Medicine Lodge: The Story of a Kansas Town* by Nellie Snyder Yost (Chicago: Swallow Press, 1970).

† For more information about the Red Hills, including a description of the region's subterranean world (there are more than 400 caves in Barber and Comanche Counties), see "The Red Hills: Good Medicine" by Bob Mathews in *Kansas Wildlife and Parks*, March/April 1996.

THE HIKE

GYPSUM HILLS SCENIC WALK: Our favorite piece of the Gypsum Hills Scenic Drive is a 5.5-mile section starting at the west end of the loop, at the turnoff from U.S. 160. The last 8.8 miles along the gravel section of the scenic drive are more agricultural and less scenic. (If you are traveling with one car, we suggest parking off the road near the entrance to the scenic drive and hiking 1.9 miles to the first bridge, for a round-trip of 3.8 miles.) Beginning at the western entrance to the scenic drive, the road forks after a mile—the right fork is a private drive. The next mile of road passes through a valley, where the vistas of the Red Hills are spectacular. Wildflowers bloom profusely along the roadbed, and the reflection of the afternoon sun on the plumes of the mixed tall and short grasses create a silvery haze across the hills. The Red Hills are in a transition zone where eastern and western vegetation are intermixed.

The terra-cotta–colored soil contrasts vividly with the eastern red cedar trees, wildflowers, and native grasses that cover the hills. To the delight of our children, we found layers of gypsum along the roadbed. Diamond-shaped crystals of gypsum, called selenite, are also commonly found here. The rocks exposed here are part of a series of Permian deposits that geologists call "red beds," colored by iron oxide (rust), which turns bright red when exposed to oxygen. At 1.9 miles, the road crosses a bridge and veers right, up a hill. In another .5 mile, the road passes a quonset hut and then a farm to the left. For the next 2 miles the hills are strenuous, but the exceptional views of the unique landscape are worth the effort.

At 5.1 miles from the start, the road veers east and continues to wind through the hills. By the time the road reaches the oil rigs at 6.6 miles, the scenery is not as dramatic, and the Red Hills can only be seen in the distance. More of the valleys are planted to crops and the terrain is flatter. Just when you may be losing interest at 10.3 miles, the road reaches another panoramic view of the Red Hills, but then flattens as it passes through a valley. At 14.4 miles from the start, the gravel road intersects with a paved road.

Cheyenne Bottoms Wildlife Area

Cheyenne Bottoms Wildlife Area

C heyenne Bottoms Wildlife Area, covering 19,857 acres, is located in a 41,000-acre elliptical natural sink near Great Bend. This sink was part of an ancient migratory flyway long before pools, levees, and canals were built to control and conserve water and to maintain the swampy marshlands in periods of drought. Although there are no designated hiking trails at the Cheyenne Bottoms Wildlife Area, you can hike for miles on the gravel roads and dikes that border the marshes and the five manmade pools. In spring and summer, verdant marsh grasses provide a beautiful backdrop for showy wildflowers. There is birdwatching year-round at the Bottoms, but spring and fall migrations bring concentrations of a large number of different species. Three-quarters of a million birds may land at the Bottoms during spring migration. Of the 650 species of birds in the United States, 320 have been spotted at Cheyenne Bottoms. In 1988, Cheyenne Bottoms was the first non–federally-owned land in the United States to be designated a "Wetlands of International Importance" under a worldwide treaty. Ownership: KDWP (316) 793-3066. (The 24-hour hotline at Cheyenne Bottoms Wildlife Refuge is [316] 793-7730.)

HUNTING REMINDER: Approximately 13,150 acres at Cheyenne Bottoms are open to hunting and trapping. Pools 1, 5, and a portion of 2 are designated refuge areas and are closed to all activities, including hunting. If you plan to hike off the roads, be sure to pick up the map available at headquarters, which shows the public hunting areas. It is always advisable to wear bright colors when you hike—preferably an orange hunting vest and hat.

DIRECTIONS

Cheyenne Bottoms is located northeast of Great Bend and southeast of Hoisington. Several roads provide access. We entered at the first of two entrances off of K-156, about 6 miles from the junction with K- 56/96 and about 9 miles northeast of Great

Bend. This road leads to the observation tower near Pool 1. Alternatively, you can travel 5 miles north from Great Bend, or 8 miles south from Hoisington, on U.S. 281, and then 2 miles east on a county blacktop road to the Cheyenne Bottoms Headquarters and Check Station. Also, from Redwing, on K-4, watch for a gravel road just east of town, leading south to Pool 3, or the gravel road .75 mile west of Redwing, leading south to Pool 2.

[i] GENERAL INFORMATION

The large sink in which the Cheyenne Bottoms Wildlife Area is located is said to have been discovered in 1806 by Zebulon Pike, who was sent by James Wilkinson to explore the headwaters of the Arkansas River and descend the Red River. Bounded on the north by high rock bluffs, this natural basin was rich in wildlife and a prized hunting ground. The basin was named Cheyenne Bottoms after an 1825 battle over hunting rights between the Cheyenne Indians, the victors, and the Pawnee, or Kiowa.

Cheyenne Bottoms is a federally designated critical habitat for the endangered whooping crane. In the fall of 1994, mild weather and favorable water levels in the Bottoms caused the cranes to linger for an unprecedented 48 days (their normal stay is less than a week). On November 1, 1994, 18 whooping cranes (of the approximately 175 that exist in the wild) were spotted at Cheyenne Bottoms. The migratory route of the whooping crane covers about 2,500 miles, from Aransas National Wildlife Refuge in southern Texas to Wood Buffalo National Park in the Northwest Territories. The cranes usually cover this route over several weeks, averaging about 250–300 miles per day with 12–15 stops, typically landing in Kansas the first week of November on their fall migration, and during April on their spring migration. Draining of marshes and loss of habitat along the migratory route, together with human encroachment on their nesting grounds, nearly led to the extinction of the extremely shy whooping crane. In Kansas alone, approximately 40% of the wetlands were drained and converted to other uses between 1955 and 1978.

Twelve thousand acres of this 20,000-acre wildlife area are usually covered by shallow waters. In the summer heat, it becomes very apparent why the diversion of water into Cheyenne Bottoms is critical for the maintenance of the wetlands. About 60 inches of water is lost annually to evaporation, but annual rainfall averages only 24 inches. The Nature Conservancy has purchased over 6,500 acres of land adjacent to, and primarily to the west of, the state-owned Cheyenne Bottoms Wildlife Area.

🏃 THE HIKE

CHEYENNE BOTTOMS WILDLIFE AREA: There are few hiking areas in Kansas as flat as Cheyenne Bottoms, but this serves only to enhance the beauty of the marshes and the channels of water that slice through the tall cattails, reeds, and sedges. The large expanses of water mirror the sky. Birds in flight against the backdrop of a colorful sunrise or sunset create unbeatable photo opportunities. Wildflowers line the roads

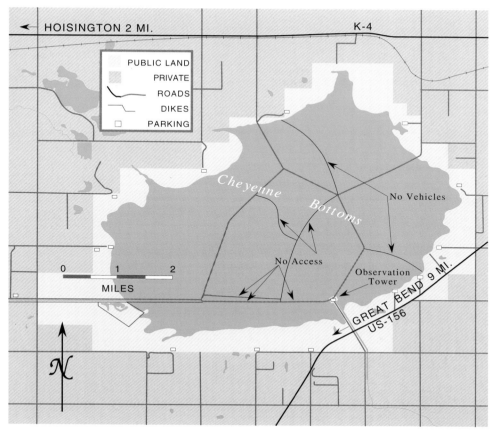

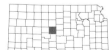

Cheyenne Bottoms Wildlife Area

and dikes from spring through fall. Unlike the neighboring Quivira National Wildlife Refuge, Cheyenne Bottoms has no hiking trails or designated wildlife drives. Because water levels in the pools are constantly manipulated, and some pools are completely drained from time to time (for planting, weed control, and other reasons), we cannot recommend a particular route. The water in most areas is shallow, below the shoulders of a deer running through, except in certain ditches along the dikes and in Pool 4.

Dikes are generally open to hiking, but may be closed depending on nesting activities. Certain dikes, such as on the south side of Pool 1, are closed to all activities, including hiking. We advise calling ahead to determine which pools are full and where there is the most bird activity. Otherwise, we recommend simply parking your car and walking the dikes between the pools. In the warmer months, Massasauga rattlesnakes frequently sun on the roads. Watch your step.

Big Basin Prairie Preserve

Big Basin Prairie Preserve

The beauty of the Big Basin Prairie Preserve caught us all by surprise. As we approached from the west, the terrain changed abruptly. Creeks cut paths through hills, exposing whitish-gray layers of rock, part of the Ogallala Formation, and red shale and siltstone, part of the Big Basin Formation. Before we entered the preserve, we traveled across the floor of Big Basin, a mile-wide, 100-foot-deep sinkhole, whose rocky walls rise almost vertically. Bison roam freely across this 1,818-acre preserve. Long after we finished exploring Big and Little Basins, the short trail down to St. Jacob's Well, the Living Water Monument, and the 3.5 miles of gravel road that wind through the Preserve, we lingered to watch a herd of buffalo in a distant valley and to watch the sun set on the surrounding hills and canyons. Ownership: KDWP (316) 227-8609.

BISON WARNING: While hiking at Big Basin Prairie Preserve, always be alert for, and stay clear of, bison. Bison are wild animals that should not be harassed or approached. They are unpredictable and can charge without provocation. We recommend driving into the preserve to see where the bison are before hiking.

HIKE LENGTH
The only designated hiking trail at Big Basin Prairie Preserve is the short St. Jacob's Well Foot Trail. The entire preserve, however, is open to hiking, and the park brochure encourages it. If you leave your car at the entrance and hike the scenic gravel road around the Big and Little Basins to the Living Water Monument, the round-trip hike is 5 miles.

DIRECTIONS

Big Basin Prairie Preserve is in Clark County, 36 miles south of Dodge City. From Dodge City, take U.S. 283 south to the entrance, on the east side of the highway (3

miles past the intersection with U.S. 160). There is an information sign about the preserve at the entrance.

ⓘ GENERAL INFORMATION

From a geological perspective, the Big and Little Basins are not old sinks. They were formed before historical record, however, probably in the past few thousand years. The forces that created these sinks were set in motion long before, as rain and artesian waters found their way down crevices in the surface of the earth somewhere west of Big Basin. Seeking an exit, these waters flowed downhill, east and south, descending in some places as deep as 1,000 feet. Soon the waters penetrated, eroded, and weakened the massive gypsum and salt beds that lay several hundred feet below the earth's surface. (These minerals had been deposited over 250 million years ago by inland seas that repeatedly flooded and receded, leaving layers of salt and anhydrite as the ocean waters evaporated.) Eventually, the weakened underlayer of salt, gypsum, and other minerals gave way, and the overlayer of sandstone, shale, and siltstone collapsed into the void, perhaps even overnight, creating Big and Little Basins.*

When Big Basin subsided, it exposed mortarbed of the Ogallala Formation, seen in the almost vertical walls. Wind and water continue to change the preserve. In 1944, a small sink appeared about 200 feet east of St. Jacob's Well, and other small depressions have since formed in Little Basin. The walls of Big and Little Basins are eroding. "Soon, geologically speaking, these walls will be breached and Big and Little Basins will no longer be separate features but will be continuous with the Ashland-Englewood Basin to the south."†

🥾 THE HIKE

BIG BASIN PRAIRIE PRESERVE: We parked at the first scenic overlook, .4 mile from the entrance. This is a good spot to hike down the walls of Big Basin, and once you reach the floor, you can hike across or explore the corral and windmill to the northeast. Watch for the several small and usually dry ponds that dot the basin floor. They catch but only temporarily hold the water that flows into the basin. After hiking back out of Big Basin, we followed the gravel road another 1.1 miles to the next scenic overlook, before continuing .2 mile to the entrance to Little Basin. Here you can turn right (south) and travel .4 mile to the Living Water Monument or turn left (northeast) and

---

* The fascinating history of Big Basin is found in "The Ancient Mystery of Big Basin" by Mark Shoup, *Kansas Wildlife and Parks*, January/February 1993. Equally fascinating is the guide to this area in *Roadside Kansas: A Traveler's Guide to Its Geology and Landmarks* by Rex C. Buchanan and James R. McCauley (Lawrence: University Press of Kansas, 1987). In the chapter "From the High Plains to the Coal Fields," the description of miles 118–39 on U.S. 160 describes the western approach to Big Basin.

† *Roadside Kansas*, p. 40.

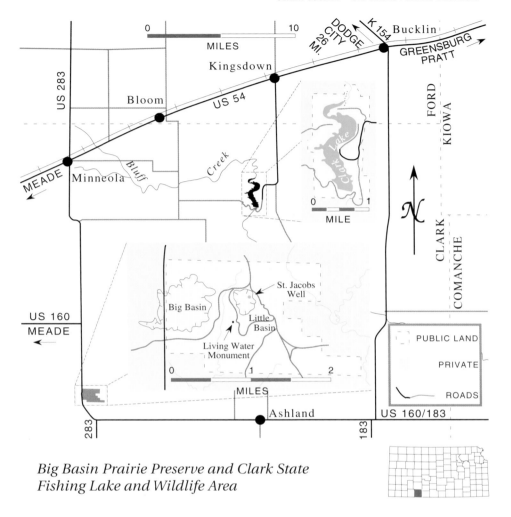

Big Basin Prairie Preserve and Clark State Fishing Lake and Wildlife Area

travel .25 mile to Little Basin and the foot trail down to St. Jacob's Well. We followed the road northeast to Little Basin.

Little Basin is only about 280 yards in diameter and 35 feet deep. Parking is available, and the trail to St. Jacob's Well starts at the parking. While the trail is short, it is steep and rocky. St. Jacob's Well is a spring-formed well that served as a landmark and water-stop for settlers as well as cowboys on cattle drives. Some thought it was bottomless, and others thought it was connected to an underground stream that could carry away anything that fell in its depths. In fact, the funnel-shaped well, which is 84 feet in diameter and 58 feet deep, has never been known to go dry. There is no fence around the actual perimeter of the well, and children, who may scramble down the trail faster than adults, should be cautioned to wait at the gate to the well area.

Our next stop was the Living Water Monument. We suggest returning to the entrance to Little Basin and traveling .4 mile west, then south to the monument. (We do not recommend driving the gravel road heading southeast from the parking area—it is rugged and rutted. We do note that as we traveled this unmapped road, we stopped to watch a tarantula cross.) The limestone Living Water Monument (whose plaque was missing) stands at the top of a hill overlooking much of the preserve and commemorates the importance to early settlers of St. Jacob's Well and other watering sites on the preserve. The view in all directions is spectacular.

Clark State Fishing Lake and Wildlife Area

Those who have seen and judged western Kansas only from their car windows, driving I-70 to Colorado, need to leave the highway to see places such as Clark State Fishing Lake. This beautiful lake sits deep in the rocky canyon of Bluff Creek. The miles of flat, treeless landscape we crossed between Dodge City and Clark State Lake gave no clue as to what lay ahead. While the park brochure includes a map of a 1-mile nature trail at the north end of the lake, high water on Bluff Creek had washed out the last half of the trail before we hiked here in September 1996. We recommend hiking the 2.2-mile section of gravel road at the north end of the lake and from there hiking out to the scenic grassy knobs overlooking the lake. Note: for map see Big Basin Prairie Preserve. Ownership: KDWP (316) 227-8609.

HUNTING REMINDER: Most of the area surrounding the lake is open to hunting—check hunting schedules before you hike. It is advisable to wear bright colors (e.g., orange hunting vest and hat) when you hike in multiple-use areas.

HIKE LENGTHS
Jay Wood Memorial Nature Trail.. 1 mile
Gravel Road from trailhead to K-94 .... 2.2 miles

DIRECTIONS AND TRAIL ACCESS

Clark State Fishing Lake is about 45 miles southeast of Dodge City and about 15 miles north of Ashland, the seat of Clark County. Take U.S. 54 to Kingsdown and turn south on K-94. This highway travels 8.4 miles south before it turns west. Watch for the lake sign at this turn. It is an additional 1.4 miles to the first park entrance, a gravel road marked by a large sign. Travel north, then west on this gravel road for 2.2 miles to the trailhead for the nature trail, on the north side of the road. There is no trailhead sign, and the mowed path from the gravel road to the pedestrian

Clark State Fishing Lake

bridge over Bluff Creek may be difficult to spot. Take time, when you return to K-94, to turn south, toward the main entrance to the lake. K-94 travels south for about .75 miles before curving west around a rocky bluff and descending into the canyon. The hills and bluffs to the west and north of this section of road are not open to hunting.

ℹ️ GENERAL INFORMATION

When construction began in 1934 at Clark State Fishing Lake, a Civilian Conservation Corps (CCC) project, the unique features of this 1,240-acre site were well recognized, as reflected in an article in the *Clark County Clipper:*

> The location is unsurpassed for rugged grandeur and scenic beauty anywhere in the state. It is in a setting which those who have not been privileged to see would [not] believe existed in Kansas. It is approached by winding road up the south escarpment of the plateau between the Arkansas and Cimarron rivers about half way to the top of the divide, which raises nearly six hundred feet above the valley at Ashland. On either side of the site are abrupt almost

precipitous bluffs two hundred forty feet high and where the dam will be built these approach each other within little over a half mile.*

Henry Alonzo Ford, a resident of Ashland and a member of the board of the Pioneer Museum, was in CCC Company 729, which was one of two CCC companies assigned to the project. He sent to me several newspaper articles about the project, including the *Clipper* article, as well as pictures of the barracks that housed more than 400 men in Bluff Creek canyon. The camp resembled a town, and included a hospital, mess hall, recreation hall, company headquarters buildings, officers' quarters, bathhouse, garages, waterworks, electric-light plant, and U.S. Forestry Department headquarters. Initially, mules and horses were used in the construction.

THE HIKES

JAY WOOD MEMORIAL NATURE TRAIL: This trail follows the tree-lined, sandy-bottomed waters of Bluff Creek, north of the lake. We did not find a trailhead sign but followed a mowed path leading north from the park road to a beautiful wooden pedestrian bridge over Bluff Creek. Beyond the bridge, the trail was overgrown, especially with a healthy crop of poison ivy. The trail is not marked. At the first fork past the bridge, we continued straight. At .2 mile, we crossed a creek and traveled through the woods. Based on the large number of fallen trees and the water-swept vegetation, heavy storms must have recently moved through, probably interfering with trail maintenance. About .3 mile from the start, we could not find any evidence of the trail. We crossed a small creek into a weedy field, then lost the trail altogether and retraced our steps back to the road. While the nature trail provides a cool, shaded retreat in warm weather, we preferred the panoramic views and breeze on the bluffs overlooking the lake.

GRAVEL ROAD HIKE: From the mowed path leading to the nature trail, the park road climbs a steep hill. Take time to walk across the hills surrounding the lake, through the mixed prairie grasses. Interspersed in the tall and short prairie grasses are yucca, white-flowered tenpetal mentzelia, sunflowers, sandhill sage, and aromatic sumac. You can't miss the scenic point overlooking the lake, where you can clearly see the outcroppings of buff-colored rock at the tops of the bluffs that tower over the lake. This rock, including the spectacular bluff at the main entrance to the lake, are part of the Ogallala Formation, an accumulation of naturally cemented sands, silts, and clay carried by rivers from the Rocky Mountains during the Pliocene epoch. At the base of the dam and surrounding the lake, you will see Permian red beds. Hundreds of fossils have been found south of the lake.

* "1500 Foot Dam Will Make Clark County Lake," *Clark County Clipper,* November 2, 1934.

Cimarron National Grassland

Cimarron National Grassland

As you hike the Cimarron National Grassland, you walk through history. The 19-mile Santa Fe Companion Trail parallels the Cimarron Cut-off of the historical Santa Fe Trail. Twenty-three miles of the 1,200-mile Santa Fe Trail cross the Cimarron National Grassland, the longest section on public land. The limestone posts that mark its route can be seen from the Companion Trail. The Point of Rocks, a beautiful rocky bluff overlooking the Cimarron River Valley at the southwestern end of the Companion Trail, was the last landmark on the Santa Fe Trail before it left Kansas and crossed into Colorado. At one time, Indians stood here watching for buffalo or intruders. When we hiked here in late summer, sunflowers bloomed so profusely that the distant hills were blanketed with a yellow haze. The 10.5-mile Turkey Trail offers a different perspective of the Cimarron Grassland, winding through cottonwoods and grasslands in the Cimarron River corridor. Ownership: United States Department of Agriculture (316) 697-4621.

SAFETY REMINDER: All of the Cimarron National Grassland is open to public hunting. Wear bright colors when you hike—preferably an orange hunting vest and hat. Although there is water at many windmills along the trail, this water is not known to be safe for drinking. Carry plenty of water with you.

HIKE LENGTHS
Turkey Trail .... 10.5 miles (one-way)
Santa Fe Companion Trail .... 19 miles (one-way)

DIRECTIONS

The Cimarron National Grassland is in the southwest corner of Kansas in Morton and Steven Counties. The office is at 242 U.S. 56 East in Elkhart.

▼︎ TRAIL ACCESS

Turkey Trail

COTTONWOOD PICNIC GROUND ACCESS: From Elkhart, take K-27 7.5 miles north to the Cottonwood Picnic Ground, just south of the Cimarron River Bridge. Park at the east end by the entrance to the trail. Restrooms and drinking water are available.

CIMARRON RECREATION AREA ACCESS: This is approximately 5.6 miles northeast of the Cottonwood Picnic Ground. From K-27, take FS 700 (South River Road, less than .25 mile south of the entrance to the Cottonwood Picnic Ground) east 4 miles to the Cimarron Recreation Area, on the north side of the road. Parking, restrooms, and drinking water are available.

WILBURTON CROSSING ACCESS: The trail east from the Cimarron Recreation Area to Wilburton Crossing was overgrown but could be followed. We could not find the last mile east of the crossing. Follow FS 700 about 3 miles east past the Cimarron Recreation Area. Wilburton Crossing (County Road 16) is the first paved road east of K-27. Turn left (north) and look for a roadside parking area next to a grove of cottonwoods, just north of FS 700 on the west side of County Road 16. There are no facilities.

Santa Fe Companion Trail

MURPHY TRAILHEAD: From Elkhart, take K-27 about 8 miles north to the first gravel road (FS 600) past the Cimarron River Bridge. Turn west and travel 7 miles to the trailhead. (This road also leads to the historic Point of Rocks.) Parking, restrooms, and drinking water are available.

CONESTOGA TRAILHEAD: Follow the directions to the Murphy Trailhead, but turn east on FS 600. Travel 7 miles to Wilburton Crossing (County Road 16), a paved road that leads to Wilburton, if you turn south. FS 600 jogs north a short distance on County Road 16, then turns off east and returns to gravel. Follow FS 600 another 3 miles to the gravel road leading north 2 miles to the Conestoga Trailhead. Parking, restrooms, and drinking water are available.

FS 600 parallels much of the Santa Fe and Companion Trails and can be hiked, biked, or driven to view and enjoy the Santa Fe Trail. It also can be used to access the Companion Trail, as shown on the map.

⒤ GENERAL INFORMATION

The acquisition of the 108,175 acres that comprise the Cimarron National Grassland was prompted by the devastation suffered by Morton County during the Dust Bowl of the 1930s, when erosion badly damaged 78% of the land. The Dust Bowl could not have come at a worse time. Following a period of droughts and declining population in the 1890s, Morton County had reached a turning point in 1905 with the beginning of a 25-year wet cycle. Eight years later, the A.T. & S.F. railroad extension finally reached the southern boundary of the county, allowing farmers to transport and market their crops. Advances in farm equipment allowed farmers to cultivate larger tracts, and thousands of acres of pasture were plowed and planted to wheat. In 1931, 103,787 acres of wheat were harvested in Morton County, compared to 33,009 in the prior year. When the duststorms began in 1933, there were no grasses, sand sage-brush, or cacti to anchor the dirt in the plowed fields. Strong winds hurled dirt 20,000 feet into the air. Static electricity produced during the duststorms damaged the roots of young wheat. On "Black Sunday," April 14, 1935, the dust storm that crossed the high plains was 1,000 miles wide.* The devastation prompted Congress to acquire and manage thousands of acres of damaged farmland in Morton County. Native grasses were planted to stabilize the soil, and eroded lands were taken out of cultiva-tion. Between 1936 and 1939, the government purchased a total of 107,000 acres. In 1954, the U.S. Forest Service took over the management of the land, which in 1960 became part of the National Forest system as the Cimarron National Grassland.

"Walks and Rambles on the Cimarron National Grassland" is an informative booklet covering the Turkey and Companion Trails as well as other trails. By Stephen Hayward and Martha Hayward, it was a helpful source for this chapter and can be purchased at the Cimarron National Grassland office on U.S. 56 in Elkhart.

THE HIKES

TURKEY TRAIL: The trail is named for the wild turkey that inhabited this river cor-ridor before the trail was developed. We began at the Cottonwood Picnic Ground and had no difficulty following the 5.6-mile section leading to the Cimarron Recreation Area. The trail follows a two-track primitive road that was once open to, or may have been created by, off-road vehicles, now prohibited. At times, the weeds between the tracks were high. A good rule to follow when the trail branches (side trails intersect with the Turkey Trail) is to follow the track most traveled.

Generally, the terrain along the Turkey Trail is flat and a representative riparian habitat. Sections of the trail wind through tall and short native grasses, inter-spersed with wildflowers. A common plant is sandhill sage, a distinctive gray-green bush that flourishes in this area. Ranchers may consider it a weed, but sandhill sage anchors and stabilizes highly erodible sands and soils like those at the grassland and provides cover and nesting sites for wildlife. You will also see the tamarisk tree, also called "salt cedar." While tamarisk is actually native to southern Europe, it thrived when it was introduced in Texas in the late 1800s. Spreading along river sys-

* These facts, as well as a succinct history of Morton County, are found in "The Cornerstone of Kansas" by Joe Hartman and Mechele MacDonald, *Kansas Wildlife and Parks*, September/October 1988.

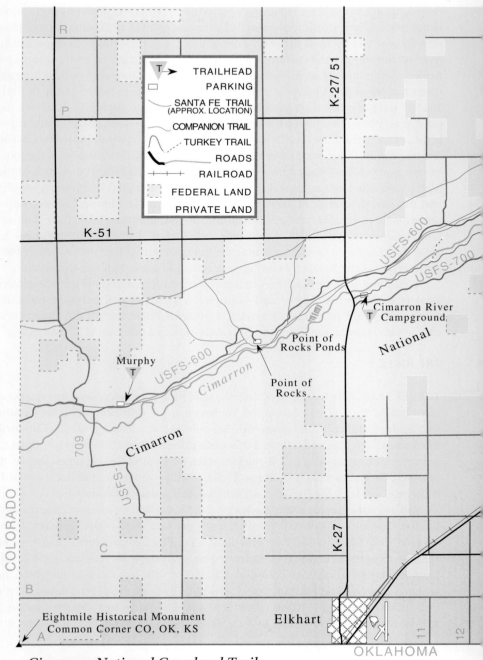

TRAILHEAD
PARKING
SANTA FE TRAIL
(APPROX. LOCATION)
COMPANION TRAIL
TURKEY TRAIL
ROADS
RAILROAD
FEDERAL LAND
PRIVATE LAND

K-27/51

R

P

K-51   L

USFS-600

USFS-700

Cimarron River
Campground

Point of
Rocks Ponds

National

Murphy
T

USFS-600

Cimarron

Point of
Rocks

USFS-709

Cimarron

COLORADO

C

K-27

B

Eightmile Historical Monument
Common Corner CO, OK, KS

Elkhart

11   12

A

OKLAHOMA

Cimarron National Grassland Trails

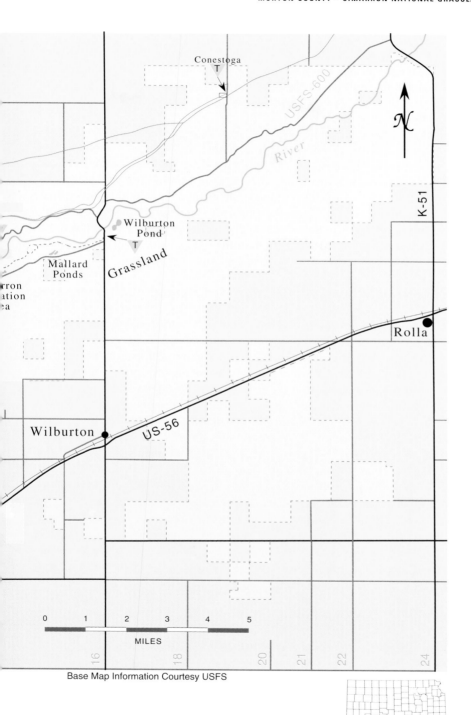

Conestoga

USFS-600

River

N

K-51

Wilburton
Pond
T

Mallard
Ponds

Grassland

rron
ation
ea

Rolla

Wilburton

US-56

0   1   2   3   4   5

MILES

16   18   20   21   22   24

Base Map Information Courtesy USFS

tems, the deep-rooted tamarisk currently infests about 1 million acres in the arid southwestern United States and guzzles 5 million acre-feet of water a year, sometimes sucking springs dry. There is some concern that the tree may excrete salt from its leaf glands, inhibiting growth of native vegetation around it. During the construction of the Suez Canal, excavators encountered tamarisk roots at depths of nearly 100 feet.*

About a mile west of the Cimarron Recreation Area, the trail rounds a bend after passing through a scenic grove of trees and comes in view of a windmill. In late summer, the approach to the windmill was lined with sunflowers that towered over our heads. At the windmill, turn left (north). If you continue straight through the gate, you will intersect FS 700. Less than .5 mile further, the trail intersects with a gravel road leading right (south) to the Cimarron Recreation Area. To continue, cross the road and follow the trail east. I stopped here, but John Young braved the chest-high weeds along the remainder of the Turkey Trail. He described it as similar to what we had seen to the west, but with a climb up a sand dune.

SANTA FE COMPANION TRAIL: The U.S. Forest Service appropriately describes this trail as a "grassy trace" across the prairie. When we visited the grassland in late August, the trail had not been mowed and could only be followed by spotting the brown flex-markers. The Forest Service clears the trail of sand sagebrush and cacti, which helps make the trail apparent to hikers with a minimal impact on the prairie. Generally, the Companion Trail runs within 150 feet of the historical Santa Fe Trail. Where the ruts of the Santa Fe Trail are no longer visible, due to erosion or subsequent cultivation, the Companion Trail may overlap it. The Santa Fe Trail is marked by limestone posts, easy to spot even from a distance. The Forest Service requests that hikers use the Companion Trail, and not the Santa Fe Trail, so as to preserve the historic ruts created by the caravans of wagons that traveled here from 1821 to 1880. This section of the Santa Fe Trail, while originally part of the main route to Santa Fe, came to be known as the Cimarron Cut-off, or the dry route ("La Jorda"), after the mountain route was opened across Colorado in the 1840s.

The Conestoga Trailhead derives its name from the Conestoga wagons that traveled the Santa Fe Trail. From the trailhead to Wilburton Crossing (County Road 16, the first paved road you cross traveling west) is about 4 miles. About .5 mile west of the trailhead, the Companion Trail splits from, and travels slightly north of, the Santa Fe Trail. Less than a mile further, the Santa Fe Trail itself branches. The Companion Trail follows the south branch, eventually crossing it to run parallel on the south side until Wilburton Crossing.

The 8.25-mile section of the Companion Trail from Wilburton Crossing (County Road 16) to K-27 is especially scenic. The hills offer vistas of the surrounding prairie and the many windmills that dot the horizon. At several points, the trail crosses FS

---

* *Roadside Kansas: A Traveler's Guide to Its Geology and Landmarks* by Rex C. Buchanan and James R. McCauley (Lawrence: University Press of Kansas, 1987).

600, the gravel service road that runs to the north of the Cimarron River corridor. Several miles west of County Road 16, the Companion Trail joins the Santa Fe Trail, then travels just north of it to K-27. Less than 1.25 miles before the trail crosses K-27, watch for a rocky bluff to the west. This is False Point of Rocks, which may have been mistaken by travelers on the Santa Fe Trail for Point of Rocks, about 4.25 miles further west.*

Several historical landmarks are located off of the 6.5-mile section of the Companion Trail between K-27 and Murphy Trailhead. The first is Middle Spring, on the Cimarron River, where travelers on the Santa Fe Trail were assured of good water year-round. The wagon ruts are very visible. Travelers frequently camped here, after a dry 36 miles from the last water source, Lower Spring, near Ulysses, Kansas. Point of Rocks, about 3 miles west from K-27, is capped by the younger layers of the Ogallala Formation, which overlies some reddish sandstones and shales of the Jurassic period (between 200 and 150 million years ago). Point of Rocks may be the only place in Kansas where these red Jurassic shales are visible. From Point of Rocks to the Murphy Trailhead, the Companion Trail runs south of, and parallel to, the Santa Fe Trail. At Murphy Trailhead, you are only 2.5 miles from Colorado and about 6 miles from Oklahoma.

* *Walks and Rambles on the Cimarron National Grassland,* Stephen Hayward and Martha Hayward, 1989.

Lake Scott State Park

Lake Scott State Park

When we rounded the curve at the north entrance to Lake Scott and saw the blue lake in the deep canyon below, surrounded by semi-arid buttes and mesas, we thought we had driven into a John Wayne western. In 1995, the National Geographic Society's *Traveler* magazine ranked Lake Scott State Park among the top 50 state parks in America. The unique features of this canyon-land, which include a 100-acre spring-fed lake set in Ladder Creek Canyon, have been known for hundreds of years. In 1664, the Taos Indians built a pueblo and spring-fed irrigation ditches in this area, now a 1,280-acre park. Ownership: KDWP (316) 872-2061.

HIKE LENGTH

Bridle and Mountain Bike Trail.. 7 miles

Additional mileage can be added by climbing the steep foot paths up the buttes. The Big Springs Nature Trail is about .25 mile.

DIRECTIONS AND TRAIL ACCESS

From I-70 take the Oakley Exit (Exit 76) and follow U.S. 40 west for a short distance until it intersects with U.S. 83. Travel south on U.S. 83 for about 30 miles to the junction of K-95. Travel 3 miles west to reach the park. The Bridle and Mountain Bike Trail circles the lake and can be accessed at many points. We started from the Big Grove Camping Area: from K-95, take the park road south (the road leading right, or west, crosses the dam) to the south end of the lake. Turn northwest and watch for the park's self-pay station. Take the first park road northeast to the Big Grove Camping Area. The trail is marked by signs. The Big Springs Nature Trail is just north of the self-pay station and is accessed from the Bridle and Mountain Bike Trail.

ⓘ GENERAL INFORMATION

The site of Lake Scott State Park has a unique history. Fossils dating from 45 million to 140 million years ago have been found in this area, once an inland sea. Just off the trail on the west side of the lake are the ruins of a seven-room pueblo identified in 1898 as El Cuartelejo (old barracks or building). This is the northernmost pueblo discovered in the United States. Spanish records indicate that two groups of Pueblo Indians from New Mexico fled here to escape Spanish rule. The first group, the Taos Indians, settled here around 1664 with a band of Plains Apache. The Taos Indians occupied the village, which came to be known as El Cuartelejo, for 20 years. The local band of Apache became known as the Cuartelejo band. In 1717, Juan de Uribarri, known as Jean Iturbi (who also led the French fur-trader and explorer La Salle to an ambush where La Salle was fatally wounded) established a trading post at El Cuartelejo, and French traders were reported there in 1727. Shortly thereafter, Comanche, Ute, and Pawnee attacked the settlement and forced the Apache southward.

The abandoned settlement was lost almost entirely to weather and erosion before Herbert Steele, who homesteaded the land, discovered it over 160 years later. The first Steele family home was a dugout, which they later renovated and expanded to a four-room home, faced with native sandstone. Their home is now a museum, but when we visited the park it was boarded up and defaced by vandalism. Across the park road, at the top of the bluff to the west, stands a granite monument honoring the Steeles, who hoped that their land would one day become a public park. In 1928, the Kansas State Forestry, Fish, and Game Commission acquired the 640-acre Steele homestead and an additional 640 acres to establish the present-day park.*

🚶 THE HIKE

The Bridle and Mountain Bike Trail circles the lake and is wild, craggy, and untamed. At several points, steep footpaths climb to the tops of buttes, from which you can view Ladder Creek Canyon and other outlying canyons. By far the most scenic and untouched section is on the west side of the lake. The trail on the east side travels closer to the park road and picnic/camping areas. In the warmer seasons, watch for rattlesnakes. The trail is not shaded, except for a few picnic areas. Carry twice as much water as you think you will need.

From the Big Grove Camping Area, we headed southeast across the park road to the trail. At .1 mile, the trail crosses the park road by the self-pay station and heads toward the bluffs. A short distance from here, it intersects with the .25 mile Big Springs Nature Trail. The bluffs at Lake Scott are mostly capped by the Ogallala Formation, naturally cemented sands and gravels (locally referred to as "mortarbeds") that provide an aquifer in the western third of the state. At Big Springs, water moving down through

---

* For more information, read "Pearl on the Plains: Scott Lake State Park" by Marc Murrell in *Kansas Wildlife and Parks*, July/August 1995.

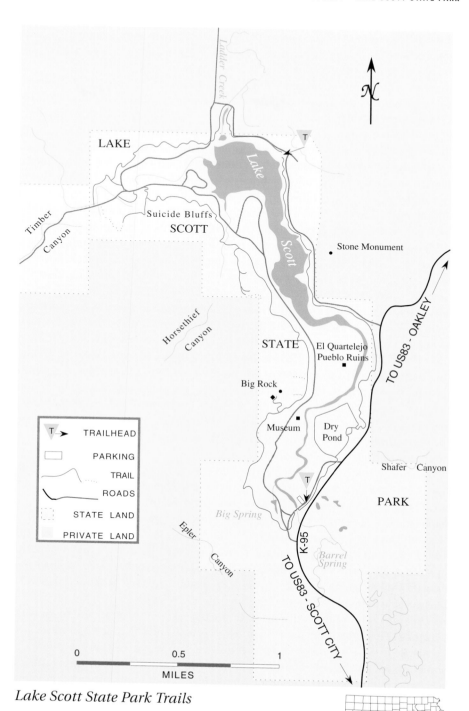

Lake Scott State Park Trails

the Ogallala Formation encounters Niobrara chalk, then moves laterally to where erosion has exposed the spring. Big Springs is home to a number of insect species that are unusual on the High Plains.

From here, the terrain becomes rougher and more arid. In less than a mile, we saw the Steele home across the park road. Watch for the steep footpath leading up the bluff to the stone park shelter and monument. The view from the top is worth the climb—to the east, the pyramidal monument at the top of a ridge across the lake honors Grover E. McBride, a Scott City businessman instrumental in the establishment of Lake Scott State Park. We passed at least three more footpaths (some with railroad-tie steps) leading up to the tops of buttes along the west side, before we reached Horsethief Canyon. We climbed one of the last paths and followed it for about half a mile along the top of the ridge overlooking Horsethief Canyon and the lake. The view from here was even more spectacular than that from the Steele monument.

At 1.75 miles from the start, the trail crosses a gravel road with a sign for Horsethief Canyon. Just past this road is a shaded picnic area. As you cross the dam of a dry pond, look to the west to see Suicide Bluffs. About .5 mile from the picnic area, we came to a split in the path, overlooking Timber Canyon. The branch to the left travels down the hill to an area that appeared rather mucky, probably due to the 4 inches of rain that fell at the park the night before. We took the trail on the higher ground, to the right. About 100 yards after this, we had some difficulty finding the trail. The trail through the grassy horse camping area was not well defined. One of the footpaths climbs to the top of Suicide Cliff. As soon as we crossed the paved park road across from the horse camping area, we realized that we had to find a detour to avoid the standing water (heavy rains frequently flood this spot). We traveled a short distance northeast on the paved park road to a gravel service road next to the restrooms. Traveling uphill on the service road, we rejoined the trail at a point just north of Timber Canyon.

The next .5 mile to the road near the dam is scenic. The colors of the surrounding buttes and mesas change with the sun and clouds. After the trail crosses the road, it travels downhill, passing between wood posts, parallel to a gravel road outside of the park. We caution that this part of the trail is on private property. When the trail intersects with an east-west gravel road, follow the road east and then south. In June 1996, after heavy rains, the crossing at the creek was closed because of high water. Even in January 1997, the water at the crossing was about 5 inches deep. We had some difficulty following the mowed trail after it reentered the park. Watch for the trail on the lake side of the road, just past the first primitive camping area.

The remainder of the trail travels on the lake side of the road and often within view of it. This side of the park is more developed, and the trail is not as secluded or rustic. It travels through several primitive camping areas and meadows and some timber. At about 5 miles from our start at the Big Grove Camping Area, we reached a campsite across from the Methodist Church Camp. About .5 mile later, the trail loops around a dry pond through young timber before the final stretch to Big Grove.

Quivira National Wildlife Refuge

T he beauty of these wetlands caught me by surprise. When we visited the refuge in March 1996, the winds were howling, dust and sand blew fiercely against our faces, and the flat, nondescript landscape was colorless. Yet when we rounded the corner and caught sight of the Little Salt Marsh, where white-capped waves broke against the shore, and acres of cattails and water grasses bent in the wind, we thought we had been transported to another part of the country. The Quivira National Wildlife Refuge covers 21,820 acres of salt marshes, sand dunes, dikes, canals, woodlands, and prairie. All of the refuge is open to hiking, and two short nature trails were recently built. The dikes, trails, and roads provide hikers a unique opportunity to view hundreds of species of birds. Ownership: U.S. Fish and Wildlife Services (316) 486-2393.

HUNTING REMINDER: While the areas surrounding the Big Salt Marsh, the Little Salt Marsh, and the Migrant Mile Nature Trail are not open to hunting, other sections of the refuge, such as the area surrounding Horseshoe Lake and the area north of Marsh Road (north of Wildlife Drive) are open to hunting. If you plan to hike off the roads, be sure to pick up the map available at the refuge headquarters, which shows the public hunting area. It is always advisable to wear bright colors when you hike—preferably an orange hunting vest and hat.

HIKE LENGTHS
Birdhouse Boulevard Nature Trail .... .2 mile
Migrant Mile Nature Trail .... 1.25 miles

The Wildlife Drive by the Big Salt Marsh is not a designated trail, but we recommend hiking it. If you have two vehicles and can park one at each end, the hike is 3.4 miles. If you have one vehicle, add 1.75 miles to loop back on Marsh Road. Unless otherwise marked, all other roads and dikes in the refuge are open to hiking.

Quivira National Wildlife Refuge

 ## DIRECTIONS AND TRAIL ACCESS

The Quivira National Wildlife Refuge covers much of the northeast corner of Stafford County. It is 13 miles northeast of Stafford, 32 miles southeast of Great Bend, and 28 miles northwest of Hutchinson. The refuge headquarters, at the southern edge of the refuge, is 8 miles north of Zenith. From Great Bend, take U.S. 281 to U.S. 50 and travel 14 miles east, past Stafford, to Zenith. (From Hutchinson, take K-61 south to U.S. 50 and travel west to Zenith.) Watch for the refuge sign at Zenith—turn north and travel 8 miles to the headquarters.

The Birdhouse Boulevard Nature Trail is by the refuge headquarters/visitors center. To reach the Migrant Mile Nature Trail, continue north past the headquarters. This road wraps around the Little Salt Marsh, then heads west. Turn right (north) at the first refuge road past the Little Salt Marsh (3.5 miles from the headquarters). Continue on this road for 2.9 miles and watch for the trail sign on the south side.

To reach the Wildlife Drive by the Big Salt Marsh, continue north on the refuge road leading from the Migrant Mile Nature Trail. In 1 mile, you will stop at County Road 484, marked by a sign to the "Big Salt Marsh Wildlife Drive." The Wildlife Drive is 3 miles north and 1.5 miles west of this intersection and is well marked.

GENERAL INFORMATION

For thousands of years, hundreds of species of birds have depended upon the salt marshes in Quivira National Wildlife Refuge for food and habitat. The Quivira Refuge and Cheyenne Bottoms, only 30 miles away, are halfway down the Central Flyway, a major route for migrating birds. For some species, the refuge is critical to reproduction and migration. For example, the white-rumped sandpiper winters on the northern shores of South America, then flies directly to the refuge. Here, it fattens up on blood worms (the larval stage of the midge fly) and other insects to enable it to complete its journey to breeding grounds in the north, below the Arctic Circle. Whooping cranes, the tallest North American birds and among the rarest, may stop for food at the refuge on their 2,500-mile journey from Alberta, Canada, to southern Texas. This 5-foot snow-white crane with a red face, 7.5-foot wingspan, and a loud "whooping" call in flight, is hard to mistake for any other bird. At one time on the brink of extinction, whooping cranes in the wild now number about 175. Sandhill cranes use the refuge as a staging area—flocks that can number 70,000–75,000 congregate here to feed, regroup, and wait for appropriate conditions before continuing their migration.

While the salt marshes themselves are ancient, the land for the refuge was not acquired until the Migratory Bird Commission approved the purchase in 1955. The last acres of the 21,820-acre refuge were purchased in 1969. The Quivira National Wildlife Refuge is one of 508 refuges forming the national wildlife refuge system. The Quivira Refuge is unique in that most of its marshes are salty due to the salt bed that underlies the area. This salt bed covers 27,000 square miles of Kansas and in places is 400 feet thick. It was deposited during the Permian period (about 250 million years ago) and remains largely intact because a thick layer of shale covers it.

THE HIKES

BIRDHOUSE BOULEVARD NATURE TRAIL: This is a short, concrete-surfaced trail through a stand of cedar trees west of the refuge headquarters/visitors center. Examples of birdhouses and bird feeders are along the trail, and eventually plans will be made available for building them.

MIGRANT MILE NATURE TRAIL: This is a loop that winds through timber, grasslands, and the wetlands designated "wetland unit 22." The first .75-mile loop is wheelchair accessible. The impressive 310-foot boardwalk that crosses the marsh is excellent for viewing wildlife. Markers direct your attention to points of interest. If you travel the west side of the loop first, and wish to continue on the additional .5-mile loop, do not turn left (east) at the boardwalk—continue straight. The second loop travels through woodlands and tallgrass areas, crossing another short bridge before intersecting with the east side of the first loop, at the east end of the boardwalk.

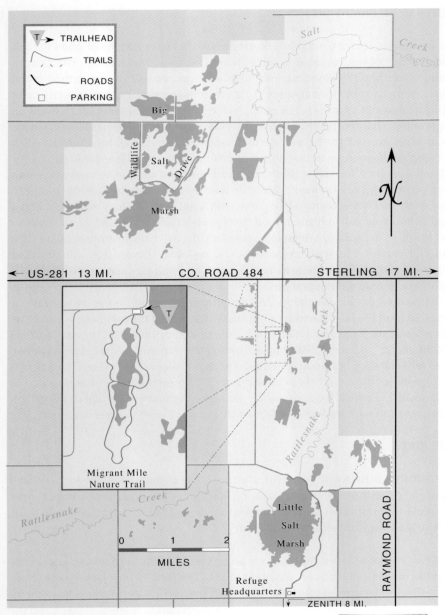

TRAILHEAD

TRAILS

ROADS

PARKING

Salt Creek

Big

Wildlife Salt Drive

Marsh

N

← US-281 13 MI. — CO. ROAD 484 — STERLING 17 MI. →

T

Creek

Migrant Mile
Nature Trail

Rattlesnake Creek

Rattlesnake Creek

Little Salt Marsh

RAYMOND ROAD

0   1   2

MILES

Refuge
Headquarters

ZENITH 8 MI.

Quivira National Wildlife Refuge

WILDLIFE DRIVE: One of the birds' favorite hangouts is the Big Salt Marsh. In the 1.5 hours that I spent on the drive, I saw only one other car (although I understand that traffic increases significantly during fall migrations), but hundreds and hundreds of birds. While many of the birds fled as I approached, by fall there are so many birds at the refuge that they don't pay much attention to humans. By walking this drive, you have a better chance of seeing the birds that are camouflaged by the wetland grasses and cattails. You will be amazed at the cacophony of sounds that might otherwise be muffled by a car's engine. At the south end of the drive, the 1,500 acres of the Big Salt Marsh are a beautiful backdrop for birds in flight.

ROADS AND DIKES: Using the map included in this chapter, you can create your own hike through the refuge. Unless specifically marked otherwise, all parts of the refuge are open to hikers, and hiking is encouraged. You can hike the roads around the marshes or the dikes. There are also designated foot-trails that lead to smaller wetland units. The refuge suggests following the foot-trails to Horseshoe Lake (wetland unit 10b) and the foot-trail to wetland unit 10c next to Horseshoe Lake. These are northeast of, and across the road from, the Little Salt Marsh. Public photo blinds are located on the Little Salt Marsh and by the Migrant Mile Nature Trail.

If you are interested in seeing a particular bird species, check with refuge headquarters before hiking. The refuge staff follows the migrations closely and can tell you what birds are at the refuge at any particular time.

1 CHEYENNE 1	RAWLINS 2	DECATUR	NORTON	PHILLIPS	SMITH
SHERMAN	THOMAS	SHERIDAN	GRAHAM	ROOKS	OSBORNE
WALLACE	LOGAN	GOVE	TREGO	ELLIS	RUSSELL 3

NORTHWEST REGION

1. Arikaree Breaks
2. Lake Atwood
3. Wilson Lake

NORTH

Northwest
REGION

WEST

Arikaree Breaks

T he Arikaree Breaks, near "Three Corners," where Nebraska, Colorado, and Kansas meet, are often called the badlands of Kansas. While the name "badlands" appropriately conjures up an image of a stark landscape, it does not convey the unusual beauty of the Breaks' yawning gorges and canyons, where fragile loess walls rise almost vertically from the ground. Sage-covered hills, sculpted by weather, sometimes hide chasms that have broken from the earth. There is no public access or hiking trails, but there are miles of remote, seldom-traveled, narrow dirt roads that are better hiked than driven. Many, when wet, are impassable by car. The views of the Arikaree Breaks, especially through an area called Devil's Gap and along the road to the Lookout Point, are spectacular.

HIKE LENGTHS
Horse Thief Cave Hike .... 1.6 miles (one-way)
Lookout Point Hike .... 2.3 miles (one-way)
Devil's Cap Hike... 2.5 miles (one-way)

DIRECTIONS

The Arikaree Breaks are northwest of St. Francis. Take I-70 west to K-27 (Exit 17), by Goodland. Travel about 30 miles north to U.S. 36 and turn west, to St. Francis. Be sure to stop in St. Francis to pick up an auto-tour pamphlet, which includes information about the numbered red signs along the roads through the Breaks. The pamphlet can be found in gas stations and stores.

ACCESS

HORSE THIEF CAVE HIKE: Turn north on Benton Street in St. Francis and follow it out of town. Benton Street becomes FAS 115 outside of St. Francis and 2.2 miles

Arikaree Breaks

past the railroad tracks outside of St. Francis reaches a fork, marked by a round red sign numbered "2." Bear right (northeast) but not far right to the G.A.R. Cemetary. In another mile, FAS 115 veers right (east). At this point, continue north on FAS 876 for 9 miles to FAS 891 (marked by signs 9 and 10) and turn east. Travel east 2 miles and watch for a row of red cedars and grain bins marking the road north to Horse Thief Cave. (Note: driving-tour sign 14, which marks this road, was missing when we visited in January 1997.) We suggest traveling 1.5 miles north on this road and parking near the "Winding Road" sign to walk to the Nebraska border. About .8 mile from the "Winding Road" sign, the road passes Horse Thief Cave.

LOOKOUT POINT HIKE: Follow the directions to Horse Thief Cave, except at the intersection of FAS 876 and FAS 891 (marked by driving-tour signs 9 and 10), continue north on FAS 876. We suggest traveling .9 mile north and parking near the "Winding Road" sign to walk to the Nebraska border. Lookout Point is .3 mile from the "Winding Road" sign.

DEVIL'S CAP HIKE: About 1.25 miles west of St. Francis, turn north off of U.S. 36 onto K-27, which travels about 5.75 miles north/northwest before it veers west for

5 miles, and then north again for 3.1 miles. Watch for the sign on the west side of the road marking the turnoff for Devil's Cap. Turn west and continue for 4 miles, then turn north. Continue north for 2.3 miles and watch for a sign for the "Route of the Cheyenne—1865." We suggest parking here and hiking 2.5 miles to the second sign for Devil's Cap.

GENERAL INFORMATION

The Arikaree Breaks were named after the Arikaree River, which enters Kansas from Colorado and travels diagonally about 2 miles before crossing into Nebraska. The Breaks in northern Cheyenne County cover an area approximately 36 miles east to west and several miles north to south. The Breaks also extend about 15 miles west into Colorado and several miles east into Rawlins County. A thick layer of buff-colored loess, a silty, porous sediment deposited by wind during the Ice Ages, covers the area, in places 100 feet deep. Over time, streams carved paths through the loess, which has a remarkable ability to remain vertical and withstand cave-ins. Nonetheless, Rex Daniels, a native of Cheyenne County, recounted a collapse that occurred in 1913:

> They thought it was an earthquake, judging from all the noise. Window panes rattled and plates fell off the table onto the floor. Then it stopped as suddenly as it started. It wasn't until six months later that some cowhands were riding that part of the range looking for strays and they saw it. Acres of range land just collapsed into the earth.*

The sink described by Daniels is near Devil's Cap, described below.

THE HIKES

HORSE THIEF CAVE HIKE: If you judged this road by the terrain at the turnoff from FAS 891, you probably would not bother to travel much further. The road is completely flat and nondescript for the first 1.4 miles. At 1.5 miles from the turnoff, the terrain changes dramatically as you enter the Breaks. Suddenly, the road descends and winds, cutting a deep channel into the loess. The deep loess canyons and land bridges are unique. Small soapweed (yucca), sand sage, little bluestem, and other grasses provide some ground cover and anchor the loess, and in August the road was lined with sunflowers. Two species of sage here do not grow in any other place in Kansas. At .8 mile from the "Winding Road" sign, on the east side of the road, watch for driving-tour sign 15, marking the location of Horse Thief Cave, once used by rustlers to hide stolen horses. Before the cave collapsed beneath the heavy machinery of a county road crew, who unknowingly drove over it, the cave was

---

* Quoted in "The Cheyenne Breaks" by Lee Ann Stephens, in *Kansas!* (3) 1995.

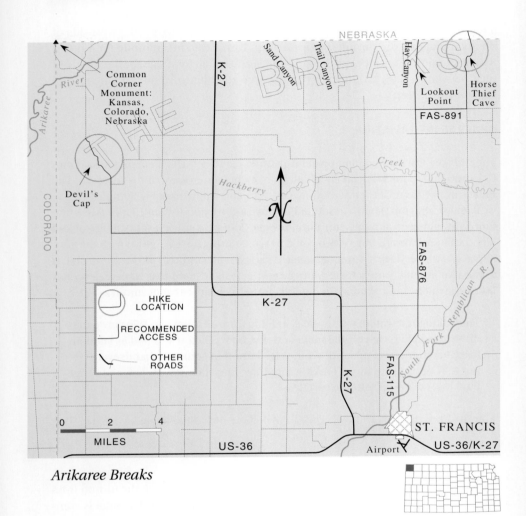

Arikaree Breaks

large enough to accommodate six horse stalls in a back chamber and living quarters (including a small kitchen) in the front. The cave is located in a "blind" canyon and was so well camouflaged by the surrounding terrain that residents who lived as close as a mile did not know it existed. Only the entrance is intact today. The Kansas-Nebraska border is another .8 mile past the cave.

LOOKOUT POINT HIKE: The road to Lookout Point, only 2 miles west of the road to Horse Thief Cave, offers a spectacular, panoramic view of the Breaks. Like the approach to Horse Thief Cave, the first mile is completely flat and offers no clue of the dramatic terrain that lies around the bend. Lookout Point is just .3 mile from the "Winding Road" sign. Even in winter, copper clusters of little bluestem, gray-green sage, golden grasses, and yucca made this a colorful landscape.

DEVIL'S CAP HIKE: The scenery along the 2.5-mile section of road from the sign marking the 1865 route of the Cheyennes to the last marker for Devil's Cap is extraordinary. The narrow, winding dirt road is steep in places and provides an unbeatable view of the deep canyons and gorges. The road is completely isolated—we were never passed by a vehicle during the afternoon we spent by Horse Thief Cave and Devil's Cap. As we neared Devil's Cap, we came in view of Devil's Cap Canyon, a beautiful canyon bordered by rugged hills. A narrow ribbon of water runs through the base of the canyon, and a variegated carpet of green grasses and sage covers the hills in summer. The Cheyenne Indians passed through this canyon in 1865 on the way from their Cherry Creek encampment (about 2.5 miles northwest of St. Francis on K-27) to a raid on Julesburg, Colorado.

The first sign for Devil's Cap is on the west side of the road, and the second is a short distance further north, on the east side, 2.5 miles past the 1865 Route of the Cheyenne. To extend your hike from here, continue north on this road to Three Corners, where Kansas, Nebraska, and Colorado meet (although this will add about 5 miles to your 2.5 mile hike, for a one-way trip of 7.5 miles). To reach Three Corners, which is on private land, watch for a sign, several miles north of Devil's Cap, pointing to a two-wheel-rut path leading west into private land. Travel about 2.75 miles northwest on the private road. This land is owned by Rex Daniels, who has fenced in a 20-foot-square area where a U.S. Geological Survey marker defines the juncture. Daniels allows visitors access to this marker and keeps a guest registry in the mailbox. Be sure to sign it.

Lake Atwood

Lake Atwood

Lake Atwood, at the north end of the town of Atwood, is a delightful city lake encircled by a 1.4-mile concrete walking trail. Large cottonwoods line the small lake in this 43-acre recreational area on Beaver Creek. Decorative street lamps light the trail across the causeway, through the middle of the lake. Most of the surrounding area is developed, but outlying hills to the southwest are a reminder that this is but a small oasis on a vast prairie. In January 1997, construction was underway on the 3.6-mile Hayden Wildlife and Nature Trail (named after former Kansas Governor Mike Hayden), on the west side of the lake. By April 1997, the first phase of the trail, which includes a lookout tower and wooden bridges over a wet-lands area, was complete, and phase two of the trail, which will travel north along Beaver Creek, was nearing completion. Eventually, the trail will loop to the south side of U.S. 36 through a woodlands area. Ownership: City of Atwood (785) 626-9630.

HIKE LENGTHS
Lake Atwood Walking Trail.. 1.4 miles (round-trip)
Hayden Wildlife and Nature Trail .... 3.6 miles (round-trip, when completed)

DIRECTIONS AND TRAIL ACCESS

Atwood, a town of about 1,600 people, is located in the Beaver Creek Valley, at the center of Rawlins County. Lake Atwood is at the north edge of town, at the junction of U.S. 36 and K-25. The concrete walking trail circles the lake to the north of U.S. 36, on the east side of K-25, and the Hayden Wildlife and Nature Trail is on the west side of K-25 (eventually traveling on both sides of U.S. 36).

ⓘ GENERAL INFORMATION

Lake Atwood takes its name from Attwood Matheny, the son of one of the town's founders, J. M. Matheny. In 1882, three years after Attwood was founded, it dropped a "t" out of its name at the request of the U.S. Post Office. The original town was 2 miles east of its present location, but when it became apparent that it had been built on school land, all of the buildings (which by then included two general stores, a hotel, and a drugstore) had to be moved. While Kansas was being settled, railroads determined track and depot locations, and it was not unusual for an entire town to be packed up and moved. Atwood nearly was forced to move yet again in the late 1880s as a result of a long, bitter fight with the Burlington & Missouri River Railroad over moving the county seat, then Atwood, to Blakeman, a new town the railroad created 5 miles west of Atwood.*

🚶 THE HIKES

LAKE ATWOOD WALKING TRAIL: Lake Atwood is in a natural basin, once called Beaver Lake. When stream flow was low, the lake was dry. In 1927, the town passed a bond issue to dam Beaver Creek, and to develop the lake and surrounding recreational area. In the 1930s, the Civilian Conservation Corps completed additional projects, including a bridge; other renovations occurred in the 1940s, 1950s, and 1980s. As you enter the park off of K-25, you will be able to see most of the concrete trail that circles the eastern part of the lake, and you can enter it from any point off of the road that also circles the lake. The trail is flat and much of it is shaded by cottonwoods. Over time, the lake has silted in and is less than half the size it was 50 years ago. To the north, the lake is bordered by a nine-hole golf course. The trail on the south side passes through picnic and playground facilities.

HAYDEN WILDLIFE AND NATURE TRAIL: The portion of the lake to the west of K-25 is undeveloped. The Hayden Wildlife and Nature Trail, which will be surfaced with wood chips, is intended to provide opportunities to observe a riparian ecosystem. Wooden bridges have been built over wetlands, and a tower has been built for observing wildlife. While the trail was under construction when we visited in January 1997, the second phase of the trail, which travels north along Beaver Creek, was nearing completion in April 1997. A third phase will take the trail to the south of U.S. 36 through a woodlands area.

* For more information about Rawlins County and Atwood, see *History of Rawlins County*, compiled by the Rawlins County History Book Committee (Rawlins County Genealogical Society, 1988).

Wilson Lake

F ew places in Kansas rival the beauty of the Konza Prairie. Wilson Lake is one of them. Unlike most lakes in Kansas, it is clear and blue, lying in the Saline River Valley, among the Smoky Hills. When we hiked the trails in early June, dark green prairie grasses provided a dramatic backdrop for the soft white bloom of the small soapweed that covered many of the hills. On the Rocktown Trail, a deep canyon slices through a hill close to the lake and massive red sandstone formations rise out of the water. Ownership: USACE (785) 658-2551.

HIKE LENGTHS

Dakota Trail .... 1-mile loop
Bur Oak Nature Trail .... .75-mile loop
Rocktown Trail .... 3-mile loop

DIRECTIONS

Take I-70 to K-232 (Exit 206, about 47 miles west of Salina and about 20 miles east of Russell). Travel north on K-232 to Wilson Lake.

TRAIL ACCESS

DAKOTA TRAIL TRAILHEAD: Turn left (west) off of K-232 at the entrance to Wilson State Park (the South Shore Drive), approximately 5.2 miles north of I-70. The Dakota Trail is in the eastern section of the Hell Creek Area of Wilson State Park. Cross the Hell Creek Bridge and continue to the park entrance on your right. The trailhead is 1.3 miles northwest of the park office. Take the turnoff to the Big Bluestem Campground. The trailhead is just past the restroom.

Rocktown Trail, Wilson Lake

BUR OAK NATURE TRAIL TRAILHEAD: Take K-232 north to K-181. (If you cross the dam, you've gone too far.) Take a short jog to the right (southeast) on K-181 and turn left into the Sylvan Park entrance. Shortly after you pass the Administrative Area for the Corps of Engineers, veer left (northwest) at the Y intersection and watch for the parking area at the trailhead.

ROCKTOWN TRAIL TRAILHEAD: Take K-232 across the dam and turn left (southwest) just past the dam, to Lucas Park. The turnoff to Lucas Park is 9.1 miles north of I-70 and 3.9 miles from the Wilson State Park turnoff. Remain on this park road for 1.43 miles, until you reach a T intersection, then turn left (south). The trailhead is another 1.7 miles. Immediately after passing the Corps of Engineers booth, veer right. Continue until you see the sign for the Rocktown Trail, on the right (west) side of the road. There is parking at the trailhead.

GENERAL INFORMATION

Wilson Lake is in the heart of the Smoky Hills physiographic region, formed by three overlapping layers of sediments, each capped by a different rock. The lowest, the eastern range, sometimes referred to as "Dakota Hills Country," is capped by the thick red sandstone of the Dakota Formation, prominently exposed both here and at Kanopolis Reservoir. To the west, the next level of uplands—"Fence Post Limestone Country"—is capped by Greenhorn Limestone. This rock layer is made up of alternating beds of thin, chalky limestone and thicker beds of shale, topped by a foot-thick layer of the distinctive post rock that underlies many fields in Russell, Ellis, and other counties. (The rock fenceposts seen from the trails were quarried locally from the Greenhorn Limestone layer, located just beneath a shallow covering of soil. The Smoky Hills contain 30,000 to 40,000 miles of post-rock fence lines.) The highest and westernmost range of the Smoky Hills region—"Niobrara Chalk Country"—is capped by thick chalk beds of the Niobrara Formation, seen in Gove (where Castle Rock and Monument Rocks are located), Logan, Trego, and other counties. Outcroppings of the sandstone of the Dakota Formation and Greenhorn Limestone can be found in the hills surrounding Wilson Lake.*

The unusual sandstone formations on the Rocktown trail were created by differing rates of erosion of the thick sandstone cap. As ground water circulated through the sandstone, it deposited a limey cement. These deposits, dispersed throughout the sandstone, grew outward in all directions, cementing the sandstone and making it almost impervious to erosion. The uncemented sandstone weathered away, leaving the sandstone concretions, at times perched perilously on pedestals of softer rock. The angled lines in the Dakota Sandstone are called crossbedding.

* For more information, see "Landscapes: A Geologic Diary" by Frank Wilson, in *Kansas Geology: An Introduction to Landscapes, Rocks, Minerals, and Fossils,* edited by Rex Buchanan (Lawrence: University Press of Kansas, 1984).

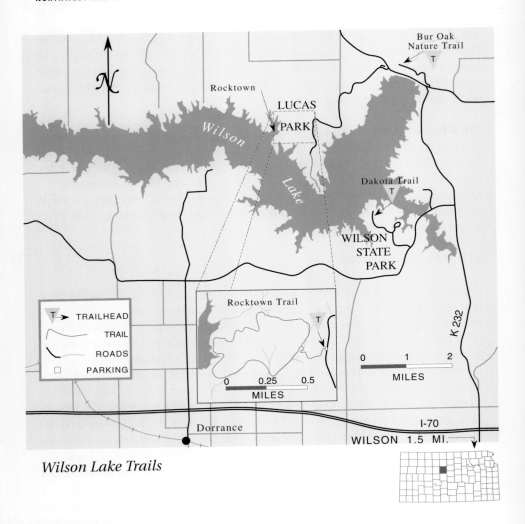

Wilson Lake Trails

🚶🚶 THE HIKES

THE DAKOTA TRAIL: This nature trail can be hiked as a 1-mile or .5-mile loop. The 1-mile loop includes 12 interpretive stations. If you hike the .5-mile loop, turn right (south) at station 4 to return to the start. While there are some steep inclines, the sandy surface provides sure footing. The vistas of the lake and surrounding hills, where wildflowers grow in abundance, should tempt even serious hikers who might bypass this short trail. Brochures are available at the trailhead.

BUR OAK NATURE TRAIL: This shorter, flatter trail behind the dam was named after the only oak native to western Kansas. Look for the trail brochure at the trailhead. The .75 mile loop includes 23 interpretive stations.

ROCKTOWN TRAIL: This 3-mile loop travels primarily through native prairie. The mowed trail heads west from the parking lot for about .25 mile. At that point, the trail branches right (northeast) and left (southwest). Because this trail is a loop, you can take either branch. We took the trail to the right. The views of the Smoky Hills are spectacular. Eventually, the trail crests at an overlook above the lake and the large sandstone formations called Rocktown. When we hiked this trail in June 1995, the lake was high from spring floods, and part of the trail leading down to the formations was under water. Before reaching the overlook, watch for the canyon on your right. You may need to step off the trail onto the rocks for a full view. After the trail leaves the lake and heads back east, it cuts through an area that after heavy rains can be marshy. In late spring and early summer, wildflowers bloom profusely here.

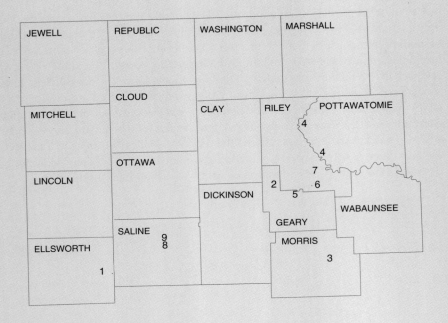

NORTH CENTRAL REGION

1. Kanopolis Lake
2. Milford Lake
3. Council Grove Lake
4. Tuttle Creek Lake
5. Kaw River Nature Trail
6. The Konza Prairie
7. Manhattan Linear Park Trail
8. Indian Rock and Salina Levee Trails
9. Lakewood Park

NORTH CE

North Central

REGION

NTRAL

Kanopolis Lake

K anopolis Lake sits in the Smoky Hill River Valley, surrounded by the hills and buttes characteristic of Dakota Sandstone country. The deep, tree-lined canyons, red and white sandstone formations, and native prairie along Horsethief and Prairie Trails are singularly beautiful. Nor is this western, semi-arid landscape without color, particularly in late spring and early summer, when the small soapweed, cobaea penstemon, blue wild indigo, pale and purple poppymallow, and western yarrow are in bloom. On a sunny day, the wind- and water-carved outcroppings of red rock along the trail are nearly incandescent. After we completed our fieldwork, the Alum Creek Trail was constructed, adding 9 miles to the network of trails at Kanopolis Lake. This trail travels through open prairie and over many water crossings on Alum Creek. It also passes by several table rocks. The 1.5-mile Buffalo Tracks Canyon Nature Trail is reserved for hiking only; the remaining trails—Horsethief Trail, Prairie Trail, and Alum Creek Trail—are open to hikers, mountain bikers, and equestrians. Ownership: KDWP (785) 546-2565.

SAFETY REMINDER: The Prairie Trail and the Alum Creek Trail are in a public hunting area and for this reason are closed to horses and mountain bikes from November 1 through January 31. Hikers are encouraged to wear blaze orange during this period. Trails inside the park, including the Rockin' K Trail, Horsethief Trail, and Buffalo Tracks Canyon Nature Trail, are open year-round, but portions may be closed during high water, when crossings become hazardous or impassable. Always approach crossings with caution. At this time, no camping is permitted on the trails.

HIKE LENGTHS
Buffalo Tracks Canyon Nature Trail .... .75 mile (one-way)
Horsethief Trail .... 5.5-mile loop
Prairie Trail .... 6-mile loop (total with Horsethief Trail loop 11.5 miles)
Alum Creek Trail............................ 8.3-mile loop (total with Horsethief Trail and
Prairie Trail 19.8 miles)

Horsethief Trail, Kanopolis Lake

⚑ ⊕ DIRECTIONS AND TRAIL ACCESS

From I-70, take I-135 (on the west side of Salina) south to K-140. Travel west approximately 20 miles to K-141 and turn south. Continue for approximately 8.1 miles and turn west at the entrance to the Venango Park Area (East Shore State Park). Continue to the Y intersection and bear right. It is .9 mile to the state park office. From the office, the road travels west, then north for a total of 1.4 miles before reaching a T intersection. Turn right (east) and continue on the road as it veers north then west to the end. Turn right (north) on the gravel road to Buffalo Tracks Canyon (trailhead C). The trails all begin in the Horsethief Area of Kanopolis State Park. Be sure to stop at the park office to pick up the large (22" x 17") full-color map and brochure for the trails provided by the Kansas Department of Wildlife and Parks. The trails have been recently blazed and color-coded.

ⓘ GENERAL INFORMATION

Jim Gray, a descendant of Buffalo Bill Cody and a farmer, rancher, and local historian, recounted to us the story behind Horsethief Canyon. According to Mr. Gray, Lieutenant Allen Ellsworth was ordered to establish an army post here after an uprising of the Cheyenne Indians in 1863–64. Fort Ellsworth was built on the banks of the Smoky Hill River, approximately 1 mile southwest of the present site of Kanopolis. Buffalo Bill Cody was stationed there, scouting the area between Fort Ellsworth and Fort Fletcher, 48 miles to the west. In 1866, Fort Ellsworth was renamed Fort Harker and relocated to the present site of Kanopolis. Harry Thompkins Anderson came in the second wave of settlement and built an inn and stagecoach station at the mouth of Horsethief Canyon, along the proposed route of a military road. Anderson was deputized to capture some horse thieves and tracked them down in Lincoln County, to the north of Ellsworth County. According to Jim Gray, the stories told by Anderson's descendants and by the descendants of the homesteaders of Horsethief Canyon diverge at this point. Anderson's family contends that Anderson shot the thieves in Lincoln County, returned to Ellsworth with the bodies for identification, and buried the thieves in Horsethief Canyon. The descendants of the homesteaders contend that the men were found guilty by a kangaroo court in Lincoln County, and that Anderson took them to Horsethief Canyon, where he pushed them over the edge to their fatal destiny.

THE HIKES

BUFFALO TRACKS CANYON NATURE TRAIL: A single trailhead provides access to both the Buffalo Tracks Canyon Nature Trail and the Horsethief Trail. The Buffalo Tracks Canyon Nature Trail, with 14 interpretive stations, is marked with yellow carsonite posts. It runs northeast through the middle of the eastern loop of the Horsethief Trail.

HORSETHIEF TRAIL: This can be followed either northwest or east from the trailhead. We headed right (east). Less than .2 mile from the trailhead, the equestrian trail leading north from the Horsethief trailhead intersects on the right. Shortly thereafter, the Rockin' K equestrian trail ("K" on the trail signs) also intersects on the right. Horsethief Trail veers left (north) at the barbed-wire fence, then passes along the edge of a box canyon. You will soon reach a fork in the trail; veer right. The trail to the left eventually leads into the canyon, and the Buffalo Tracks Canyon Nature Trail.

Horsethief Trail is laid out in a series of loops. Watch for low-water crossings at the northeastern tip of the first loop, the northern and southern ends of the second loop, and at three points in the last mile of the Horsethief Trail. Generally, the Horsethief Trail is a well-defined narrow dirt trail, marked in grassy segments by yellow carsonite posts, with orange or blue stripes. The blue stripes denote the southern and western sides of the loop. (A green-striped post designates a shortcut, and a red-striped post designates an alternative route for emergencies.) The topography along Horsethief Trail is much rougher and the scenery more varied than that of the Prairie Trail. At the northwestern tip of the fourth loop of Horsethief Trail, watch for gate 1 leading to the Prairie Trail.

PRAIRIE TRAIL: Like the Horsethief Trail, the Prairie Trail is a loop; you will return through gate 1 to complete the Horsethief Trail. Past gate 1, we headed right

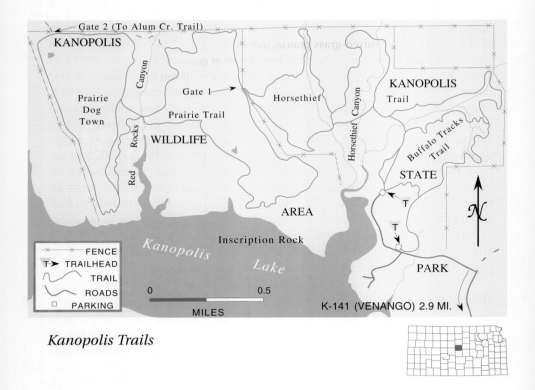

Kanopolis Trails

(north). The predominant feature of the Prairie Trail is native prairie, although another highlight is the outcroppings of the Dakota sandstone in Red Rocks Canyon. Spotting the yellow markers is critical because the trail is not well defined, particularly in the grazed areas. The low-water crossing past Red Rocks Canyon takes you to the second, shorter loop of the Prairie Trail. Watch for gate 2 at the northeastern corner of the second loop—it leads to the Alum Creek Trail.

The main feature of the second loop is Prairie Dog Town. We heard the high-pitched warning call of these creatures before we saw them. They quickly sought cover in their burrows, but poked their heads up through their mounds and yapped at us as we passed. A Hack Tower for a golden eagle reintroduction project stands nearby. Trail users should stay clear of it. We lost track of the trail where it travels around the tall, pointed knob southwest of the pond. Southeast of the southeastern-most tip of the first loop of the Prairie Trail is a 40-foot bluff known as Inscription Rock, on which Native Americans carved petroglyphs, estimated to be no more than 400 years old. Unfortunately, access has been closed to the public, due to vandalism and the instability of the rock formations. The trail takes you back to gate 1. Turn right (southeast) past the gate to complete the southern portion of the Horsethief Trail.

ALUM CREEK TRAIL: This had not been constructed when we completed our field-work. Opened in the fall of 1996, the trail starts from gate 2 at the northwest corner of the Prairie Trail. According to the Kansas Department of Wildlife and Parks, the trail winds through native mixed-grass prairie, tree-lined creeks, and canyons and passes by table rocks on the eastern side of the loop, south of gate 3. The trail has two short-cuts, marked with yellow carsonite posts, striped in green. If you follow these, you will shorten this loop to 4.3 miles. Otherwise, the loop is 8.3 miles. There is no other way to shorten the distance on this trail. The park advises all trail users to use the designated water crossings only—the creeks can be very dangerous. You will need to open both gate 3 and gate 7. In the summer of 1997, all of the trails were being marked to match the colors shown on the park map.

Crystal Trail, Milford Lake

Milford Lake

We hiked the 2.5-mile Crystal Trail at Milford Lake (the largest lake in Kansas) on a hot, humid, breezeless July afternoon (1997) and found it enjoyable—mature walnuts, hickories, and oaks provided a lush canopy. Part of the trail follows a creek, and picturesque bridges offer a dry passage over the low areas. The wide mowed path is well maintained, even in the woods. The 5.7-mile Eagle Ridge Trail, a multi-use trail in the Sunset Ridge area of Milford State Park, is one you will want to hike again. It crosses through prairie, woodlands, and hay fields, across old stream beds, and along the shoreline. The trail climbs to a scenic, grassy knob overlooking the lake for a beautiful vista. For a shorter hike, follow the .6-mile Waterfall Trail in the state park or the .5-mile Tallgrass Nature Trail near the nature center and fish hatcheries. The Tallgrass Trail connects to the Wood Duck Trail, which parallels the old Republican River channel. We were advised in July 1997 that the Wood Duck Trail was mowed, but not completed, and that there were no signs on the trail. Ownership: KDWP (785) 238-3014; USACE (785) 238-5714.

HIKE LENGTHS

Crystal Trail .... 2.5 miles (round-trip)
Eagle Ridge Trail.. 5.7 miles (round-trip)
Waterfall Trail .... .6 mile (round-trip)
Tallgrass Nature Trail... .5 mile (round-trip)
Wood Duck Trail .... 2 miles (round-trip, including the Tallgrass Nature Trail)

DIRECTIONS

Milford Lake is 4 miles north of Junction City. From I-70, take Exit 295 and follow U.S. 77 north to K-57. Turn west and follow the signs to the dam.

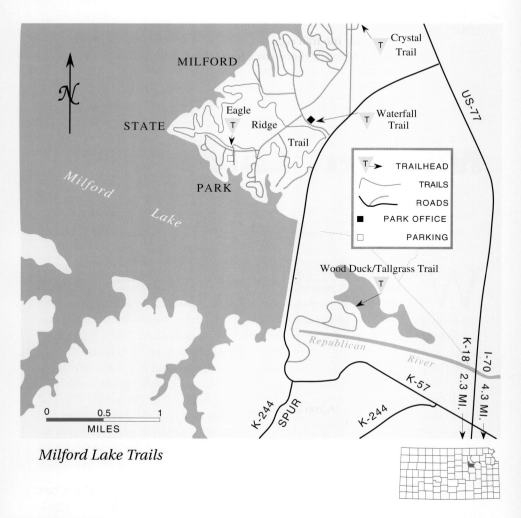

Milford Lake Trails

TRAIL ACCESS

CRYSTAL TRAIL TRAILHEAD: This trail is in Milford State Park, north of the dam. Follow the signs to the state park. Past the park office, turn right (northeast) at the road to the yacht club. Before you reach the yacht club, watch for the trail sign on the right (east) side of the road. Although there is no designated parking area, we parked our car near the trailhead, off of the road.

EAGLE RIDGE TRAIL TRAILHEAD: This trail is also in the state park. Turn left (southwest) at the first road past the park office, following the signs to the beach (now closed) and Sunset Ridge. The well-marked trailhead is just north of the shower house, with adjacent parking.

WATERFALL TRAIL TRAILHEAD: This is a short nature trail in the state park, near the park office. Watch for the trail sign on the north side of the road. (There is no waterfall on this trail—formerly there was a fountain here.)

TALLGRASS NATURE TRAIL AND WOOD DUCK TRAIL TRAILHEAD: These trails are located near the nature center and fish hatcheries. Just before you reach the dam, follow the directions to the Outlet Park. The trailhead for the Tallgrass Trail is next to the parking area for the nature center. The Wood Duck Trail is a loop off the Tallgrass Trail. According to the park office, the Wood Duck Trail was still under construction in September 1997—it was mowed, but not signed.

GENERAL INFORMATION

The small town of Milford is on the east shore of the lake, about 4 miles north of Milford State Park. Milford was once the home of Dr. John R. Brinkley, who achieved fame through the novel, albeit unproven, procedure of restoring male virility with goat-gland transplants. In 1930, he was nearly elected governor of Kansas when he ran as an independent. The Republican River is named after the Republican Pawnee, one of four bands of Pawnee Indians living in Kansas and Nebraska in the 1500s. (Apparently, French explorers thought one of these bands had a republican form of government.) Early records indicate that the Kansa and Pawnee tribes clashed, and the Pawnee were forced out.* Southeast of Milford Lake, the Republican River joins the Smoky Hill River to create the Kansas River. The Republican River was impounded by the Army Corps of Engineers in 1967 to create Milford Lake. With 16,200 surface acres of water and 163 miles of shoreline, it is the largest lake in Kansas.

THE HIKES

CRYSTAL TRAIL: This consists of two loops. The first begins at the trailhead, just past the gate, and branches to the left. There is no directional marker. The trail begins in an area that appears to have once been prairie, now invaded by immature timber, cedar, and woody vegetation. The first loop winds across a rocky slope, dotted with cedar. Even in the heat of July, wildflowers bloomed in this dry, rocky terrain. While there is a short climb, most of the trail is relatively flat, coming within view of the lake (the only view of the lake from the trail) before turning into the woods. Eventually, the trail edges a cultivated field, before linking with the second loop. An arrow for the "long loop" points left.

Don't miss the second loop, which meanders along a stream and through scenic woodlands, where the foliage of mature hardwoods filters out most of the sun. The

---

* See *Roadside Kansas: A Traveler's Guide to Its Geology and Landmarks* by Rex C. Buchanan and James R. McCauley (Lawrence: University Press of Kansas, 1987).

woods were so dark that we felt sure a summer storm was imminent and were surprised to see blue skies when we emerged. At the eastern edge of the loop, the trail leaves the woods and circles a cultivated field, in view of U.S. 77. As you reenter the woods, watch out for the healthy tendrils of poison ivy that border the trail. Near the end of the second loop, keep your bearings—you will see four trails where the two loops join. Take the trail to the far left to return to the trailhead. To be certain, watch for the "long loop" arrow and head the opposite direction.

EAGLE RIDGE TRAIL: This is a mowed loop that circles Sunset Ridge. Most of it is fairly flat, but there are a few long, gentle hills. If you hike the west edge of the loop at the end of the day, you will understand the name Sunset Ridge. The views of the lake from this ridge overlooking Milford Lake are spectacular. If you are hiking with children, be aware that the trail crosses several park roads on the east and south sides of the loop.

From the trailhead near the shower house, we followed the branch to the left, following the west side of the loop. For the most part, the trail around this ridge is through open prairie, but much of it follows dense belts of cedar trees. Not far from the start, we began to catch glimpses of the lake through the cedars. The trail weaves back between two cedar rows, a quiet, sheltered area that tempts you to return with a blanket and a book on a warm spring day. In wooded areas, moss grows on the trail, and the leaves of the bur oaks and chinquapin (chestnut) oaks are so thick they feel like rubber underfoot. As we crossed the prairie, the sumac, which had turned a brilliant shade of red, was a striking contrast to the yellow sunflowers and goldenrod. Nearing the amphitheater at the northwest end of the loop, we came to a complete halt at the top of the hill. The view is spectacular. Watch for a side-trail descending to the lakeshore, and take time to sit on the rocks by the water.

Hiking east on the north side of the loop, we left behind the views of the lake, but enjoyed the route across the prairie and along cultivated fields. The trail eventually crosses the road to the beach and takes you within view of the park office. When the trail loops back south, it climbs for some panoramic views of the lake and surrounding hills. The trail crosses several more park roads before it returns to the trailhead.

Council Grove Lake

While the trails at Council Grove Lake cannot be recommended for scenery or diversity, the fields of prairie wildflowers that border the trails provide reason enough to hike them. The Tallgrass Day Trail in Canning Creek Cove circles a field of tallgrass and prairie wildflowers that looks rather ordinary when the flowers are not in bloom, but in late spring and early summer, it explodes with color. Portions of the Pioneer Nature Trail travel through prairie, but most of it weaves through woodlands along a scenic creek. Ownership: USACE (316) 767-5195.

HIKE LENGTHS

Tallgrass Day Trail.. 2.2-mile loop
Pioneer Nature Trail .... .63-mile loop
Richey Cove Trail .... 1-mile loop

DIRECTIONS

Council Grove Lake is in Morris County, 37 miles south of Manhattan and 58 miles southwest of Topeka. From I-70, take K-177 (Exit 316) south to Council Grove Lake. Alternatively, from U.S. 56, take K-177 north.

TRAIL ACCESS

TALLGRASS DAY TRAIL TRAILHEAD: From K-177, turn southwest at the entrance to Council Grove Lake, 1.8 miles north of the intersection with U.S. 56. Take this road 3.2 miles across the lake dam to the Canning Creek Cove entrance on the north side of the road. Continue 1 mile to the trailhead just east of the park entrance station.

PIONEER NATURE TRAIL TRAILHEAD: Follow the directions to the Tallgrass Day Trail, but turn left (south) just past the lake dam to the trailhead by a small stand of trees on the west side of the Corps of Engineers project office.

Tallgrass Day Trail, Council Grove Lake

RICHEY COVE TRAIL TRAILHEAD: The entrance to Richey Cove is directly off of K-177, about 1 mile north of the entrance to Council Grove Lake and .6 mile south of the entrance to Custer Park. After entering Richey Cove, turn left past the park pay-station and take the next park road left. The trailhead is at the south end of Richey Cove, close to the outhouses. The trail can also be accessed from Kit Carson Cove, south of Richey Cove.

GENERAL INFORMATION

Council Grove was the last outfitting post on the 1,200-mile Santa Fe Trail, which linked Franklin (now Boonville), Missouri (and later, successively, Arrow Rock, Fort Osage, Independence, and Westport Landing, Missouri) to the Mexican provincial capital of Santa Fe. It was one of the greatest and most exotic highways across the West for the first three-quarters of the nineteenth century, and traders told colorful stories of Indian ambushes, Mexican outlaws, army rescues, blizzards, and other adventures. The Santa Fe Trail opened in 1821, after Mexico won independence from Spain, when William Becknell, a Missouri trader, traveled from Franklin, Missouri, to Santa Fe, carrying calico, clothes, trinkets, and equipment. Becknell was one of the first traders to use wagons to transport his goods instead of pack mules or horses. On his second trip in 1822, he had difficulties with the Osage Indians, whose lands he crossed in what is now Kansas. In 1825, the government appointed a commission to survey the trail and negotiate treaties for unmolested passage across Indian lands. On August 10, 1825, a treaty with the Osage Indians was signed at a grove of trees, which one of the commissioners dubbed "Council Grove." The occasion was memorialized by an inscription on a suitable oak tree, which stood until 1958, when it was blown down in a windstorm. By that time, the tree was approximately 70 feet tall and 16 feet in circumference.

THE HIKES

TALLGRASS DAY TRAIL: This flat mowed path circles a field just inside Canning Creek Cove. The first part travels through an area that in late spring and early summer is filled with wildflowers. It appears that at one time the trail continued through the woods that border the field, but high waters washed out the lower parts of it. The fence posts that marked the old trail still stand, but the trail was overgrown when we hiked. The mowed trail edges the woods, then enters a tallgrass area. From here, there is a scenic view of the lake and the distant Flint Hills. The trail parallels the park road as it returns to the trailhead.

PIONEER NATURE TRAIL: A map and interpretive trail guide is available at the project office. Initially, this trail travels through a grassy area bordered by wildflowers. Just before the woods, it branches—the trail guide directs you left (east). The trail enters a wooded area, where it weaves back and forth across a stream leading from the Grand (Neosho) River. The poison ivy leaves here rank among the largest I have seen on any trail. The woods, watered by the meandering stream, are lush, a sharp contrast to the prairie that borders the lake. The western end of the trail passes through prairie, which is especially colorful from late spring through early fall. Past the prairie, the trail comes full circle just after crossing the stream.

RICHEY COVE TRAIL: The entrance is not well marked. The first part of the trail is mowed and parallels K-177. Wildflowers bloom profusely in this area. Before the trail reaches the entrance to Kit Carson Cove, it curves west into the woods, toward the lake. The trail is marked by fence posts. When we hiked it in June 1995, the western section close to the lake was underwater.

Tuttle Creek Lake

The trails at Tuttle Creek Lake offer spectacular views of the surrounding Flint Hills and the lake. The vistas along the upper loop of the Carnahan Creek trail are as beautiful as those at the Konza Prairie, about 18 miles south. Parts of the Carnahan Creek Horse Trail travel through woodlands dominated by red cedars and oaks, but most of it winds through the open tallgrass prairie. The Randolph State Park Horse Trail is more strenuous, leading through scenic, tree-covered hills. After 11.5 miles of knee-grinding climbs and descents, my legs were mush. One of our favorite spots on the state park trail is an overlook on the east side of the outer loop, south of K-16. After meandering through a grove of tall cedars, where even the fiercest Kansas winds are quieted, the trail climbs to a rocky ledge overlooking miles of the Flint Hills. The trails at Carnahan Creek Park and Randolph State Park were designed for equestrian use, and some sections, especially at Randolph State Park, frequently double back to maximize mileage. Ownership: USACE (785) 539-8511; KDWP (785) 539-7941.

HIKE LENGTHS
Carnahan Creek Horse Trail .... 5 miles
Randolph State Park Horse Trail .... 11.5 miles

DIRECTIONS AND TRAIL ACCESS

CARNAHAN CREEK HORSE TRAIL: Tuttle Creek Lake is about 4.5 miles north of Manhattan. From Manhattan, take Tuttle Creek Boulevard (U.S. 24) north. Turn east on K-13, cross the dam, and continue for 5.5 miles to County Road 43 (Prairie Parkway). Take Prairie Parkway west 5.2 miles to the gravel road entrance to Carnahan Creek Park. (This entrance, on the south side of Prairie Parkway, is marked only by a small wooden sign that is not well secured and blends in with the rock behind it. We miss it every time.) Follow the gravel road for 1 mile to the large

Carnahan Creek Horse Trail, Tuttle Creek Lake

sign at the entrance to the park. Continue straight and watch for the parking area by the restrooms. We started the hike across the road.

RANDOLPH STATE PARK HORSE TRAIL: Follow the directions to Carnahan Creek Park, but remain on County Road 43 (Prairie Parkway) until it intersects with K-16 (about 12 miles from the K-13 turnoff, or 6.5 miles past the Carnahan Creek Park entrance). At K-16, turn west and go 5.5 miles to the Randolph State Park entrance. Turn right (north) at the entrance and park near the restrooms. As you drive in, watch for the white post and mowed trail along the park-boundary fence.

ⓘ GENERAL INFORMATION

The decision to build Tuttle Creek Lake, a flood-control project on the Big Blue River, was vigorously opposed by many whose homes and communities now lie beneath the lake. The original town site of Randolph, also beneath the waters to the west of Randolph State Park, was a headquarters for the citizen crusade against the dam. Randolph was relocated 2 miles southeast. Residents of the Fancy Creek Valley and Blue River Valley had been accustomed to floods long before the U.S. Army Corps of Engineers initially recommended a dam in 1937. In 1903, after heavy rains, the Big

Blue River left its banks, carrying away homes, crops, livestock, and bridges of the town of Irving, located at the north end of the Reservoir and now part of a wildlife refuge. (Irving had endured many other hardships, having been virtually destroyed on May 30, 1879 by two tornadoes from two different storm systems.) In October 1915, heavy rains undermined the Union Pacific railroad bridge over Fancy Creek, near Randolph. The bridge collapsed beneath the weight of a train, which catapulted into the embankment and tumbled into the high waters of Fancy Creek. Eleven of the 50 people on the train died. After the devastating floods of 1951, the Corps of Engineers selected the Big Blue River as the site for a large dam, and by 1962 the project was complete.*

THE HIKES

CARNAHAN CREEK HORSE TRAIL: From the shelter across from the restrooms, we walked up the hill to the outer loop. We headed right (west) on the trail, across the rocky hillside shaded by oaks and cedars. The trail wraps around the ridge, with views of the wetlands and then the lake below. The wetlands are within the flood-control pool of the reservoir and are covered by water after heavy rains. After the trail rounds the bend and turns south, it crosses an area covered by flood debris. We had some trouble following the trail through here, but it is marked by a white "horse trail" marker a short distance up the hill from the lake. The trail parallels the lakeshore, and the views of the lake and outlying sculpted hills are hard to beat. As the trail rounds the end of the peninsula and turns north, the spectacular Flint Hills vista will bring you to a halt (the view from the upper trail is even better).

When we hiked in mid-May 1997, the wildflowers were just beginning to show their colors amid the verdant tallgrasses. The remainder of the trail travels along the base of the ridge through open prairie. While the trail continues north across the road, we do not recommend hiking this section—parts are overgrown and the remainder, through the silt plain, is not scenic. Turn left (west) instead at the road, and watch for the upper loop which actually intersects twice with the road. If you follow the trail at the first intersection, you will hike the upper loop clockwise (having traveled the lower loop counterclockwise). We suggest waiting for the second intersection, a short distance further west. Here, the trail climbs through a grove of cedars up the hill, for a panoramic view of the Flint Hills. While the scenery and terrain on the upper loop are similar to the lower loop, the vistas are far more dramatic.

RANDOLPH STATE PARK HORSE TRAIL: The 11.5 miles of horse/hiking trail at Randolph State Park were completed by the Kansas Trails Council in late 1996. The trail is split by K-16, with 4.5 miles of trail to the north of the highway and the remainder to the south. The 1-mile Randolph Bridge, which you will see from the

---

* See *Ghost Towns of Kansas: A Traveler's Guide* by Daniel C. Fitzgerald (Lawrence: University Press of Kansas, 1988) for these and other fascinating stories about Randolph and Irving.

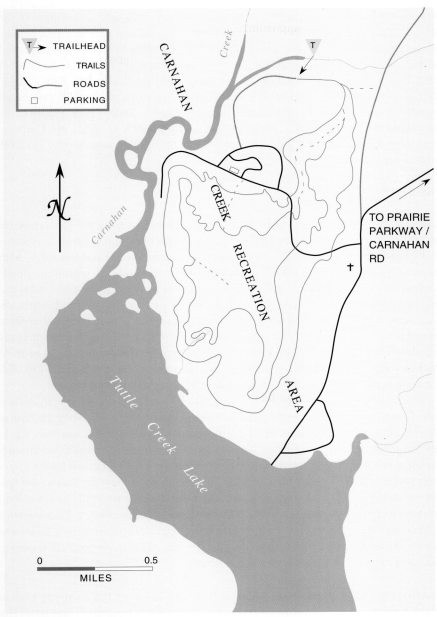

- T→ TRAILHEAD
- TRAILS
- ROADS
- □ PARKING

CARNAHAN

Creek

T

Carnahan

CREEK

RECREATION

AREA

TO PRAIRIE
PARKWAY /
CARNAHAN
RD

†

Tuttle Creek Lake

0   0.5
MILES

Carnahan Creek Horse Trail

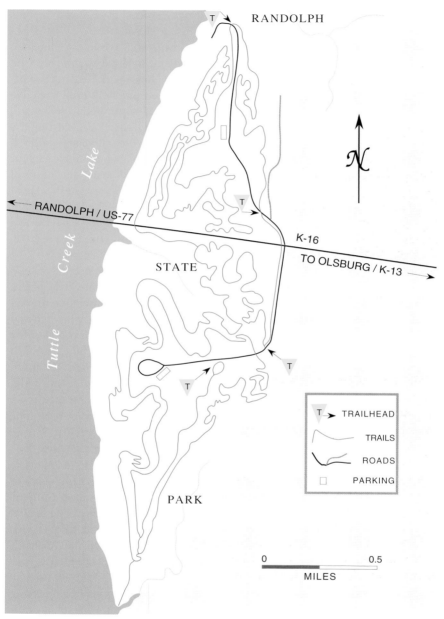

RANDOLPH

RANDOLPH / US-77

K-16

TO OLSBURG / K-13

Tuttle Creek Lake

STATE

PARK

T → TRAILHEAD

TRAILS

ROADS

□ PARKING

0   0.5

MILES

Randolph State Park Horse Trail

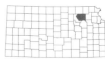

trail, crosses Tuttle Creek Reservoir on K-16 and is the longest in Kansas. When we hiked, the road leading into the park south of K-16 was closed.

We first hiked the northern section of the trail, which has white trail markers. The first mile winds along a wooded, rocky hillside and backtracks almost to the trailhead before jogging back north. When the trail reaches a park road at the bottom of the hill, it turns south and makes a steep ascent, parallel to the road. We missed the mowed cut-over path near the restrooms and continued to follow the road. The trail jogs southwest from the road to reach the upper level, skirting the edge of the woods on the ridge overlooking the lake. Before the trail reaches a small brick building, it turns left (east) and enters the woods. Here it winds above a beautiful valley, where we saw red quartzite rock, deposited by the Kansas glaciations of about 750,000 and 250,000 years ago. Randolph State Park is on the eastern edge of the Glaciated physiographic region, while the land across the lake is in the Flint Hills physiographic region. The terrain is rough and hilly along the easternmost point of the trail, near the park entrance. As you emerge on the bluff above K-16, keep your distance from the edge.

When the trail turns north, you start the second of five layers of trail that ascend the ridge overlooking the lake. According to the Corps of Engineers, bald eagles usually appear in north Randolph State Park during their fall migration and remain through the winter, sometimes for three to four months. The trail folds back on itself yet again, but travels further north, coming close to the northern end of the first mile of the trail. At this point, the trail turns south again for .6 mile, closer to the lake than before, crossing under the Randolph Bridge to the trail on the south side of K-16. About 200 yards from the bridge, the trail intersects with the "blue-blazed" section. If you continue straight 1 mile, the trail intersects the park road. Turn right (south) to follow the trail to its end (5.5 miles, plus an additional 1 mile if you pick up the section you missed by turning right at the intersection).

After turning south, we climbed to the top of a ridge overlooking a scenic wooded valley, the first of many climbs south of K-16. The trail then winds west for a vista of the Randolph Bridge and the lake. For the next 1.3 miles, it travels within view of the lake to a point on a hook-shaped peninsula. Here, the trail moves away from the lake—brace yourself for several steep climbs and some of the most spectacular views of the Flint Hills on the trail. We especially enjoyed a dense stand of cedars, where the wind was still and the sun could not penetrate. From here, the trail leads to a rock ledge, then on for two more steep climbs before intersecting with the park road. This is not the end—cross the road to complete the final 2 miles. From here the trail occasionally jogs into the woods but mostly crosses open prairie, following the top of the ridge overlooking the lake. The route of the upper trail is not as interesting (or as strenuous) as the lower loop, but the views of the lake and Flint Hills are beautiful.

Kaw River Nature Trail

The Kaw River Nature Trail is in the southeastern corner of the Fort Riley Military Reservation, behind the First Territorial Capitol Building. The trail travels along the Kansas River, through woodlands and a thick and tangled understory of woody vegetation that typifies a riparian habitat. While the outstanding views of the Kansas River and the distant Flint Hills are reason enough to hike this trail, the massive cottonwood trees make it unique. Some of these trees must be close competitors of the state's largest tree. Ownership: Kansas State Historical Society (785) 784-5535.

HIKE LENGTH
Kaw River Nature Trail .... 1.75 miles

DIRECTIONS AND TRAIL ACCESS

From I-70, take K-18 (Exit 303, just east of Junction City) northeast 4 miles to Walnut Street in Ogden. Turn left (west) and continue for .8 mile to Riley Road (the main road through Ogden) and turn left (southwest). Remain on Riley Road for 3.5 miles to the First Territorial Capitol Building on the east side of the road. Riley Road becomes Huebner Road when you enter Fort Riley Military Reservation. The trailhead is just behind the capitol building. Parking is available at the historical trail marker just off of Huebner Road.

GENERAL INFORMATION

It is not hard to imagine this area as it was in 1855, when the first legislature of the Kansas Territory met in the unfinished stone warehouse overlooking the Kaw River. The territory, created by Congress with the passage of the Kansas-Nebraska Act, had been in existence one year. Under the act, Congress left it to the new territories

Kaw River Nature Trail

to decide whether they would become free states or slave states. Andrew Reeder, a Democratic lawyer from Pennsylvania, was appointed by President Franklin Pierce as the territory's first governor.

The town of Pawnee, where the first session was to be held, was a settlement of only two houses in 1854. Nevertheless, it was considered a real-estate investment because of its location on the north bank of the Kaw and its close proximity to the Fort Riley Military Reservation. The military road, in fact, ran through the town. At that time, the Kaw River was considered to be navigable, and steamboats and barges traveled the river, at least when high waters permitted. Among the investors in the new town was Governor Reeder, who told the town company in December 1854 that he would convene the first legislature at Pawnee on July 2, 1855, if suitable buildings and accommodations were provided. Settlers moved in and houses and buildings were hastily erected, as news spread that Pawnee might be the capital of the Kansas Territory. The roof of the capitol building was completed the day before the legislature was to convene. Legislators sat at unpainted tables on kegs and boxes and had to avoid stepping on floorboards that hurried carpenters had left unnailed. The legislature was later dubbed the "Bogus Legislature" because of election fraud by proslavery Missourians. Only four months later, the town was found to be located on the Fort Riley Military Reservation. All Pawnee citizens were evicted, and the town was razed except for the capitol building, used by the military as a storehouse. The Kansas State Historical Society now operates the First Territorial Capitol as a historical site.

THE HIKE

KAW RIVER NATURE TRAIL: After descending the steps, you can either veer right at the trail sign, to hike the first leg, or go straight and then left, to hike the second leg. The trail is clearly marked by orange arrows. While the trail travels along relatively flat river-bottom, several sets of steep stairs lead in and out of gullies. The first leg travels along the upper level of the river-bottom before it descends to and parallels the riverbank. Benches have been placed at several observation points. Across the river, the Flint Hills meet the horizon.

Markers along the trail identify certain trees, bushes, and wildflowers. The tangled understory of vegetation is typically riparian. Wild gooseberry, easily identified by its prickly stem, five-leafleted virginia creeper, and riverbank grape, whose soft fruit ripens and turns dark blue in the fall, create a dense cover for wildlife and protect the river-bottom soil from erosion. The eastern cottonwood, the state tree, towers over the other trees along the trail, including bur oak, box elder, hackberry, and green ash. On the second leg of the trail, take time to examine the wide growth-rings (indicative of rapid growth) of the cottonwood that has fallen across the trail. A section has been removed to allow hikers to pass through the massive trunk. The second leg of the trail exits up a path east of the First Territorial Capitol Building.

The Konza Prairie

RILEY COUNTY

The Konza Prairie

We hiked the Konza long before we thought about writing this book, and it has continued to be one of our favorite trails. Each branch offers beautiful panoramic views of this tallgrass prairie in the middle of the Flint Hills. The chiseled hills, the outcroppings of sun-bleached limestone, and the tall oaks along the pristine waters of Kings Creek make this a memorable hike. Kansas State University, Division of Biology, which manages the Konza, cautions that this is a research preserve. To avoid interference with ongoing research, hikers are restricted to the established trails. The Nature Trail has numbered stops keyed to descriptions in the brochure available at the parking area. Ownership: The Nature Conservancy (785) 539-1961 or (785) 587-0381.

HIKE LENGTHS

Nature Trail .... 2.8-mile loop
Kings Creek Loop .... 4.7 miles (includes the Nature Trail loop)
Godwin Hill Loop .... 6.1 miles (includes the Nature Trail Loop and the Kings Creek Loop)

DIRECTIONS AND TRAIL ACCESS

The Konza Prairie is north of I-70 and south of Manhattan. Exit off of I-70 onto McDowell Creek Road (Exit 307) and travel north on McDowell Creek Road (Riley County 901) 4.9 miles. If you are traveling from Manhattan, take McDowell Creek Road 6.3 miles south of K-177. A sign on the east side of McDowell Creek Road marks the entrance to the Konza Prairie. Take the gravel road to the parking area. The trailhead is just across the bridge.

ℹ GENERAL INFORMATION

The Konza Prairie Research Natural Area, named after the Kansa Indians, is an 8,616-acre tract of land purchased by the Nature Conservancy in 1977. At one time, this land was part of the 10,000-acre Dewey Ranch. Recently, the limestone barn, built in 1910, the limestone farmhouse, built in 1911, and the bison-handling facility were renovated with a grant from the National Science Foundation and a matching grant from Kansas State University. Access to many parts of the preserve is restricted because of ongoing research. With careful observation, you can distinguish the watershed-sized areas burned at varying intervals to study the effects of fire and grazing on the preserve's plants and animals. Once, tallgrass prairies stretched from southeastern Texas to Canada. As these areas were settled and cultivated, the tallgrass prairies nearly disappeared. The Flint Hills prairies survived because the shallow, rocky soils, underlain by limestone, were not suitable for cultivating but were ideal for grazing. The Konza is one of the largest parcels of surviving tallgrass prairie in the United States. The predominant grass of the Konza Prairie is big bluestem, the flowering stalk of which may rise 10 feet above the ground. Other grasses include Indian grass, switchgrass, little bluestem, and several species of grama grass. Wildflowers are abundant on the Konza in the spring and summer.

🥾 THE HIKES

For a short distance, the trail runs adjacent to a cultivated field, parallel to a tributary of Kings Creek, until it reaches Kings Creek. Water usually flows here, even when other parts of the creek are dry. The water is clear and cold, and the dense shade of the gallery forest provides a brief respite from the heat on summer days. The trail crosses Kings Creek by a narrow plank bridge, then begins to climb into the Flint Hills, where the terrain is uneven and rocky. This is one of the more strenuous hikes in this book.

The field immediately past Kings Creek was once forested but was cleared in the 1970s and planted to smooth brome grass. Native grasses, wildflowers, honey locust trees, and woody vegetation such as smooth sumac and dogwood have since invaded. In the absence of fire, this field may eventually return to forest. As you climb to the top of the ridge, the trail becomes a narrow corridor through the tallgrasses characteristic of the prairie. The views of the rolling hills and the patchwork of planted fields beyond the boundaries of the preserve are spectacular. Few vistas, however, can match those from the top of the ridge. The grassy hills to the southeast stretch for miles without any sign of a manmade structure. The rocky trail then follows the ridge north for about .5 mile and veers east at the radio tower, which is used for communications on the preserve. To your left lies the Kansas River Valley, the rich soils of which were once cultivated by the Kansa Indians. A sign then directs those on the Nature Trail to turn right to return to the parking area or to take the Kings Creek Loop and the Godwin Hill Loop by continuing ahead. The trail here is one of many firebreaks marking the boundaries of the research areas on the preserve.

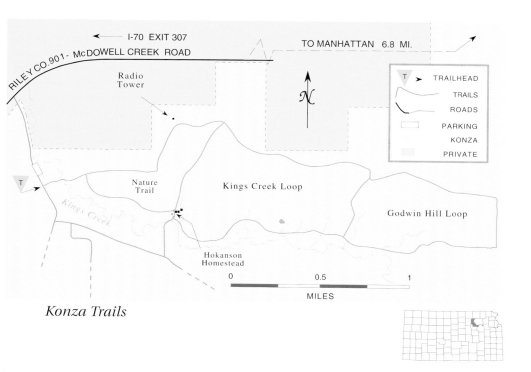

Konza Trails

The Kings Creek Loop and the Godwin Hill Loop are not strenuous and are well worth traveling. The trail continues east along the ridge for about a mile before reaching the Kings Creek Loop turnoff on your right. Outcroppings of weathered limestone dot the ridge. The Kings Creek Loop descends into the beautifully shadowed valley you have seen from the ridge and eventually intersects with the Godwin Hill trail and then the Nature Trail. The Godwin Hill Loop skirts the northern boundary of the preserve for approximately .75 mile before it turns south into the valley, crossing two tributaries of Kings Creek before merging with the Kings Creek Loop on your right. The trail then passes in and out of the gallery forest along Kings Creek, crossing several tributaries before it reaches the Hokanson Homestead, which was added to the Dewey Ranch in 1948. Before you reach it, you will see a concrete bridge over Kings Creek to your left. Because of ongoing research on the waters, wading in the creek is prohibited. The trail does not cross the bridge but continues straight toward the old stone barns of the Hokanson Homestead on your right. Shortly after, the trail intersects with the Nature Trail and leads you back to the parking area.

Manhattan Linear Park Trail

Manhattan Linear Park Trail

T he 9-mile Linear Park Trail that skirts the southern edge of Manhattan show-cases the scenic riparian corridors of the Kansas and Big Blue Rivers and Wildcat Creek. This urban trail is remarkably natural and serene in spots and offers many opportunities to see deer, turkey, pheasants, and songbirds. The first 5 miles follow the levee along the Big Blue and Kansas Rivers. Industrial develop-ments border parts of the trail along the Kansas River, but the panoramic views of the river and outlying Flint Hills make this section one you will not want to miss. From South Manhattan Avenue to the Pecan Circle Entrance, the trail parallels the woodlands along scenic Wildcat Creek. In June 1996, the golden wheat fields to the south shimmered in the hot afternoon sun. From Poliska Lane to Anderson Avenue, the trail follows an abandoned railroad bed through a tunnel of trees and over two old railroad bridges. Ownership: Manhattan Parks & Recreation (785) 587-2757.

HIKE LENGTHS

Linear Park Trail .... 9.4 miles (one-way)
   Casement to S. Manhattan Ave. .... 5.0 miles
   S. Manhattan Ave. to Ft. Riley Blvd. .... 1.7 miles
   Ft. Riley Blvd. to Anderson Ave. .... 2.0 miles
   Anderson Ave. to Anneberg Park .... .7 mile

DIRECTIONS

The Linear Park Trail runs from Casement Road on the east side of Manhattan to Anneberg Park on the west. The only available parking is at the entry off of U.S. 24; Griffith Park, just north of the South Manhattan Avenue entrance; Anneberg Park; on Hayes Drive, south of the intersection of Casement and Hayes; and at Truth Park.

◄┤ TRAIL ACCESS

CASEMENT ROAD ACCESS: From K-177, take Tuttle Creek Boulevard (U.S. 24) north to Casement Road; turn right (east) and watch for the trail entrance at Hayes Drive.

U.S. 24 ACCESS: This is off of U.S. 24, just west of the bridge over the Big Blue River (U.S. 24 branches north of K-177, with one branch, Tuttle Creek Boulevard, traveling north to Tuttle Creek Dam, and the other branch traveling northeast toward the Big Blue River and this access point).

SOUTH MANHATTAN AVENUE ACCESS: From K-177, take K-18 (Fort Riley Boulevard) west to 4th Street; turn left (south). Remain on 4th Street to Pottawatomie Avenue; turn west and continue to South Manhattan Avenue (watch for the "South Manhattan Entrance" trail sign).

TRUTH PARK ACCESS: This park is between South Manhattan Avenue and 11th Street, on Pottawatomie Avenue (parking is at the west end of the park).

PECAN CIRCLE ACCESS: From K-177, take K-18 (Fort Riley Boulevard) west to Rosencutter Road; turn left (south) and watch for Pecan Circle. Turn left, then right, and watch for the large sign and map at the trail entrance.

ANNEBERG PARK ACCESS: From K-177, take K-18 (Fort Riley Boulevard) west to K-113 (Seth Child Road); turn north and continue to Anderson Avenue. Turn west and watch for Anneberg Park, on the south side of Anderson Avenue, just west of Hudson Avenue.

[i] GENERAL INFORMATION

It is not surprising that the area traversed by the Linear Park Trail, which borders two major rivers, was inhabited long before Manhattan was founded or Kansas was a territory. An important settlement of the Kansa Indians—the Blue Earth Village— once lay at the confluence of these rivers, on the north bank of the Kaw (Kansas), and the east bank of the Big Blue (Earth), two miles east of Manhattan. One hundred twenty-eight bark-covered, circular earth-lodges, bordered by 100 acres planted in corn, beans, and pumpkins, made up the village. George C. Sibley, a trader, visited this village in 1811 and wrote in his journal that the surrounding land was a "very wild but extremely beautiful and high prairie country." He described the Flint Hills as "ranges of lofty, rugged, naked hills, overlooking extensive tracts of meadow ground." Eight years later, a company of 13 men, detached from an expedition led by Major Stephen H. Long, spent four days at the same village, collecting information about the Kansa. One of the men made a drawing of a Kansa Indian dance, believed

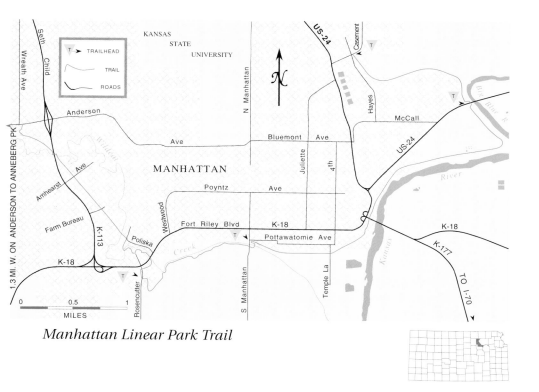

Manhattan Linear Park Trail

to be the first printed depiction of a Kansas scene. As a result of the explorations of Zebulon Pike, Stephen Long, and others, and the popular belief among easterners that treeless land was not fit for plowing, this region, extending west to the Rockies, was dubbed desert wasteland, and maps used through the end of the Civil War labeled it the "Great American Desert."

THE HIKE

We started the trail at Casement Road, following the direction in which the trail was built over the past ten years. Eventually, the City of Manhattan hopes the trail will encircle the city. From Casement to South Manhattan Avenue, the trail travels the levee, first along the Big Blue River and then along the Kansas River. This part, through fertile river valley, is flat. Wildflowers bloom from spring through fall in the adjacent meadows. The trail skirts, but never enters, the dense woodlands along the river. Watch for bald eagles after you pass under the U.S. 24 bridge and near the confluence of the Big Blue and Kansas Rivers. Over 140 years ago, you would have seen the Blue Earth Village of the Kansa Indians across the river. The trail travels within view of an industrial area, but this did not detract from our enjoyment of the beautiful views of the river and bridges. After the trail travels under the K-177 bridge, it remains on the levee but turns southwest, away from the river.

The trail from South Manhattan Avenue to Poliska Lane is surfaced with concrete; the levee and "Rails to Trails" portions are surfaced with limestone screenings, which are regraded and compacted each year. At South Manhattan Avenue, the trail jogs left (south) over Wildcat Creek, then parallels the creek to the Pecan Circle access point. This was one of our favorite sections, meandering along the edge of the scenic gallery forest and providing brief glimpses of the waters that mirror the overhanging trees. There are pastoral views of the fields and hills to the south, east, and west. Wildcat Creek once provided a natural highway to buffalo-hunting grounds on the prairies.* George S. Park, the first settler on Wildcat Creek, established a town site in 1854 at the mouth of the creek, naming it Poleska (from which Poliska Lane derives its name).

We had some difficulty following the trail from the Pecan Circle access point to Poliska Lane. This should be remedied by August 1997, upon the completion of the bypass over Fort Riley Boulevard, leading directly to the "Rails to Trails" section. From Poliska Lane to Anderson Avenue, the city has incorporated about 2 miles of an abandoned railroad right-of-way into the Linear Park Trail. The most scenic parts of this corridor are an old railroad bridge suspended over Wildcat Creek and a long tunnel of trees that even the hot summer sun cannot penetrate. The northwestern end of the trail eventually emerges in a more developed part of the city. Before the trail reaches Anderson Avenue, it crosses another railroad bridge over Wildcat Creek. At Anderson, turn left (west) to Anneberg Park—the end of the trail for now.

* See *Riley County, Kansas* by Winifred N. Slagg (Winifred N. Slagg, 1968).

Indian Rock and Salina Levee Trails

I t had been at least 30 years since I scrambled across the rocks at Indian Rock Park in Salina. I found the cliff as high and steep as I remembered, but the large "lake" below turned out to be only a 2-acre fishing pond (stocked). The scenic overlook, to which we once climbed by toe-holds and prayers, has been fenced to prevent falls. There is still a certain mystique to the park—according to legend, the large rock south of the pond marks the site of the 1857 Battle of Indian Rock, between the Kansa, Delaware, and Potawatomie (the eastern tribes) and the Cheyenne, Arapaho, and Sioux (the western tribes), over hunting grounds. Immediately adjacent to Indian Rock Park is Bill Burke Park, where the 3.1-mile Salina Levee Trail originates. While the Indian Rock Nature Trail offers several panoramic views of the Smoky Hill River, the Levee Trail actually follows the river from Crawford Street to Magnolia Road. When I hiked at the end of May 1997, foliage blocked all but a few views of the river from the Levee Trail, which travels within view of several housing developments, farms, and fields. Ownership: Salina Parks & Recreation (785) 826-7434.

HIKE LENGTHS
Indian Rock Nature Trail .... .75 mile (round-trip)
Salina Levee Trail .... 3.1 miles (one-way)

DIRECTIONS AND TRAIL ACCESS

Indian Rock Park and Bill Burke Park are in northeast Salina, only a few miles from downtown. Take the Ohio Street Exit (Exit 253) off of I-70 and travel south. To reach Indian Rock Park, turn east on Gypsum Avenue and proceed to Indiana Avenue. Indian Rock Park is bordered by Gypsum Avenue on the north and Indiana Avenue on the west. Alternatively, from I-35, take the Crawford Street Exit (Exit 92) and travel east to Ohio. Turn north and proceed to Gypsum Avenue, then turn south on Indiana

Indian Rock Trail

Avenue. The trailhead is just off of Indiana Avenue. The numbered markers follow the loop counterclockwise.

Bill Burke Park is immediately south of Indian Rock Park, at the base of the hill overlooking the old Smoky Hill River channel. It is bordered on the west by Indiana Avenue and on the south by Crawford Street. Parking is available. The concrete trail starts at the north end of the park.

While there is no trail that connects the trail at Indian Rock Park and the Levee Trail, you can easily access Bill Burke Park from Indian Rock Park by following Indiana Avenue south from Indian Rock Park. Salina Parks and Recreation provides a fascinating guide to the Indian Rock Trail, "Indian Rock Trail: Where the Past and Present Come Together," which includes a description of 15 points of interest and facts about the history, geology, flora, and fauna of the park. The booklet is available at trailhead boxes or at the Salina Parks and Recreation Office, 300 W. Ash, Room 100.

ℹ️ GENERAL INFORMATION

Small as it is (35 acres), Indian Rock Park has a rich history. Legend has it that the Battle of Indian Rock in 1857 occurred near the rock identified by marker 15 on the west side of the loop, just south of the lake. The Kansa Indians won the battle, after the arrival of reinforcements from Council Grove. With the defeat of the Cheyenne, Arapaho, and Sioux Indians, the Salina area was opened to white settlement. In 1870, the water-powered Gower Mill (or Upper Mill) was built across the old Smoky Hill River channel, at the base of the hill (marker 3) at the south end of the loop. The mill closed only 4 years later, but in its time, wheat, corn, and rye flour were milled here and packaged under the names "Pride of Salina" and "Prairie Flower." The lake at the park is not a natural feature. From 1899 to 1954, various brick companies quarried the extensive deposits of blue shale to make bricks, many of which were used to pave streets and build homes and other buildings in Salina. Eventually, water filled the deeper part of the quarry. At the south end of the Indian Rock Nature Trail, you will see the old channel of the Smoky Hill River and across it, Bill Burke Park. At one time, the Smoky Hill River cut through the center of Salina, but because of extensive and frequent flooding, the Army Corps of Engineers diverted the river to the east side of the city in the 1950s. The river now runs on the east side of Indian Rock Park and Bill Burke Park.

THE HIKES

INDIAN ROCK NATURE TRAIL: From the trailhead take the trail to the right (south) to follow the markers in sequence (counterclockwise). The trail winds south toward the old Smoky Hill River channel, where it climbs the hill overlooking the river. (If you are hiking with children, be aware that the trail crosses the park road just past marker 2.) The views of the river are beautiful. The east side of the loop travels through a 6-acre restored prairie by the new channel of the Smoky Hill River. After the trail leaves the prairie, it crosses the park road again. (Be sure to take a short detour here, up the road south to the overlook, near the shelter. From this spectacular point, you can see for miles.) After you cross the park road, the trail descends and circles the 2-acre pond, home to a variety of frogs, salamanders, crayfish, and mussels. As the trail turns south to return to the trailhead, it passes Indian Rock at the south end of the pond. From this point, there is a secondary trail that branches left (east) south of the pond. This secondary trail connects to marker 9 on the east side of the pond.

SALINA LEVEE TRAIL: This is a well-used, flat jogging/biking trail along the flood-control levee of the Smoky Hill River, mostly constructed of crushed limestone screenings. There are large maps at the trailhead on Crawford and at the south end of the trail, on Magnolia Road. I followed the trail south from Bill Burke Park, where it hugs the river for .5 mile before it crosses under the Crawford Street Bridge. About .25 mile past the bridge, the trail connects to the levee. From the trail south of the Crawford Street Bridge, you will see Oxbow Park, an 8.5-acre park adjacent to an oxbow of the Smoky Hill River. Beyond this point, I saw the gallery forest that lines the river, but caught no glimpse of the river itself. This may not be true in the winter. For the next 2.2 miles, the Levee Trail travels primarily through agricultural areas, including prairie, pasture, cropland, and farms, but also within view of several housing developments.

Old Forest Lane Trail, Lakewood Park

Lakewood Park

T he maze of trails through 99-acre Lakewood Park, in northeast Salina, provides a quiet retreat from the sounds of the city. The Old Forest Lane Trail, my favorite, travels through the gallery forest that lines the Smoky Hill River. It parallels the east shore of a sandpit lake and loops back along the river. Right in the middle of the trail, near the river, is an enormous, twisted cottonwood tree, its trunk so bent the top nearly touches the ground. The restored native prairie area is especially colorful in spring and early summer, when the wildflowers interspersed in the tallgrass are in full bloom. Ownership: Salina Parks & Recreation (785) 826-7335.

HIKE LENGTH

Lakewood Park trails... 2.25 miles (round-trip)

DIRECTIONS AND TRAIL ACCESS

Lakewood Park is in northeast Salina, just off Iron Avenue. From I-70, take the Ohio Street Exit (Exit 253) and travel south to Iron Avenue. Turn left (east), watch for the park sign on the north side of Iron Avenue, and turn left (north) on Lakewood Drive. Follow the old bridge over the Smoky Hill River, then turn right (east) onto the first park road, which ends at a parking area near the east trailhead. The trail can also be accessed at several other points, including the Discovery Center, just off Lakewood Drive, south of the lake and north of the park road to the east trailhead. Stop at the Discovery Center to pick up a brochure about the history of the park and its birds and trees, as well as a detailed map of the trails.

GENERAL INFORMATION

The land that is now Lakewood Park was originally part of a 160-acre tract owned by the widow of an Indian who had fought in the War of 1812. In 1861, she sold it all for $64.00. In 1918, the Putnam Sand Company began dredging operations on the northwest section of the tract, creating the basin through which most of the nature trail weaves. At one time, the lake at the north end of the park was three times larger than it is now, but after the Smoky Hill River was rerouted for flood-control, the lake no longer received the overflow from the adjacent river. As silt gradually filled the old river channel, the ground water that fed the lake was also reduced. As you hike through the basin, you will see that most of the timber is young, but eventually this area will be covered by a mature hardwood forest.

🏃 THE HIKE

Three trails diverge from the east trailhead. To the far right, traveling north, is the Old Forest Lane Trail. To the far left, traveling south, is the Cottonwood Trail. The middle trail connects to the Meadow Loop and the Willow Walk. I wandered on all of the loops, sometimes retracing my steps. The trails through the lake basin are covered with wood-chips and mostly shaded. Some were muddy and even under water when I hiked in October 1996. I especially enjoyed the aptly named Willow Walk, which cuts through the center of the basin. You might see four varieties of willows on this walk—black willow, peach-leaved willow, sandbar willow, and weeping willow. Wildlife includes white-tailed deer, red fox, bobcat, coyote, gophers, raccoons, opossum, rabbits, and squirrels. One of the more unusual, non-native trees that you should watch for along the trails in Lakewood is the ginkgo, which has distinctive, fan-shaped leaves. A living fossil related to conifers, it is the only survivor of its ancient and once widespread family. Female gingkos litter seeds that smell like rancid butter. Native trees to look for include bur oak, osage orange, green ash, hackberry, black walnut, cedar, and tamarisk (salt cedar).

The Old Forest Lane Trail is quiet and shaded, with scenic views of the 10-acre fishing lake and the Smoky Hill River. The trail loops back south at the north end of the lake, and returns along the river, parallel to, and not far from, the outbound trail. The south end of the Old Forest Lane Trail intersects with the mowed trail that circles the restored prairie area. While the mowed loop edges the gallery forest along the Smoky Hill River, it is not shaded. This is an ideal area for birdwatching. The prairie loop will return you to the parking area, by the eastern trailhead.

Bibliography

Andreas, A. T. *History of the State of Kansas.* 2 vols. Chicago: Andreas, 1883.

Bird, Roy. *Topeka: An Illustrated History of the Kansas Capital.* Topeka: Baranski Publishing Company, 1985.

Blair, Mike. "Flying in the Face of Extinction." *Kansas Wildlife and Parks,* March/April 1995, 2.

Buchanan, Rex, ed. *Kansas Geology: An Introduction to Landscapes, Rocks, Minerals, and Fossils.* Lawrence: University Press of Kansas, 1984.

Buchanan, Rex C. and James R. McCauley. *Roadside Kansas: A Traveler's Guide to Its Geology and Landmarks.* Lawrence: University Press of Kansas, 1987.

Busby, William H. "Bald Eagle Numbers Soar." *The Plains Keeper,* Winter News 1995.

Capper/MRI Quick-Fact Book of Kansas, The. Topeka: Capper Press, 1990.

Case, Stephen B. "A Piece of History Saved: The Prairie Center." *Kansas Wildlife and Parks,* Sept./Oct. 1994, 8.

Cherryvale Centennial 1871–1971, "A New Century Beckons."

Dary, David. *Lawrence, Douglas County, Kansas: An Informal History.* Lawrence: Allen Books, 1982.

Davis, Kenneth S. *Kansas: A History.* New York: W. W. Norton & Company, 1984.

DeLano, Patti, and Cathy Johnson. *Kansas Off the Beaten Path: A Guide to Unique Places.* Second edition. Old Saybrook, Connecticut: Globe Pequot Press, 1993.

Dilts, Carol. *Harvey County West Park Lakeside Nature Trail.* Newton: Harvey County Parks & Recreation Department, 1990.

Douthit, Kitty. "The Mined Lands: A Healing Experience." *Outdoor Kansas,* July 1995.

Early History of North Lawrence. Lawrence: North Lawrence Civic Association, 1930.

Eddy, William B. and Richard O. Ballentine. *Hiking Kansas City.* Third edition. Kansas City: Richard O. Ballentine, 1995.

Estes, Carol. "Sea of Grass." *National Parks,* March/April 1995, 38.

Evans, Catherine S. *From Sea to Prairie: A Primer of Kansas Geology.* Reprint. Kansas Geological Survey, 1995.

Farrah, Negele D. "County Trails Soon Will Offer a Trip to an Island in the Kansas River." *Kansas City Star* (Shawnee and Lenexa edition), 17 June 1995, 40.

Fitzgerald, Daniel C. *Faded Dreams: More Ghost Towns of Kansas.* Lawrence: University Press of Kansas, 1994.

_____. *Ghost Towns of Kansas: A Traveler's Guide.* Lawrence: University Press of Kansas, 1988.

Fox, Fred. "Restoration Work at Cheyenne Bottoms." *The Plains Keeper,* Spring News 1995.

Freeman, Craig C. and Eileen K. Schofield. *Roadside Wildflowers of the Southern Great Plains.* Lawrence: University Press of Kansas, 1991.

Great Bend Convention and Visitors Bureau. *Great Bend Wildlife Watching: Cheyenne Bottoms*

Wildlife Area and Quivira National Wildlife Refuge (available at the Quivira National Wildlife Refuge Visitors Office).

Greenwood County Historical Society. *History of Greenwood County.* Wichita: Josten's Publications, 1986.

Gress, Bob and George Potts. *Watching Kansas Wildlife: A Guide to 101 Sites.* Lawrence: University Press of Kansas, 1993.

Harter, Stan. "Kansas Ozarks? Spring River Wildlife Area." *Kansas Wildlife and Parks,* July/August 1995, 7.

Hartman, Joe and Mechele MacDonald. "The Cornerstone of Kansas." *Kansas Wildlife and Parks,* September/October 1988, 9.

Hayward, Stephen and Martha. *Walks and Rambles on the Cimarron National Grassland.* 1989.

Heat-Moon, William Least. *PrairyErth.* Boston: Houghton Mifflin Company, 1991.

Herring, Joseph B. *The Enduring Indians of Kansas.* Lawrence: University Press of Kansas, 1990.

Howes, Charles C. *This Place Called Kansas.* Norman: University of Oklahoma Press, 1952.

"Island Is New Gem for Parks." *Kansas City Star* (Shawnee and Lenexa edition), 8 November 1995.

Kansas Department of Commerce and Housing, Travel and Tourism Development Division. *Hiking the Trails of Kansas.* (Available at Kansas Travel and Tourism, KDOC&H, 700 S.W. Harrison, Suite 1300.)

Kansas Department of Wildlife and Parks. Pamphlets and brochures for each state park (available at the Kansas Department of Wildlife and Parks, 512 S.E. 25th Avenue, Pratt, KS 67124 (316) 672-5911, Ext. 141, as well as at state park offices) including the following: *Cheyenne Bottoms Driving Tour* (available at Cheyenne Bottoms Wildlife Area); *Gypsum Creek Nature Trail* (available at the Maxwell Wildlife Refuge); *Kanopolis State Park Trails* (available at the park office, Kanopolis State Park); *Lake Scott State Park & Wildlife* (available at the park office, Lake Scott State Park); *The Dakota Trail* (available at the park office, Wilson Lake State Park); *The Prairie Center* (available at the park office, The Prairie Center); *The Trails of Fall River State Park* (available at the park office, Fall River State Park).

Kindscher, Kelly. *Medicinal Wild Plants of the Prairie.* Lawrence: University Press of Kansas, 1992.

Kohlmetz, Ernst, ed. *Study of American History, The.* vol. 1. Guilford, CT: Dushkin, 1974.

Konza Prairie Research Natural Area Trail Guide. (Available at the Konza Prairie, trailhead box.)

Mathews, Bob. "Ark River Lowlands." *Kansas Wildlife and Parks,* March/April 1997, 9.

_____. "The Red Hills: Good Medicine." *Kansas Wildlife and Parks,* March/April 1996, 2.

Miner, Craig. *Wichita: The Magic City.* Wichita: Wichita–Sedgwick County Historical Museum Association, 1988.

_____. *West of Wichita: Settling the High Plains of Kansas.* 1865–1890. Lawrence: University Press of Kansas, 1986.

Miner, H. Craig. *Wichita: The Early Years, 1865–1890.* Nebraska: University of Nebraska Press, 1982.

Murrell, Marc. "Pearl on the Plains: Scott State Park." *Kansas Wildlife and Parks,* July/August 1995, 26.

_____. "Elk City's Pathways in Paradise." *Kansas Wildlife and Parks,* July/August 1993, 16.

"Nature's Palette Lights Up the Prairie: Beauty of the Z-Bar Belongs in the National Parks System." *Kansas City Star,* 23 July 1995.

Owensby, Clenton E. *Kansas Prairie Wildflowers.* Ames: Iowa State University Press, 1980.

Paramore, Shawna Bethell. "At Home on the Range." *Kansas!* (2) 1996, 12.

Parker, Martha J. and Betty A. Laird. *Historical Map of Clinton Lake.*

_____. *Soil of Our Souls: Histories of the Clinton Lake Area Communities.* Lawrence: Coronado Press, 1976.

Peterson, Cliff. "Maxwell Wildlife Refuge: A Glimpse of Kansas Past." *Kansas Wildlife and Parks,* January/February 1992, 12.

"Public to Get a Look at New Quivira Refuge's Visitor Center." *Wichita Eagle,* 13 October 1995, sec. D-1.

Rakestraw, John. "Our Natural Wonder." *Kansas!* (3) 1996, 2.

Rawlins County History Book Committee. *History of Rawlins County, Kansas.* Rawlins County Genealogical Society, 1988.

Reichman, O. J. *Living Landscapes of Kansas.* Photographs by Steve Mulligan. Lawrence: University Press of Kansas, 1995.

————. *Konza Prairie: A Tallgrass Natural History.* Lawrence: University Press of Kansas, 1987.

"Remnants of Old Dam Found." *Kansas City Star,* 9 May 1996, sec. C-1.

Richmond, Robert W. *Kansas: A Pictorial History.* Lawrence: University Press of Kansas, 1992.

Schmidt, Jerry. "Oasis in the Sand: Sandhills State Park." *Kansas Wildlife and Parks,* September/October 1990, 41.

Selcraig, Bruch. "What Is a Wetland?" *Sierra,* May/June 1996, 44.

"Shawnee Indian Mill Site Found." *Journal Herald,* 9 May 1996.

Shoup, Mark. "The Ancient Mystery of Big Basin." *Kansas Wildlife and Parks,* January/February 1993, 8.

Shoup, J. Mark. "The Maxwells' Prairie Legacy." *Kansas Wildlife and Parks,* July/August 1996, 16.

Slagg, Winifred N. *Riley County Kansas.* Winifred N. Slagg, 1968.

Stephens, H. A. *Trees, Shrubs, and Woody Vines in Kansas.* Lawrence: University Press of Kansas, 1969.

Stevens, William K. "Keepers of the Plains," *Wichita Eagle,* 6 August 1995, sec. A-17.

Streeter, Floyd Benjamin. *The Kaw: The Heart of a Nation.* New York: Rinehart & Company, 1941.

Trail Guide of Hiking and Biking in Johnson County, Kansas. (available through the Johnson County Parks and Recreation District, Shawnee Mission Park, 7900 Renner Road, Shawnee Mission, KS 66219.)

Unrau, William E. *The Kansa Indians: A History of the Wind People, 1673–1873.* Norman: University of Oklahoma Press, 1971.

U.S. Army Corps of Engineers. Pamphlets and brochures (available at the U.S. Army Corps of Engineers, Kansas City District, Technical Support Branch, Room 713, Federal Building, 601 E. 12th, Kansas City, Missouri 64106 (816) 983-3971 and at the park office for each Corps facility) include the following: *Kanopolis Lake Legacy Trail: A Self-Guided Auto Tour* (available at the park office, Kanopolis Lake); *Perry Lake Trail Brochure* (available at the park office, Perry Lake); *Rocktown Natural Area and Wilson Lake Bur Oak Nature Trail* (available at the park office, Wilson Lake).

Wallace, Douglass W. and Roy D. Bird. *Witness of the Times: A History of Shawnee County.* Shawnee County Historical Society and Shawnee County American Revolution Bicentennial Commission, 1976.

Watkins, Michael. "The Eagles Have Landed." *Kansas Wildlife and Parks,* May/June 1995, 2.

Wilson, Ray D. *Kansas Historical Tour Guide.* Carpentersville, Illinois: Crossroads Communications, 1994.

WPA Guide to 1930s Kansas, The. Reprint. Lawrence: University Press of Kansas, 1984.

Yost, Nellie Snyder. *Medicine Lodge: The Story of a Kansas Town.* Chicago: Swallow Press, 1970.

Zornow, William Frank. *Kansas: A History of the Jayhawk State.* Norman: University of Oklahoma Press, 1957.

Physiographic Regions

Source: Kansas Geological Survey

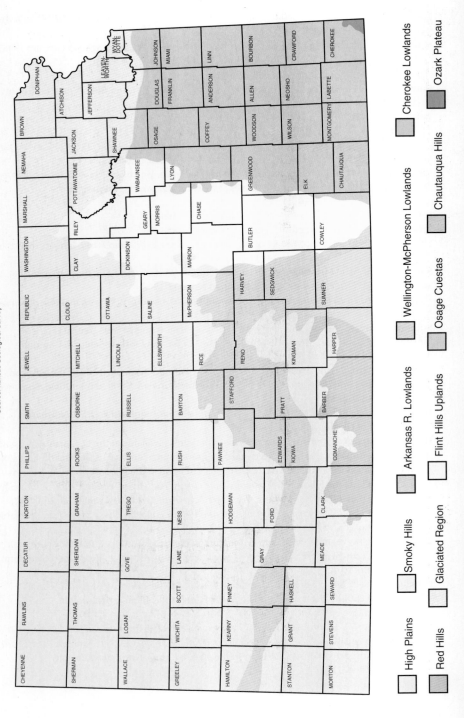

Legend:
- High Plains
- Smoky Hills
- Arkansas R. Lowlands
- Wellington-McPherson Lowlands
- Cherokee Lowlands
- Red Hills
- Glaciated Region
- Flint Hills Uplands
- Osage Cuestas
- Chautauqua Hills
- Ozark Plateau